JÜRGEN KLOPP

102 Passing, Counter-pressing Possession Games, Speed & Warm-ups Direct from Klopp's Training Sessions

PUBLISHED BY

JÜRGEN KLOPP

102 Passing, Counter-pressing Possession Games, Speed & Warm-ups Direct from Klopp's Training Sessions

First Published November 2022 by SoccerTutor.com
info@soccertutor.com | www.SoccerTutor.com

UK: 0208 1234 007 | **US:** (305) 767 4443 | **ROTW:** +44 208 1234 007
ISBN: 978-1-910491-60-7

Copyright: SoccerTutor.com Limited © 2022. All Rights Reserved.

All rights reserved. No part of this publication may be reproduced, stored in a retrieval system, or transmitted in any form or by any means, electronic, mechanical, photocopy, recording or otherwise, without prior written permission of the copyright owner. Nor can it be circulated in any form of binding or cover other than that in which it is published and without similar condition including this condition being imposed on a subsequent purchaser.

Edited by
Alex Fitzgerald - SoccerTutor.com

Diagrams
Diagram designs by SoccerTutor.com. All the diagrams in this book have been created using SoccerTutor.com Tactics Manager Software available from www.SoccerTutor.com

Cover Design by
Alex Macrides, Think Out Of The Box Ltd.
Email: design@thinkootb.com Tel: +44 (0) 208 144 3550

Note: While every effort has been made to ensure the technical accuracy of the content of this book, neither the author nor publishers can accept any responsibility for any injury or loss sustained as a result of the use of this material.

CONTENTS

Jürgen Klopp's Achievements 8
Klopp's Trophies and Records at Liverpool 9
Jürgen Klopp's Philosophy: Best Quotes 11
Diagram Key 12
Practice Format 12

Liverpool Pre-Match Warm-up 13
Part 1/6. Individual Exercises and Passing in Groups 14
Part 2/6. Group Activation Exercises 15
Part 3/6. Functional Movements + Sprints 16
Part 4/6. Passing in Pairs 17
Part 5/6. 4 v 4 (+2) End to End Possession Game 18
Part 6/6. "3-Ball" Finishing Drill + Short Sharp Sprints 19

Pre-season Training 20
1. Receive, Turn, Feint, Dribble & Pass in an End to End Technical Practice 21
2. Pass and Score Quickly vs. Speed of Middle Player Game 22
3. Juggle, Pick-up Bibs + First to Score in a Speed Race Game ... 23
4. Pass, Receive, and Dribble in a Double Triangle Connected Circuit 24
5. One-Twos on the Run in a Double Triangle Connected Circuit 25
6. Pass and Move to Receive, Dribble Through Poles + Target Goal 26
7. Pre-season Passing Circuit with One-Twos + Pass into Target Goal 27
8. Various Attacking Combinations in Threes with the Coach's Signal 28

Warm-up Exercises WITHOUT a Ball 29
1. Mobility Warm-up Circuit with Stretching + Speed & Agility Work (1) 30
2. Mobility Warm-up Circuit with Stretching + Speed & Agility Work (2) 31
3. Speed Warm-up Circuit + Static Stretching 32

4. Speed Warm-up with Quick Feet + Physical Duel 33
5. Coordination Warm-up with Dynamic Jumps and Movements 34
6. Dynamic Warm-up Circuit with All Types of Movements & Obstacles 35

Warm-up Exercises WITH a Ball 36
1. Technical Ball Control Warm-up with Various Stations 37
2. Speed of Movement Warm-up with Volleys and Headers 38
3. Dynamic Movements, Speed and Quick One-Twos Warm-up Circuit 39
4. Warm-up Competition Game with Speed, Pass, Receive + Shoot 40
5. Juggling Challenger 3-Round Relay Game (Individual, Pairs and Fours) 41
6. Football Tennis Game with Maximum of 3 Touches and 1 Bounce 42
7. Double Triangle 2-Touch Passing Warm-up 43

Speed & Agility 44
1. Fast Reactions to Coach's Signal in a Quick Feet + Sprint Race 45
2. Fast Reactions to "Left or Right" Signal to Drop Back + Sprint Race 46
3. Fast Reactions to Multiple Signals in a Speed of Movement Race 47
4. Fast Side-to-Side Reactions with Mannequins, Turn + Sprint Race 48
5. Fast Side-to-Side Reactions to Sound & Visual Signals + Sprint Race 49
6. Fast Turns, Awareness & Changes of Direction + Sprint Race 50
7. React to Signal + Sprint in 1v1 Duel 51
8. Physical Duel, React to Signal + Sprint Race 52
9. Quick Turns, React to Signal + Sprint Race to Finish Line 53
10. Rotate Position, React to Signal + Sprint Race 54
11. Spin, React to Signal + Sprint Race to Finish 55
12. Speed, Coordination & Agility Race with Signaled Fast Reactions 56
13. Speed, Coordination & Agility Circuit with Sprints 57
14. Quick Steps, Changes of Direction and Short Sprints 58
15. Quick Steps, Slalom, Plyometric Exercises & Agility Circuit 59
16. Agility Circuit with Plyometric Exercises for Speed & Explosiveness 60
17. Fast Feet, Sprints, Plyometric Exercises & Jumps in a Speed Circuit 61

Passing Combinations 62

1. One-Two, Pass and Move 3-Player Support Play Combinations 64
2. One-Two, Pass and Move 4-Player Support Play Combinations 65
3. Lofted Passing with 2-Pairs (Pass and Receive) 66
4. Passing in Fours + Quick Change of Direction to Go in Behind 67
5. Two-Touch (Pass and Receive) Triangle 68
6. Support Play and Timing of Movement Triangle with One-Twos 69
7. Central Support, Diagonal Pass, Receive and Dribble in a Triangle 70
8. Double Triangle Link Support Play in a "Passing Y" 71
9. Pass, Press, and Rotate in a 2-Ball Passing Diamond 72
10. One-Twos and Third Man Run Combinations with Switch of Play 73
11. Third Man Run Combinations + Give & Go Passing Circuit 74
12. Two-Touch "Double Triangle" Passing Circuit 75
13. Two-Touch "Double Triangle" Passing Circuit with One-Two 76
14. Open Up to Support in a Multi-Direction Passing Square 77
15. Diagonal Passes and Support Play Movements to Left and Right 78
16. Receive on Half-Turn + Diagonal Pass 79
17. Receive on Half-Turn, Diagonal Pass + One-Two 80
18. Double One-Two + Pass in Mini Goal 81
19. Quick One-Twos and Timing of Support + Switch of Pass 82
20. Give & Go + Switch in Two Connected Passing Squares 83
21. Short One-Twos in a "Double Square" with Central Support Play 84
22. Breaking the Lines with Angled Support, Lay-offs and Forward Runs 85
23. Breaking the Lines with Angled Support, Lay-offs + Third Man Run 86
24. Passing and Support Play with Quick Rotations and Movements 87
    Pattern Example 1: Receive OUTSIDE 4 Box Mannequins First 87
    Pattern Example 2: Receive INSIDE 4 Box Mannequins First 88
25. Short Possession Play + Change Direction with Sprints to Support 89
26. Possession Play + Quick Transition to Score with New Ball 90
27. Possession Play + Quick Transition to Score in Target Goals 91

Passing Diamond Combinations 92

1. Diamond with Give & Go, Switch, One-Two + Through Pass 93
2. Diamond with One-Two, Lay-offs, Give & Go + Through Pass 94
3. Diamond with One-Two, Lay-off + Final Switch Pass 95
4. Diamond with Short Combination Play + Final Switch Pass 96
5. Diamond with One-Two, Pass, One-Two, Pass 97
6. Diamond with One-Two, Give & Go + Final Pass for Third Man Run 98
7. Diamond with One-Two + Two Give & Goes 99
8. Diamond with One-Two, Lay-off, Switch + Give & Go 100
9. Diamond with Central Link Player: One-Twos & Opening Up to Receive 101
10. Diamond with Central Link Player: Lay-offs and Support Play 102
11. Diamond with Central Link Player: Support Play for Give & Goes 103
12. Diamond with Central Link Player: Support Play to Left and Right Sides 104
13. Diamond + Triangle with Quick Changes of Direction 105
14. Diamond + Triangle with Short and Quick Combination Play 106

Jürgen Klopp's Pressing and Counter-pressing Philosophy 107

Pressing and Counter-Pressing 108
Jürgen Klopp's Counter-Pressing 109
Pressing and Counter-Pressing Focus in Liverpool's Training 110

Pressing Rondos and Possession Games 111

1. 4 v 2 Rondo to Find the Free Player and Pressing to Close Passing Lines 113
2. 4 v 2 Pressing Rondo +1 Middle Floating Player 114
3. 5 v 2 Intense Pressing Rondo to "Win the Ball within 6 Passes" 115
4. Transition from Attack to Defence in Simultaneous 5 v 2 Rondos 116
5. 6 v 2 Rondo to Find the Free Player and Pressing to Close Passing Lines 117
6. 6 v 2 End to End Rondo with Support Play and Constant Pressing 118
7. 4-Team 2 + 2 + 2 v 2 Rondo with Fast Pressing and Transitions 119
8. 7 v 7 Pole Gates Possession Game 120
9. 7 v 7 Pole Gates Possession Game with End Zone Players 121

Pressing and Counter-pressing Rondos and Possession Games.... 122

1. "Hunt the Ball" 3 (+3) v 3 Tactical Rondo to Train Counter-pressing................... 124
2. High Intensity 3 (+2) v 3 Pressing & Counter-pressing Possession Game 125
3. 4 (+2) v 4 Pressing & Counter-pressing Possession Game 126
4. 4 (+2) v 4 Possession Game with Intense Counter-pressing Focus 127
5. 3 (+2) v 3 (+2) Possession Game with "Free" Outside Support Players 128
6. High Intensity Pressing 4 (+2) v 4 Possession Game in Centre Circle 129
7. High Intensity Pressing 4 (+3) v 4 Possession Game in Centre Circle 130
8. Support Play + Continuous Pressing 4 (+6) v 4 Hexagon Possession Game............131
9. Pressing & Counter-pressing in a 3-Team 4 (+4) v 4 Possession Game 132
10. Dynamic 4 v 4 v 4 Three-Zone End to End Possession Game 133
11. Pressing and Counter-pressing in a 4 (+3) v 4 Positional Possession Game 134
12. Pressing and Counter-pressing in a 4 (+4) v 4 Positional Possession Game 135
13. Pressing and Counter-pressing in a 7 (+3) v 7 Positional Possession Game 136

JÜRGEN KLOPP'S ACHIEVEMENTS

COACHING ROLES

- **Liverpool F.C.** (2015 - Present)
- **Borussia Dortmund** (2008-2015)
- **Mainz 05** (2001 - 2008)

HONOURS (Europe / World)

- **UEFA Champions League** (2019)
- **UEFA Champions League Runner-up** (2013 & 2018)
- **UEFA Europa League Runner-up** (2016)
- **FIFA Club World Cup** (2019)
- **UEFA Super Cup** (2019)

HONOURS (Domestic Leagues)

- **English Premier League** (2020)
- **German Bundesliga x 2** (2011 & 2012)

HONOURS (Domestic Cups)

- **English FA Cup** (2022)
- **EFL Cup** (2022)
- **German DFB-Pokal** (2012)
- **German DFL-Supercup** (2013 & 2014)

INDIVIDUAL AWARDS

- **The Best FIFA Men's Coach** (2019 & 2020)
- **Onze d'Or Coach of the Year** (2019)
- **IFFHS World's Best Club Coach** (2019)
- **World Soccer Awards World Manager of the Year** (2019)
- **Premier League Manager of the Season** (2020)
- **LMA Manager of the Year** (2020)
- **BBC Sports Personality of the Year Coach Award** (2019)
- **German Football Manager of the Year** (2011, 2012 & 2019)

KLOPP'S TROPHIES AND RECORDS AT LIVERPOOL

2018-2019

UEFA Champions League

2019-2020

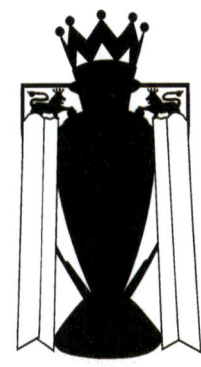

Premier League

UEFA Super Cup

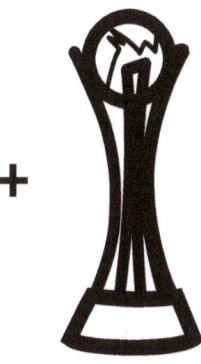

FIFA Club World Cup

In the 2018-2019 season, Jürgen Klopp's Liverpool team won the **UEFA Champions League** and also came close to winning the Premier League, finishing with a record breaking runner-up total of 97 points (losing only 1 game), just 1 point short of champions Manchester City. To win the UEFA Champions League, Liverpool beat **Bayern Munich**, **Porto**, **FC Barcelona**, and **Tottenham** with high intensity, attacking and exciting football.

In the 2019-2020 season, Jürgen Klopp's Liverpool team won the **UEFA Super Cup**, the **FIFA World Club Cup**, and the **Premier League** title with 7 games still to be played and another incredible points total of 99. Across these 2 Premier League seasons (2018/2019 & 2019/2020), Klopp's Liverpool had a record of 62 wins, 10 draws and only 4 losses (of which 2 losses were after they were already crowned Premier League Champions in 2020).

Jürgen Klopp's Liverpool have also achieved the following league records:

- Joint-record for **most Premier League wins in a season (32)** - 2019/2020.
- February 2019 to July 2020, Liverpool **won 24 consecutive Premier League home matches**.
- Joint-record for **most Premier League home wins in a season (18)** - 2019/2020.
- Joint-record for **fewest Premier League home defeats in a season (0)** - 2018/2019 and 2019/2020.
- October 2019 to February 2020, Liverpool **won 18 consecutive league matches**, a joint-record in English top-flight history.
- Liverpool remained **undefeated in 68 consecutive league games at home** (April 2017 - January 2021) - the third longest run in English top-flight history.

* Trophy images from PIXSECTOR.com

2021-2022

FA Cup + EFL Cup

In the 2021-2022 season, Jürgen Klopp's Liverpool team won the **FA Cup** and **EFL Cup** double, beating a strong Chelsea team in both finals.

They also came close to winning the Premier League again, finishing with another incredible total of 92 points after losing only 2 games, just 1 point short of champions Manchester City.

* Trophy images from **PIXSECTOR.com**

JÜRGEN KLOPP'S PHILOSOPHY:
BEST QUOTES

"Attack the opponent with, but especially without the ball - a chasing attitude over 95 minutes."

"Our way of playing is the central element in our training sessions."

"We have a team of 11 at a time, each of whom is an attacking forward and each of whom is a defender."

"We want to attack the opponent non-stop - when we have the ball, when we lose it and when the opposition have it."

"Fighting football, not serenity football - that is what I like."

"With a few new movements, with a few new passing options, you can change the whole game."

"He [Arsene Wenger] likes having the ball, playing football, passes. It's like an orchestra. But it's a silent song. I like heavy metal."

"Coaches will say that it's not important for their team to run more, and they prefer to make games the right way. I want to make games only the right way and run 10km more."

DIAGRAM KEY

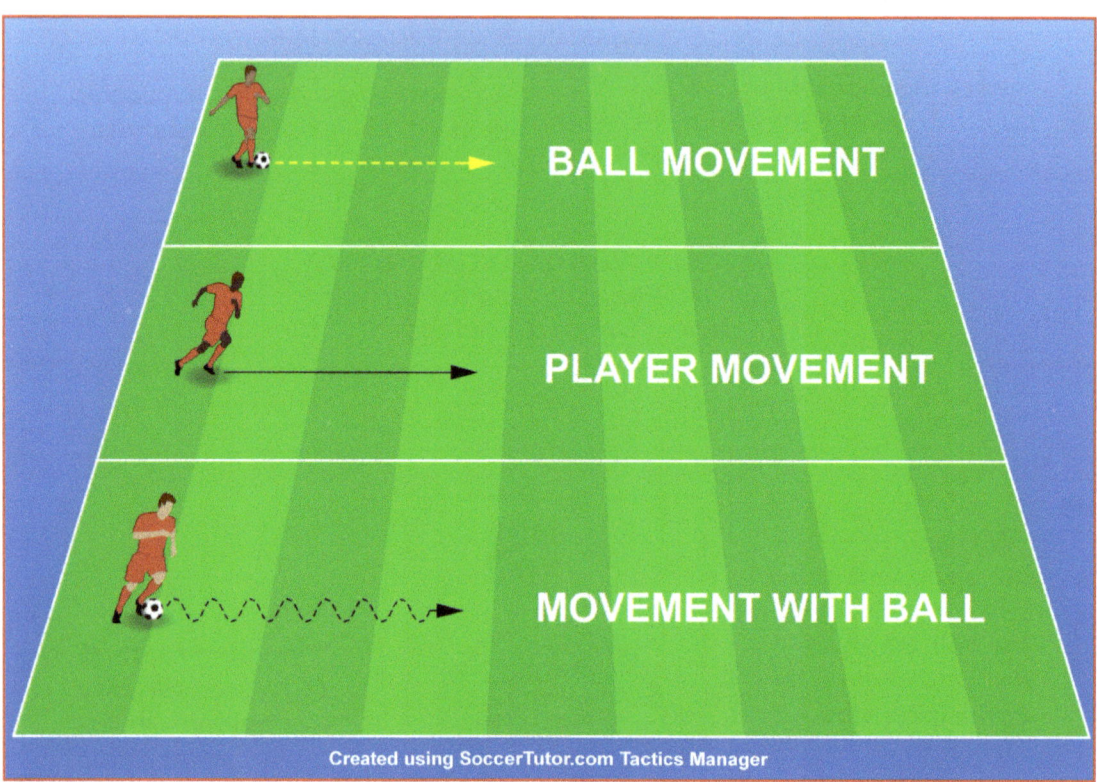

PRACTICE FORMAT

- The practices in this book are direct from Jürgen Klopp's training sessions at Liverpool F.C. between 2017 and 2022.
- Each practice includes the practice topic/name and clear diagrams with a detailed description.

Liverpool Pre-Match Warm-up

Direct from
Jürgen Klopp's
Training Sessions

©SOCCERTUTOR.COM

JÜRGEN KLOPP: PRACTICES FROM KLOPP'S SESSIONS

Jürgen Klopp Practices: Liverpool Pre-Match Warm-up

Liverpool Pre-Match Warm-up

Part 1/6. Individual Exercises and Passing in Groups

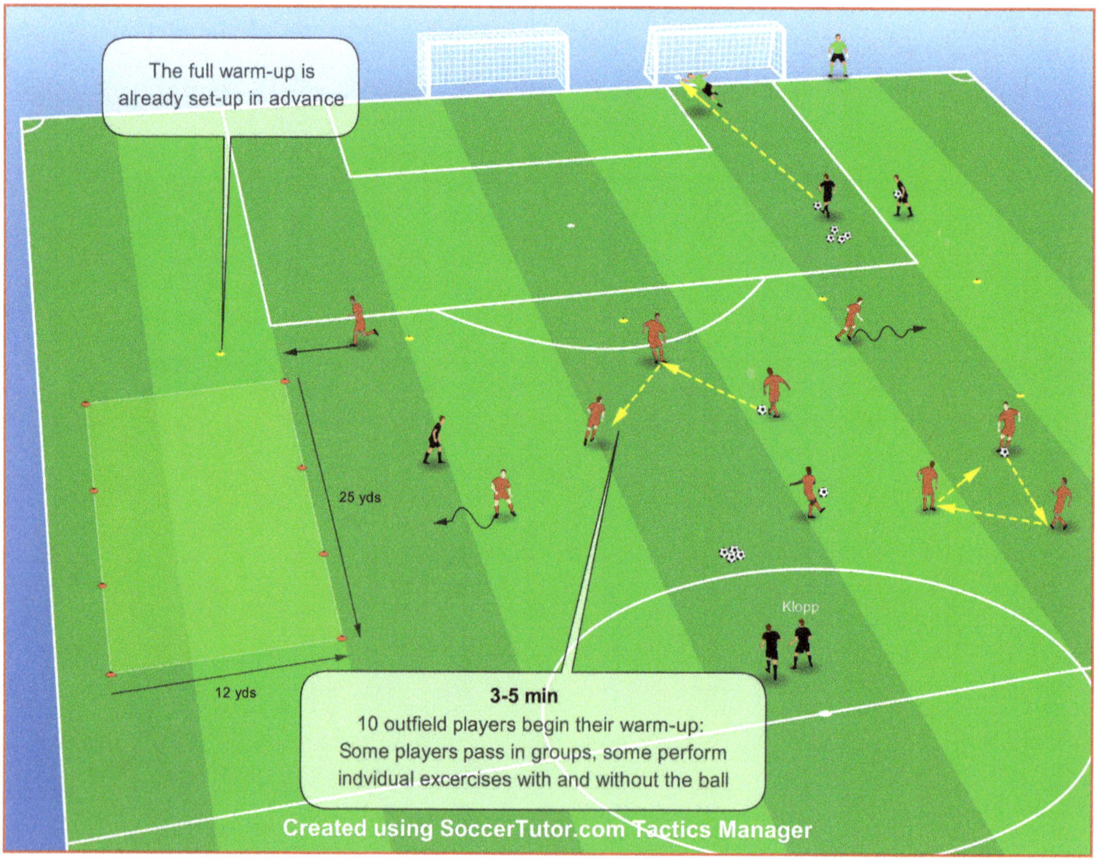

(Diagram: The full warm-up is already set-up in advance. 12 x 25 yds area marked. 3-5 min: 10 outfield players begin their warm-up: Some players pass in groups, some perform individual exercises with and without the ball. Klopp shown on pitch.)

Outfield Players

- The full warm-up is set up by the Liverpool coaches before the players enter the pitch, including a 12 x 25 yard area on one side of the pitch.

- The 10 outfield players starting the match spread out across the pitch. Some players perform individual warm-up exercises (with and without the ball).

- The other players are passing in groups.

- This phase of the warm-up lasts 3-5 minutes.

Goalkeepers

- The goalkeepers work with the GK Coaches and save shots at goal, as shown.

Source: Pre-match warm-up vs. Borussia Dortmund at Notre Dame Stadium, Indiana, USA - 20th July 2019

Jürgen Klopp Practices: Liverpool Pre-Match Warm-up

Part 2/6. Group Activation Exercises

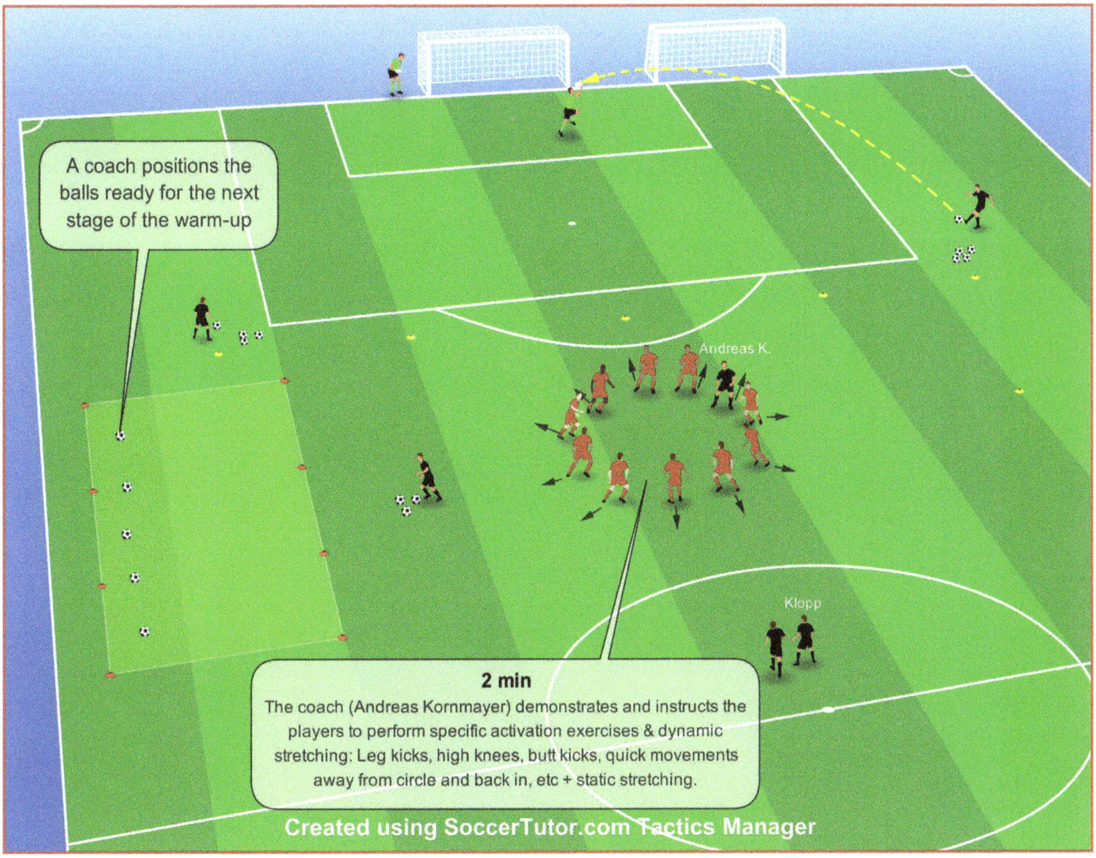

A coach positions the balls ready for the next stage of the warm-up

2 min
The coach (Andreas Kornmayer) demonstrates and instructs the players to perform specific activation exercises & dynamic stretching: Leg kicks, high knees, butt kicks, quick movements away from circle and back in, etc + static stretching.

Created using SoccerTutor.com Tactics Manager

Outfield Players

- The 10 outfield players gather in a circle in the middle of the pitch with Fitness and Conditioning Coach, Andreas Kornmayer.
- Andreas demonstrates and instructs the players to perform specific dynamic and static stretching, and activation exercises including leg kicks, high knees, butt kicks, and quick movements away from the circle and back in, etc.
- This phase of the warm-up lasts 2 minutes.
- A coach positions the balls within the marked out 12 x 25 yard area ready for phase 4/6 of the warm-up.

Goalkeepers

- The goalkeepers work with the GK Coaches and catch crosses, as shown.

Source: Pre-match warm-up vs. Borussia Dortmund at Notre Dame Stadium, Indiana, USA - 20th July 2019

JÜRGEN KLOPP: PRACTICES FROM KLOPP'S SESSIONS

Jürgen Klopp Practices: Liverpool Pre-Match Warm-up

Part 3/6. Functional Movements + Sprints

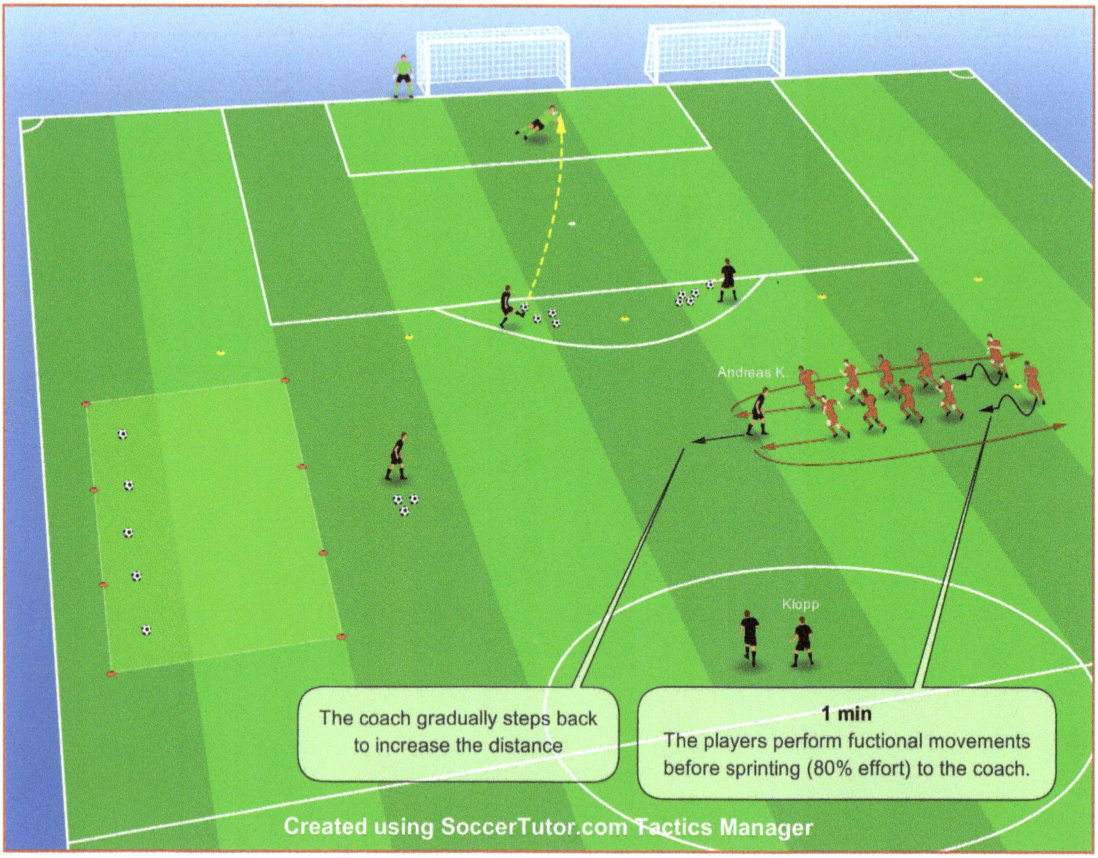

![Diagram of practice setup]

The coach gradually steps back to increase the distance

1 min
The players perform fuctional movements before sprinting (80% effort) to the coach.

Outfield Players

- The 10 outfield players form 2 lines either side of the yellow cone.
- The players work together in pairs, as shown.
- The players perform functional movements for a few yards and then sprint forward (80% speed) to the Coach.
- Fitness and Conditioning Coach, Andreas Kornmayer moves back a little after each repetition to gradually increase the sprint distance.
- This phase of the warm-up lasts 1 minute.

Goalkeepers

- The goalkeepers work with the GK Coaches and save shots at goal from just outside the penalty area, as shown.

Source: Pre-match warm-up vs. Borussia Dortmund at Notre Dame Stadium, Indiana, USA - 20th July 2019

Jürgen Klopp Practices: Liverpool Pre-Match Warm-up

Part 4/6. Passing in Pairs

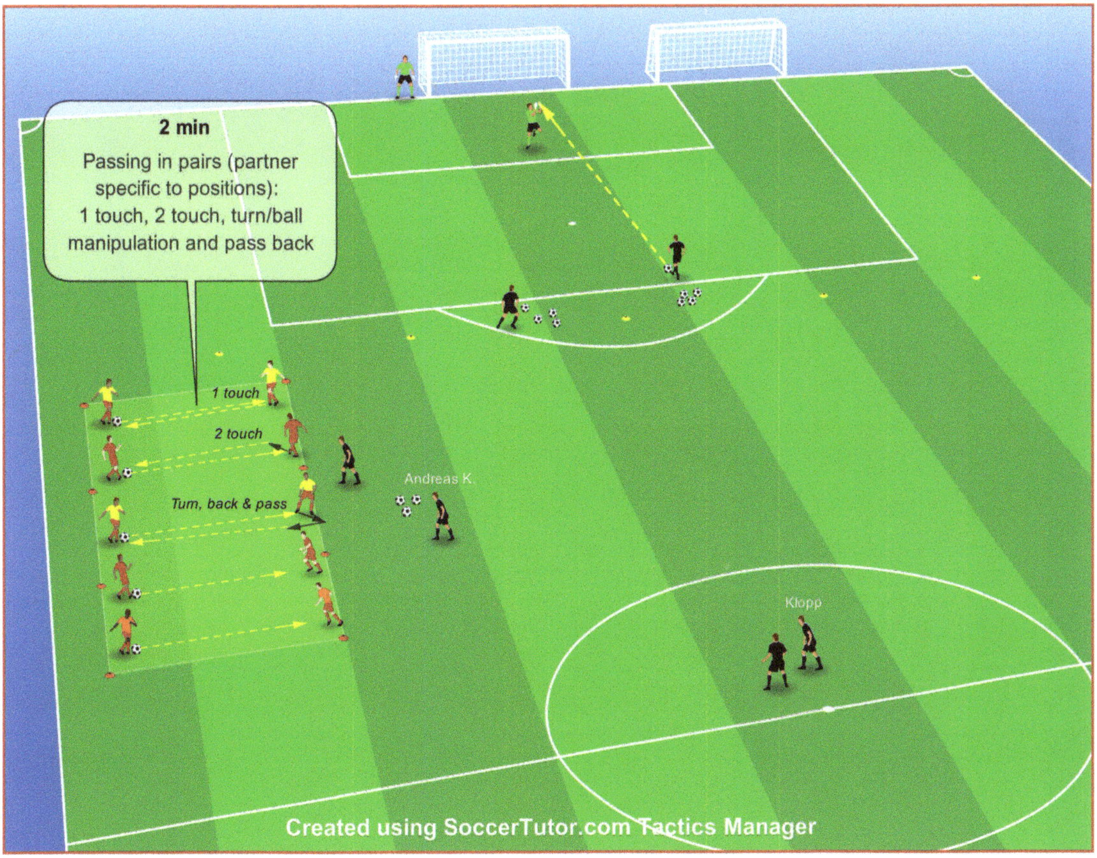

2 min
Passing in pairs (partner specific to positions):
1 touch, 2 touch, turn/ball manipulation and pass back

Outfield Players

- Within the marked out 12 x 25 yard area, the players are put into pairs and partnered to their specific positions.
- The players use a mixture of 1 touch passing, 2 touch passing (receive + pass), and receive, turn with ball manipulation and pass back.
- This phase of the warm-up lasts 2 minutes.

Goalkeepers

- The goalkeepers work with the GK and catch balls in the 6-yard area kicked from just inside the penalty area, as shown.

Source: Pre-match warm-up vs. Borussia Dortmund at Notre Dame Stadium, Indiana, USA - 20th July 2019

Jürgen Klopp Practices: Liverpool Pre-Match Warm-up

Part 5/6. 4 v 4 (+2) End to End Possession Game

3 min
4 v 4 + 2 End Game.
Mostly 1 and 2 touch.

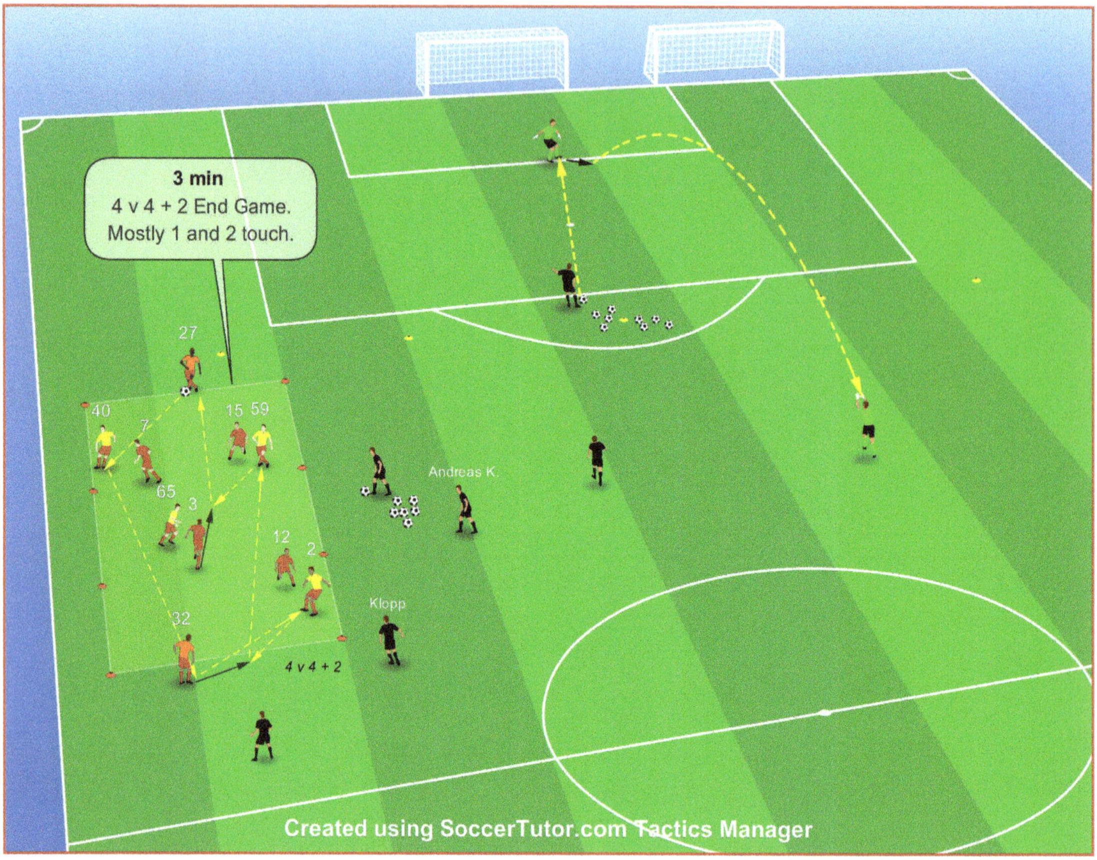

Outfield Players

- Within the marked out 12 x 25 yard area, the 10 outfield players play a **4 v 4 (+2) End to End Possession Game**.

- Klopp and 3 of his coaches observe and coach the players. The players mostly use 1 and 2 touches.

- One team starts (yellow bibs) and aims to maintain possession by moving the ball from end to end whilst utilising the 2 outside end players.

- When the reds win the ball, they have the same aim.

- The players in the yellow bibs then must make a fast transition to defence (counter-press) to try to win the ball back.

- This phase of the warm-up lasts 3 minutes.

Goalkeepers

- The GKs work together kicking and catching from a middle distance to each other, with help from the GK Coach.

Source: Pre-match warm-up vs. Borussia Dortmund at Notre Dame Stadium, Indiana, USA - 20th July 2019

Jürgen Klopp Practices: Liverpool Pre-Match Warm-up

Part 6/6. "3-Ball" Finishing Drill + Short Sharp Sprints

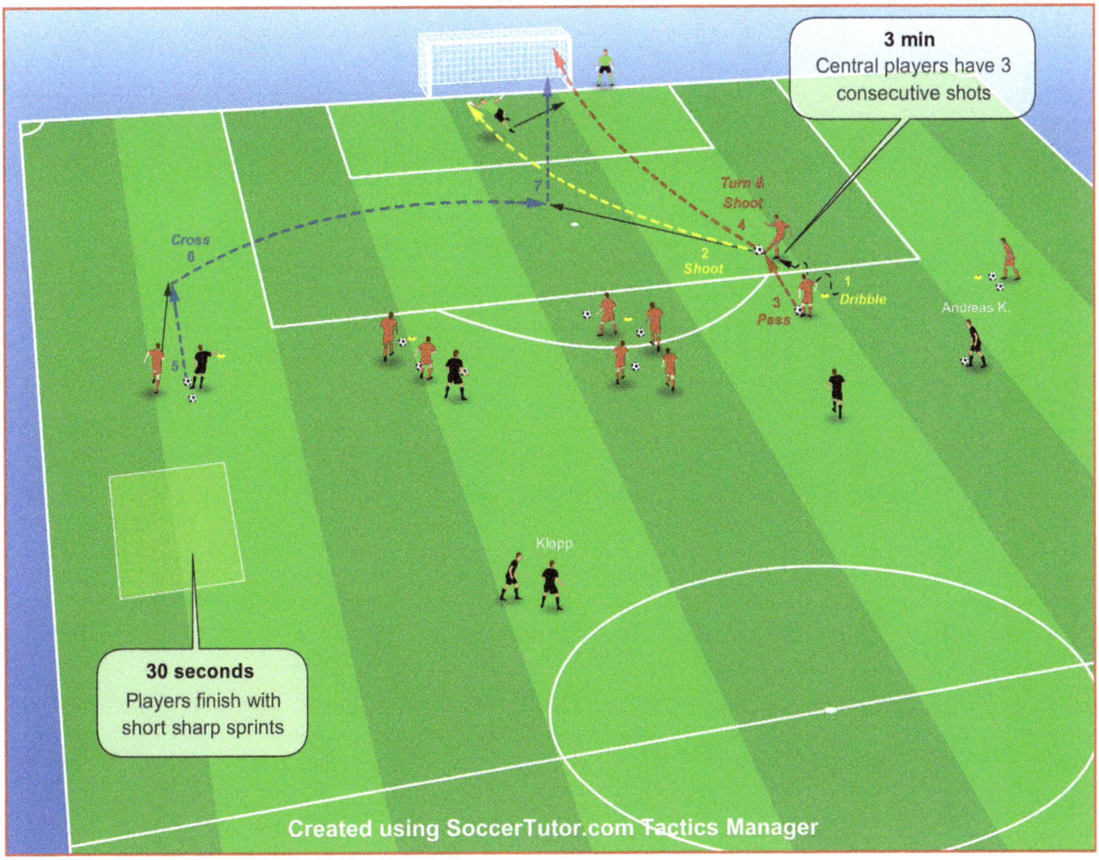

The full backs are positioned wide and the other 8 outfield players are positioned in 3 different central stations, each taking 3 consecutive shots as described below.

Description

1-2. The first central station player dribbles off their cone and shoots at goal.

3-4. They then receive a pass from their teammate or a coach, turn, and shoot again.

5-6. The Coach plays the ball ahead of the full back, for him to run onto and deliver a cross into the box.

7-8. The central player moves to meet the cross after his second shot and tries to score for a third time.

To conclude Liverpool's pre-match warm-up, the players perform short sharp sprints for 30 seconds within the area show, before leaving the pitch to go to the changing rooms.

Source: Pre-match warm-up vs. Borussia Dortmund at Notre Dame Stadium, Indiana, USA - 20th July 2019

Pre-season Training

Direct from
Jürgen Klopp's
Training Sessions

©SOCCERTUTOR.COM

JÜRGEN KLOPP: PRACTICES FROM KLOPP'S SESSIONS

Jürgen Klopp Practices: Pre-season Training

1. Receive, Turn, Feint, Dribble & Pass in an End to End Technical Practice

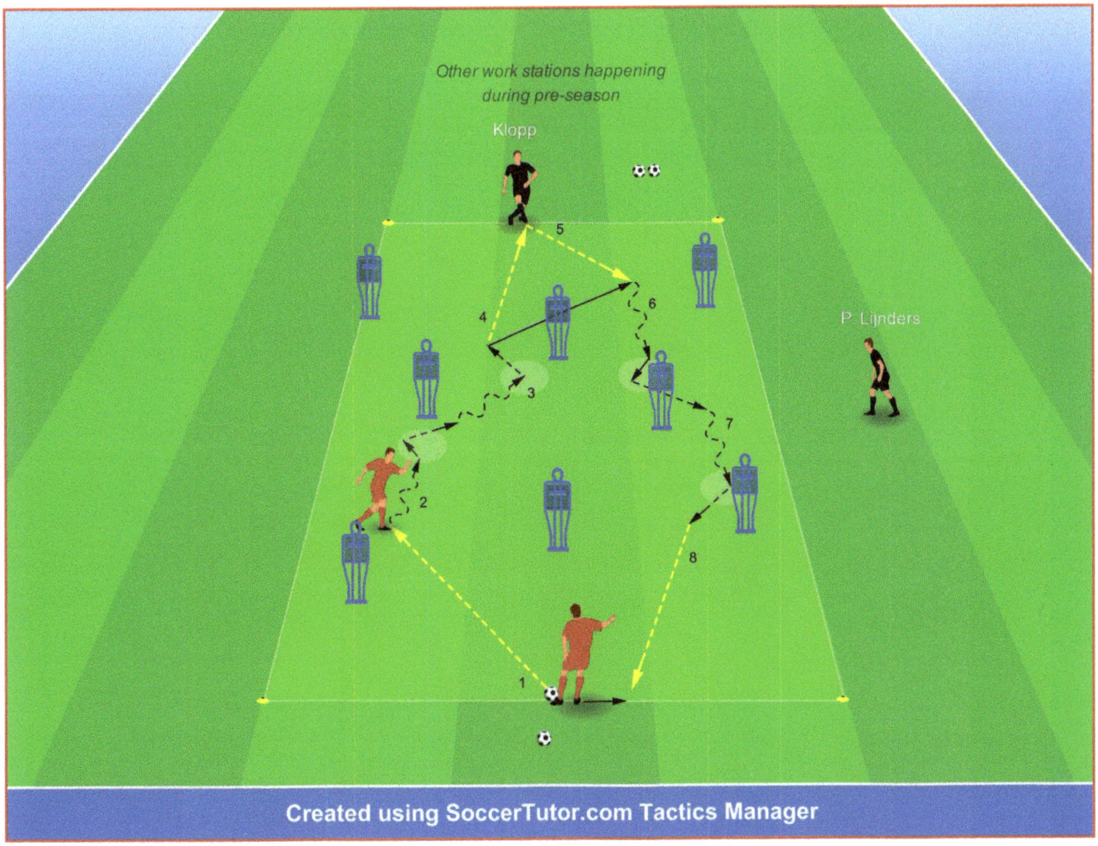

There are multiple stations set up for this practice done during pre-season.

Practice Description

1. The middle player checks away and then moves to receive from his teammate in between 2 mannequins.
2. He turns and moves forward with the ball.
3. The next step is to perform a feint and dribble past a mannequin (defender).
4. The middle player moves forward with the ball and passes to the Coach (Klopp in this example).
5-8. The exact same is repeated in the opposite direction, finishing with a pass to his teammate.

The player performs a few repetitions and then switches roles with his teammate.

Source: Jürgen Klopp's Liverpool training session at Melwood Training Ground, Liverpool - May 2020

Jürgen Klopp Practices: Pre-season Training

2. Pass and Score Quickly vs. Speed of Middle Player Game

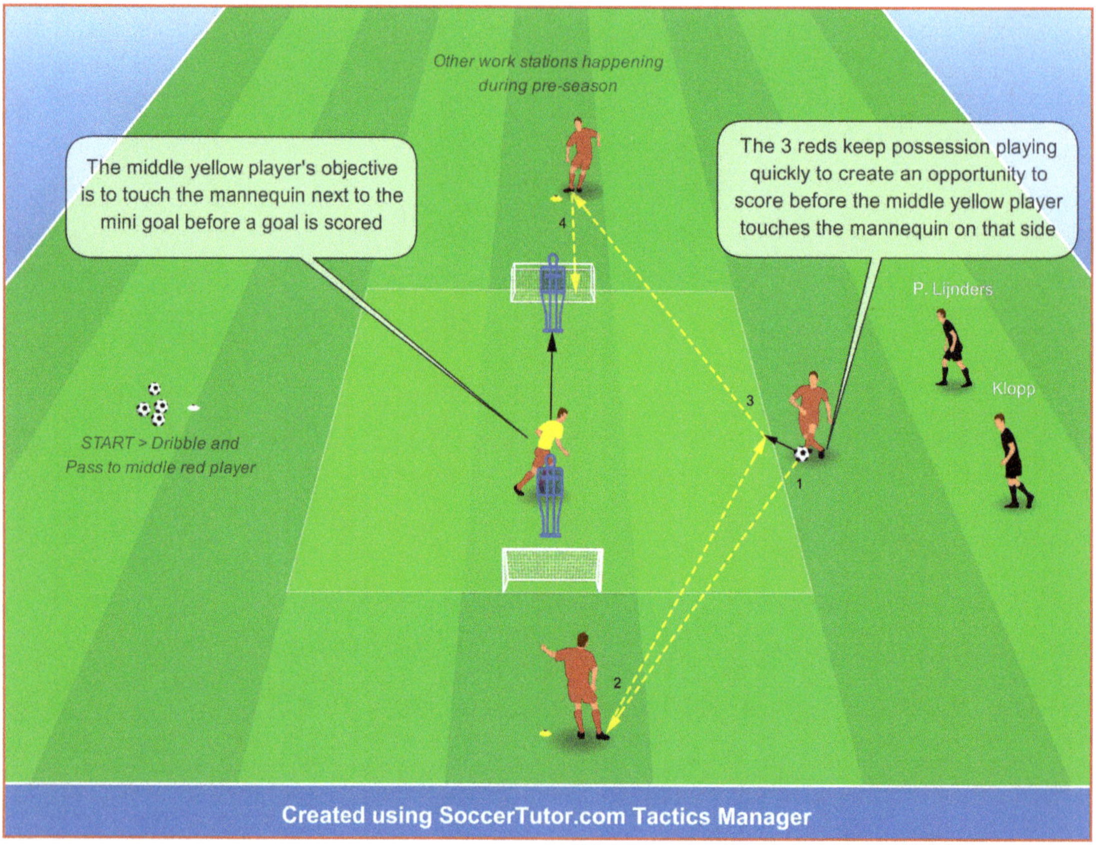

There are multiple stations set up for this practice done during pre-season.

Practice Description

1. The practice starts with the middle player (yellow bib) dribbling from the white cone and passing to the middle red player.

2. The 3 red players move the ball quickly between each other, trying to score in a mini goal before the yellow middle player can touch the mannequin next to the goal. The emphasis is on trying to move the ball quickly from one side to the other to beat the middle player.

3. The middle player's aim is to touch the mannequin before a goal is scored in the mini goal on that side, so he must keep alert to where the ball is at all times and react quickly with speed.

NOTE: Change the middle player often.

Source: Jürgen Klopp's Liverpool training session at Melwood Training Ground, Liverpool - May 2020

Jürgen Klopp Practices: Pre-season Training

3. Juggle, Pick-up Bibs + First to Score in a Speed Race Game

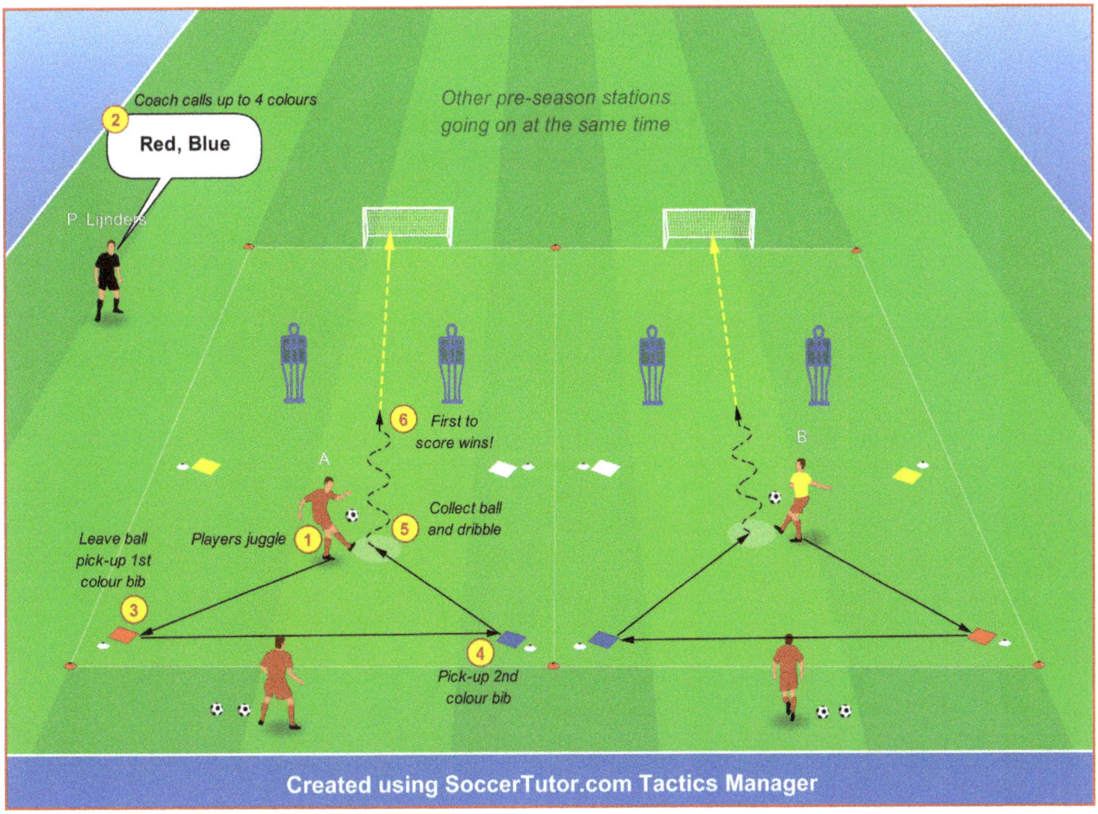

There are multiple stations set up for this practice done during pre-season.

Practice Description

1. The players start by juggling in the area, with any technique of their choosing.

2. The Coach then calls out 1, 2, 3, or 4 colours. In this example, 2 colours are called out: Red and Blue.

3. The player runs to pick up the red bib.

4. He then runs to pick up the blue bib.

5. Some players take the ball with them when picking up the bibs and other players run back to the ball after leaving it in the middle of the area. They collect the ball and dribble forward up to the mannequins.

6. As shown, the players compete with the players in the stations next to them to see who scores first!

Source: Jürgen Klopp's Liverpool training session at Melwood Training Ground, Liverpool - May 2020

Jürgen Klopp Practices: Pre-season Training

4. Pass, Receive, and Dribble in a Double Triangle Connected Circuit

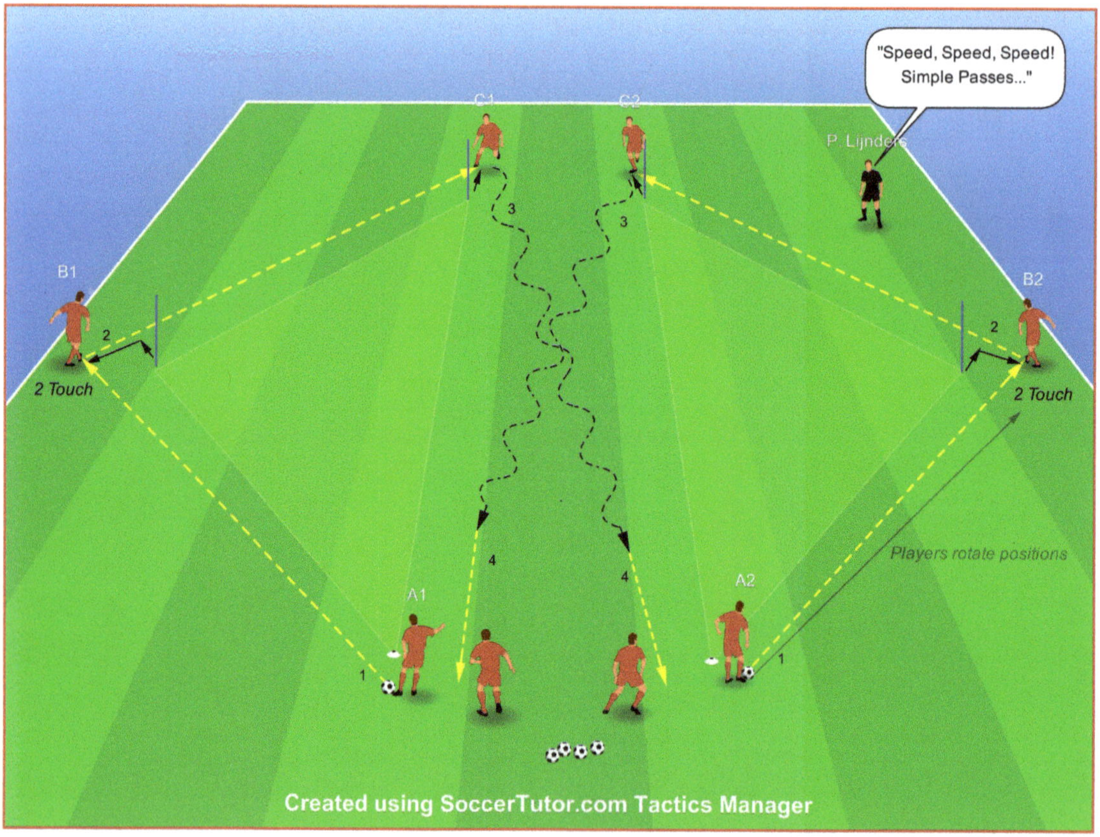

There are 2 triangles set-up in a mirror image of each other as shown, playing their sequences at the exact same time.

Practice Description

1. **A1/A2** pass diagonally to **B1/B2**, who checks off the pole and drops off at an angle to receive.
2. **B1/B2** pass diagonally to **C1/C2**, who move forward off the pole to receive beyond it.
3. **C1/C2** dribble diagonally towards the opposite group.
4. They then pass to the player waiting in the opposite group.
5. The players rotate to the next position (**A → B → C → Opposite Group**).
6. The next player waiting continues the practice in the exact same way.

Source: Jürgen Klopp's Liverpool pre-season training session in Salzburg, Austria - July 2022

Jürgen Klopp Practices: Pre-season Training

5. One-Twos on the Run in a Double Triangle Connected Circuit

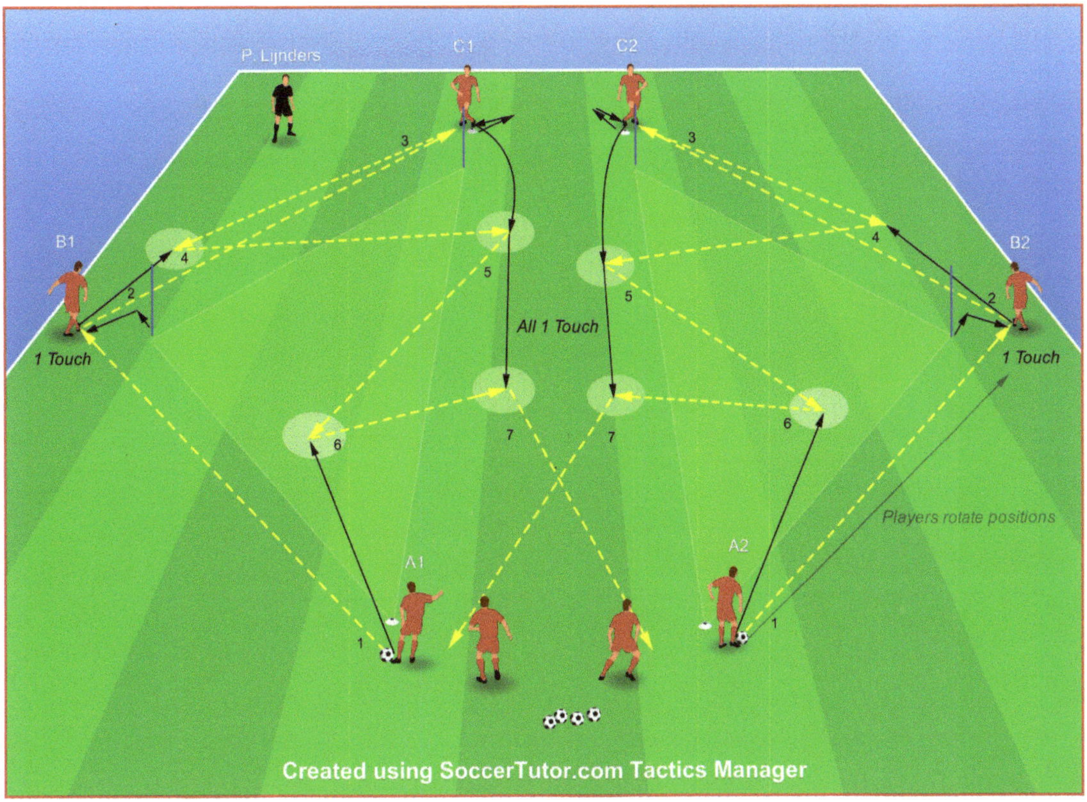

This is a variation of the previous practice.

Practice Description

1. **A1/A2** pass diagonally to **B1/B2**, who check off the pole and drop off at an angle to play the next pass first time.

2. **B1/B2** pass diagonally to **C1/C2**, who move forward off the pole to receive beyond it.

3. **C1/C2** pass back to **B1/B2**, who move forward to receive and complete the one-two.

4. **B1/B2** pass across for the run of **C1/C2** around the pole.

5. **C1/C2** pass inside for the forward run of **A1/A2**.

6. **A1/A2** complete the one-two for **C1/C2** on the run.

7. **C1/C2** pass to the player waiting in the opposite group.

8. The players rotate to the next position (A → B → C → **Opposite Group**).

9. The next players waiting continue.

Source: Jürgen Klopp's Liverpool pre-season training session in Salzburg, Austria - July 2022

Jürgen Klopp Practices: Pre-season Training

6. Pass and Move to Receive, Dribble Through Poles + Target Goal

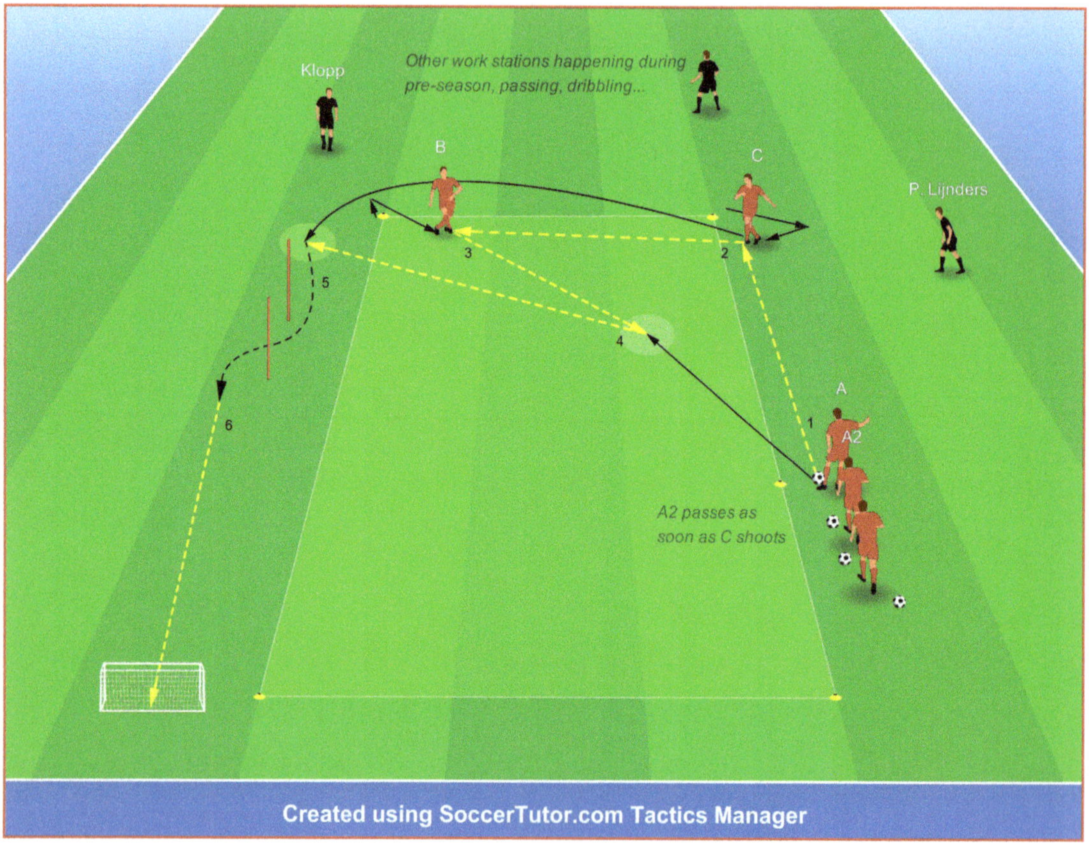

There are multiple stations set up for this practice done during pre-season.

Practice Description

1. **A** passes forward to **C**, who checks away before moving to receive.
2. **C** passes across to **B**, who also checks before receiving.
3. **B** passes back for the forward run of **A**.
4. Player **A** plays a well-timed diagonal pass for the run of **C** outside the area and around **B's** cone.
5. **C** dribbles the ball through the poles.
6. **C** passes into the target goal.
7. The players rotate to the next position (**A → B → C → A**).
8. **A2** continues with the next pass as soon as **C** shoots.

Source: Jürgen Klopp's Liverpool pre-season training session in Salzburg, Austria - August 2020

Jürgen Klopp Practices: Pre-season Training

7. Pre-season Passing Circuit with One-Twos + Pass into Target Goal

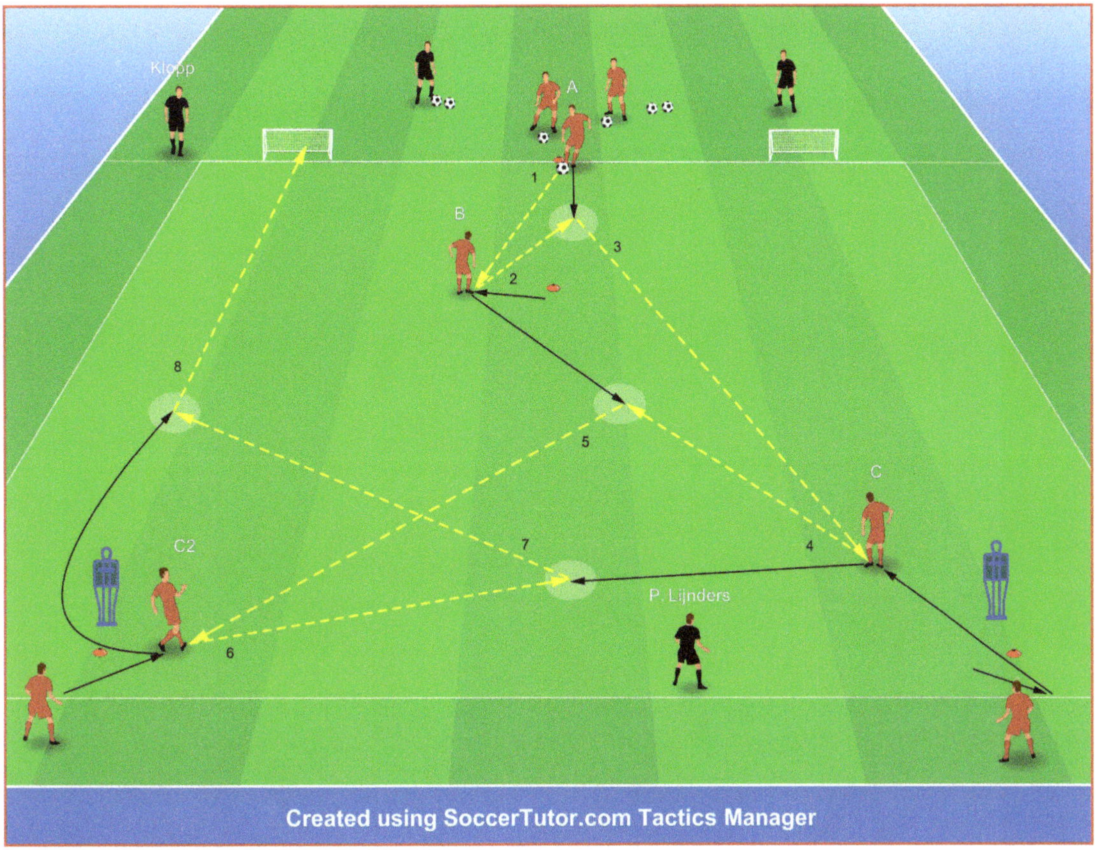

Practice Description

1. **A** passes to **B** (either side).

2. **B** returns the pass to **A**, who moves forward to receive and complete the one-two.

3. **A** passes diagonally to **C** (or **C2** if playing from other side), who checks and drops back/inside to receive.

4. **C** plays the ball back for **B** to receive on the run.

5. **B** passes diagonally to **C2**, who moves in front of the mannequin.

6. **C2** plays the ball for **C** to receive on the run.

7. **C** delivers the final pass timed for **C2's** run around the mannequin.

8. **C2** scores in the mini goal.

9. The players rotate to the next position (A → B → C → C2 → A) and the practice continues.

Source: Jürgen Klopp's Liverpool training session at Ramon Sanchez-Pizjuan Stadium, Seville - July 2017

Jürgen Klopp Practices: Pre-season Training

8. Various Attacking Combinations in Threes with the Coach's Signal

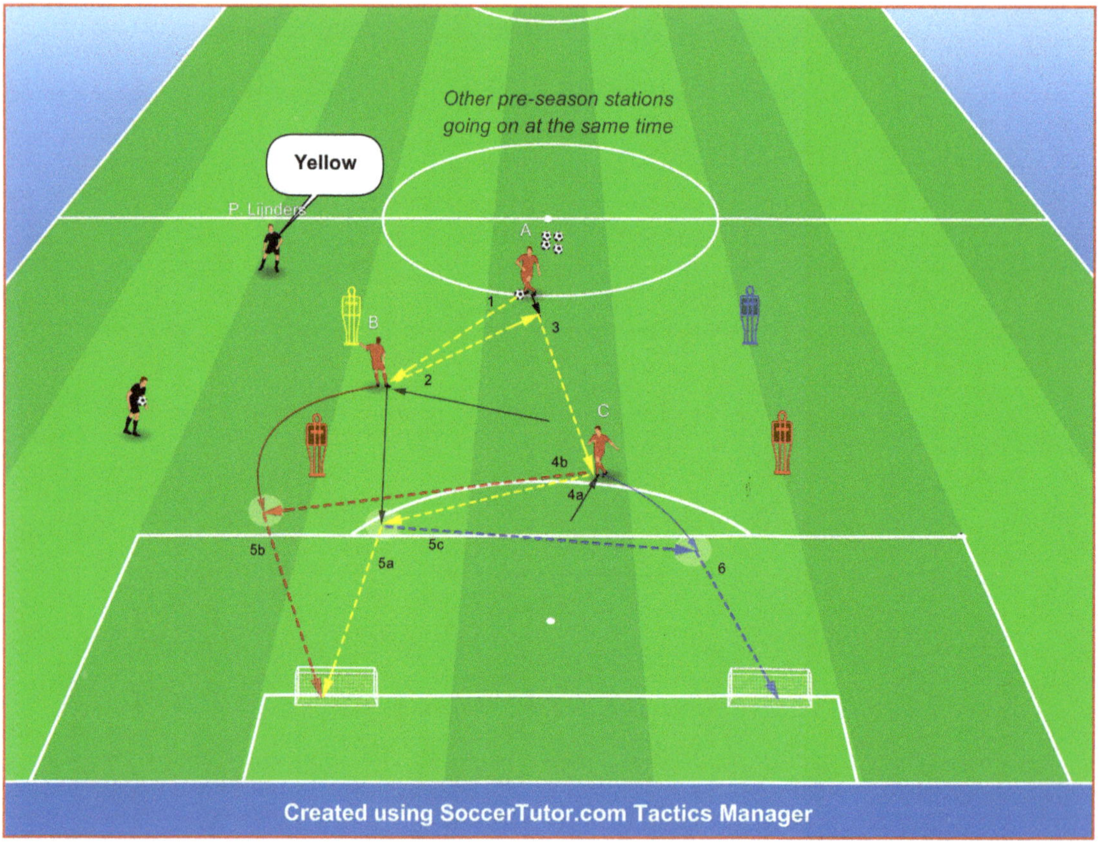

There are multiple stations set up for this practice done during pre-season.

Practice Description

1. The Coach calls out a colour which relates to the yellow, blue, red, and orange mannequins. **Player B** moves to that colour mannequin (yellow) to receive the first pass from **Player A**.

2. **Players A, B & C** then perform different attacking combination patterns which result in scoring in one of the mini goals. In the diagram, there are 3 variations shown (yellow, red & blue arrows).

3. The players rotate their positions (**A → B → C > A**) and the practice continues with the Coach calling out a new colour mannequin.

Source: Jürgen Klopp's Liverpool training session at Melwood Training Ground, Liverpool - May 2020

Warm-up Exercises WITHOUT a Ball

Direct from
Jürgen Klopp's
Training Sessions

Jürgen Klopp Practices: Warm-up Exercises WITHOUT a Ball

1. Mobility Warm-up Circuit with Stretching + Speed & Agility Work (1)

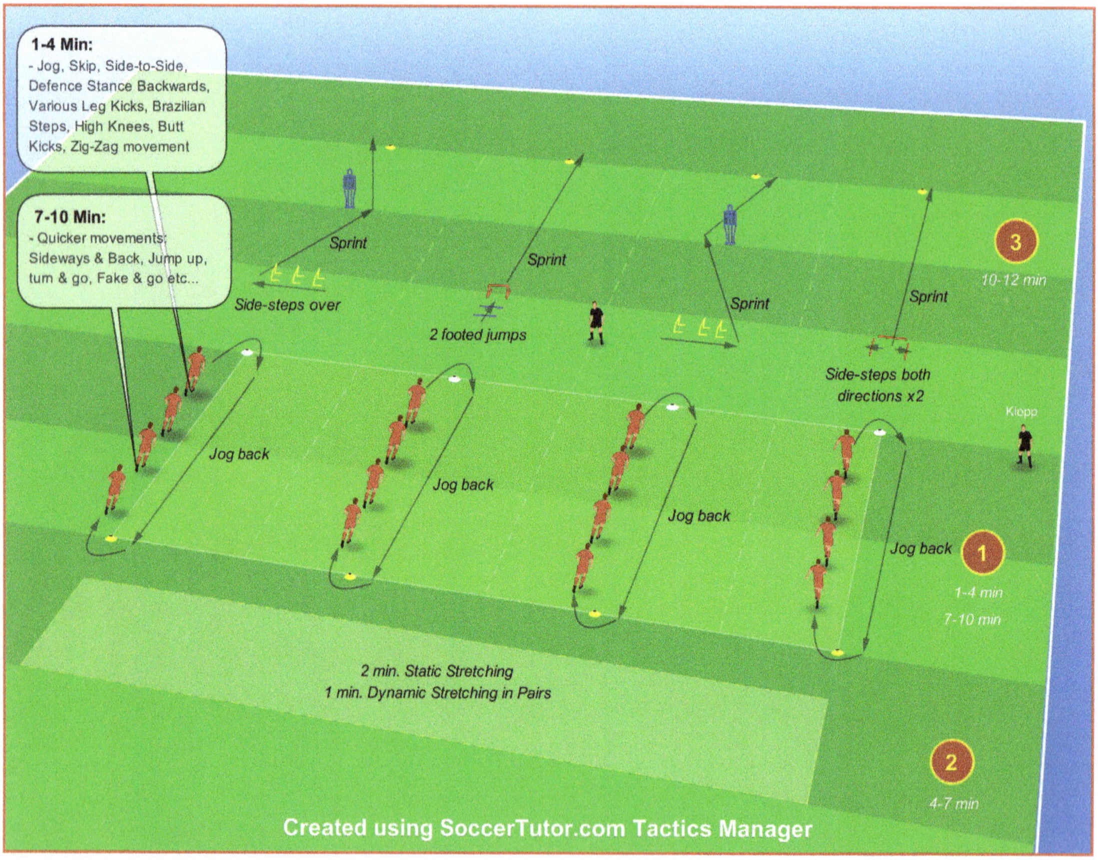

Practice Description

1-4 min. The players are in 4 groups and perform exercises from the yellow cone to the white cone, and then jog back to the yellow cone. The exercises include jogging, skipping, side-to-side, backwards defensive stance, various leg kicks, Brazilian steps, high knees, butt kicks, and zig-zag movements.

4-7 min. 2 minutes of static stretching and 1 minute of dynamic stretching in pairs.

7-10 min. Perform quicker movements/exercises in between the yellow and white cone including a sideways and back movement, jump up, turn & go, fake & go, etc.

10-12 min. The 4 groups line up across the 4 speed and agility stations and move through all of them one by one.

Source: Jürgen Klopp's Liverpool training session at Melwood Training Ground, Liverpool - March 2018

Jürgen Klopp Practices: Warm-up Exercises WITHOUT a Ball

2. Mobility Warm-up Circuit with Stretching + Speed & Agility Work (2)

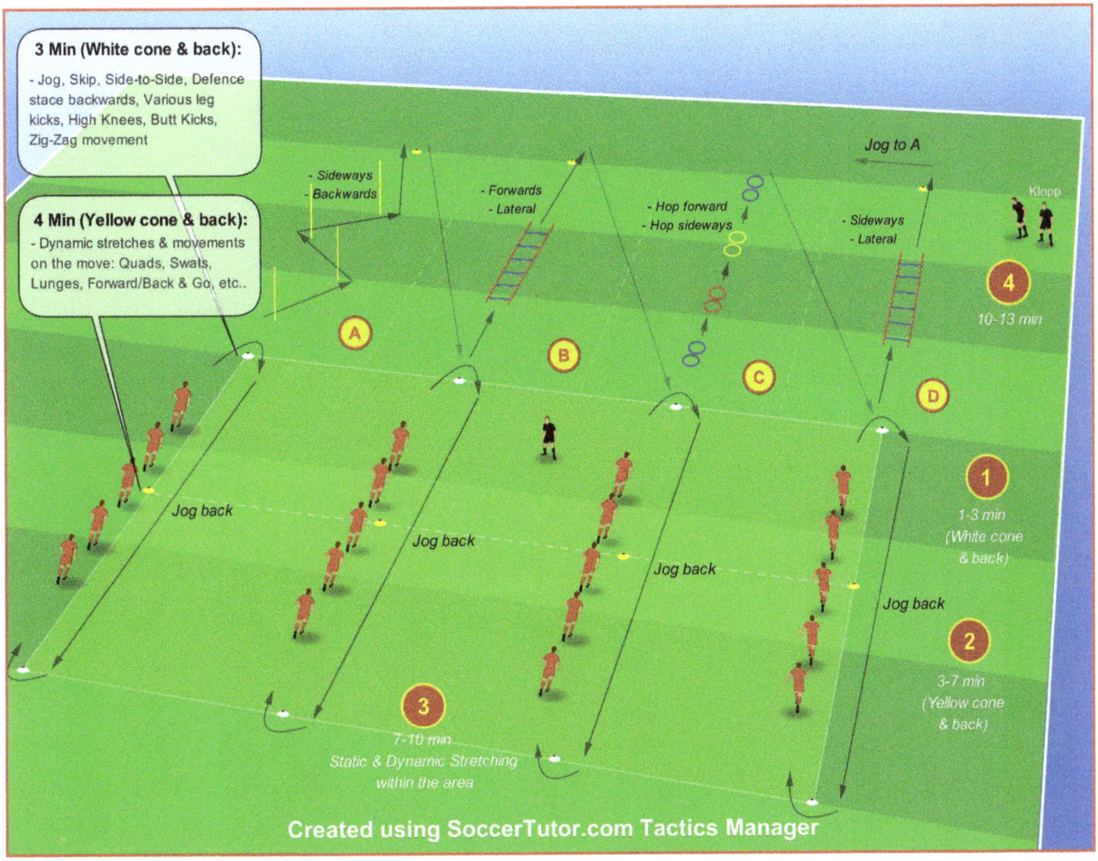

Practice Description

1-3 min. The players are in 4 groups and perform exercises between the 2 white cones. The exercises include jogging, skipping, side-to-side, backwards defensive stance, various leg kicks, high knees, butt kicks, and zig-zag movements.

3-7 min. Between the white and yellow cone, the players perform dynamic stretches/movements on the move including quads, squats, lunges, forward/back & go, etc.

7-10 min. Static stretching and dynamic stretching within the area.

10-13 min. The 4 groups line up across the 4 speed and agility stations and move through all of them one by one (**A → B → C → D → A**).

Source: Jürgen Klopp's Liverpool training session at Melwood Training Ground, Liverpool - September 2018

Jürgen Klopp Practices: Warm-up Exercises WITHOUT a Ball

3. Speed Warm-up Circuit + Static Stretching

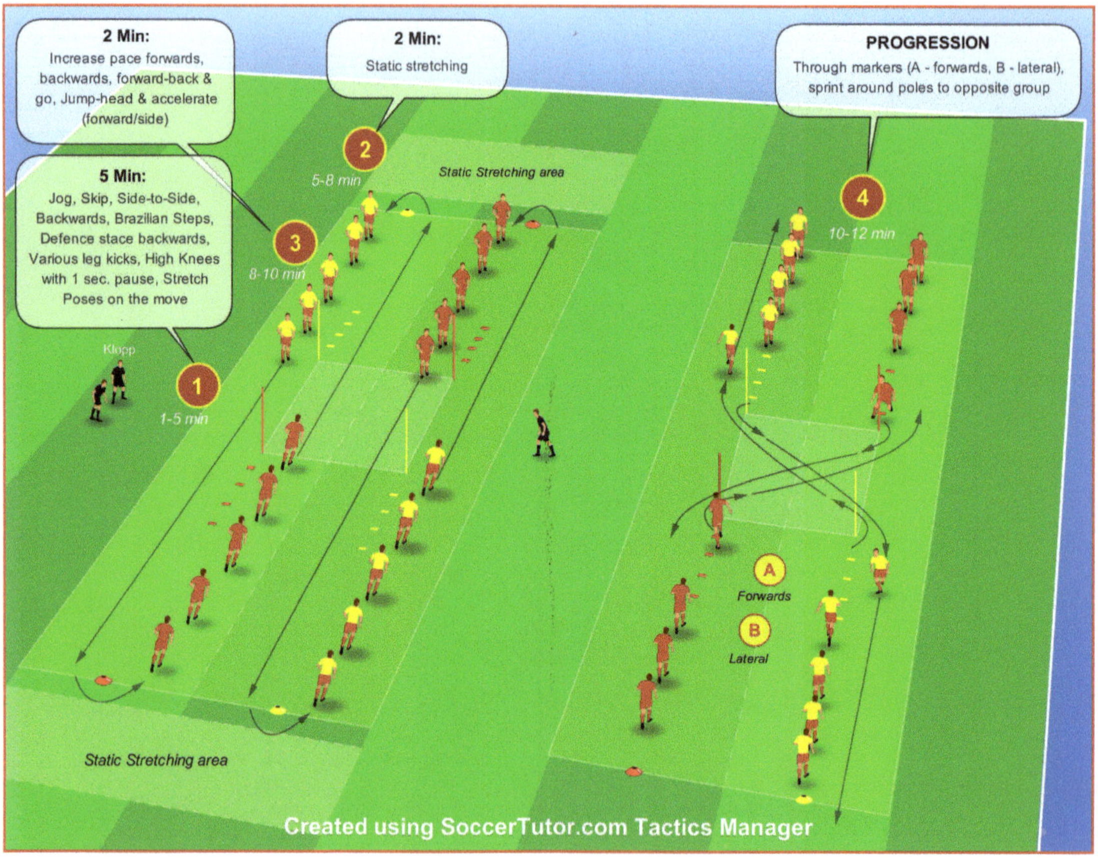

Practice Description

1-5 min. The players are in 4 groups and perform exercises around the yellow and red cones as shown. The exercises include jogging, skipping, side-to-side, backwards, Brazilian steps, backwards defensive stance, various leg kicks, high knees with 1 second pause, and stretch poses on the move.

5-8 min. The players do static stretching in the areas at either end.

8-10 min. The players now perform exercises at a higher speed, running forward, backwards, forward-back & go, jump up to head and accelerate (forward/side).

10-12 min. Progression A = Quick forward steps through the ground markers and sprint around the poles towards the diagonally opposite group, as shown.
Progression B = They do the same with quick lateral steps through the markers.

Source: Jürgen Klopp's Liverpool training session at Melwood Training Ground, Liverpool - October 2018

Jürgen Klopp Practices: Warm-up Exercises WITHOUT a Ball

4. Speed Warm-up with Quick Feet + Physical Duel

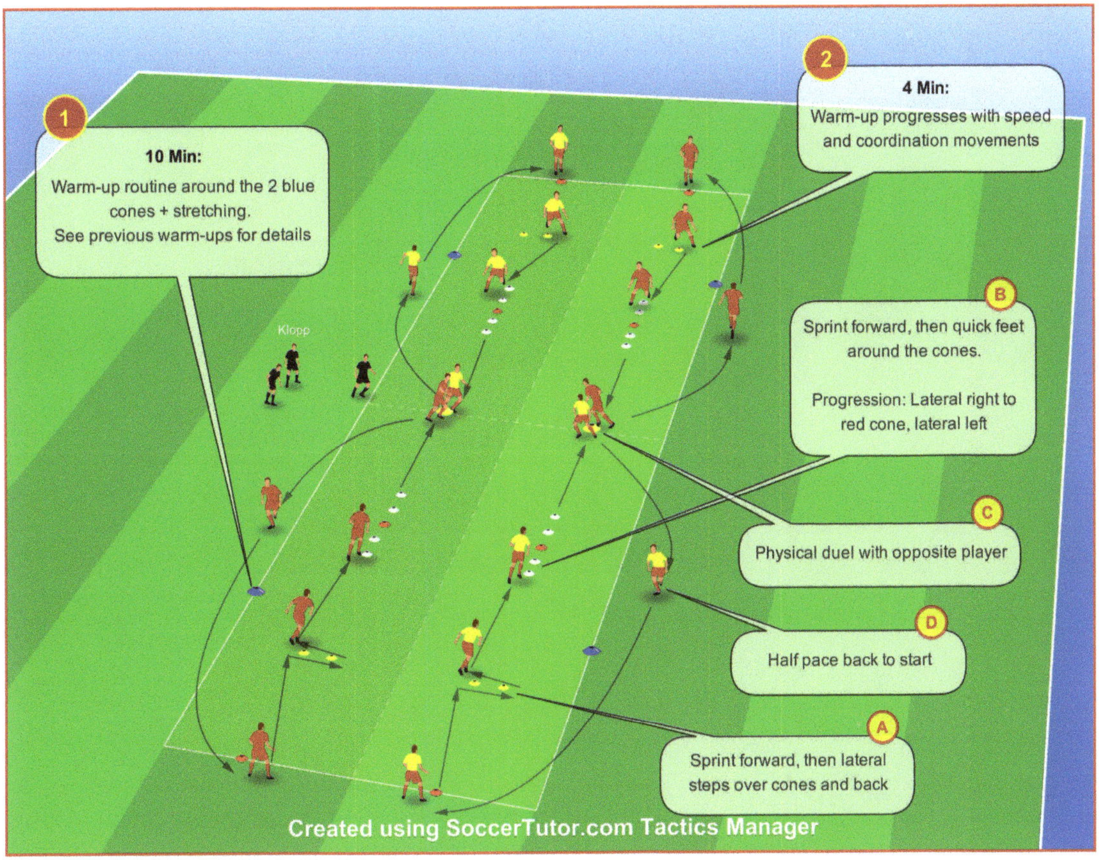

1 — 10 Min: Warm-up routine around the 2 blue cones + stretching. See previous warm-ups for details

2 — 4 Min: Warm-up progresses with speed and coordination movements

B — Sprint forward, then quick feet around the cones. Progression: Lateral right to red cone, lateral left

C — Physical duel with opposite player

D — Half pace back to start

A — Sprint forward, then lateral steps over cones and back

Practice Description

Part 1 (10 min).

The players are in 4 groups and perform a full warm-up routine around the blue cones. The warm-up includes jogging, skipping, side-to-sides, backwards defensive stance, various leg kicks, high knees, butt kicks, zig-zag movements, static stretching, dynamic stretching, jump up, turn & go, fake & go, etc.

Part 2 (4 min).

A = Sprint forward, lateral steps over the 2 cones and then back.

B = Sprint forward, quick feet around the 5 cones.

C = Physical duel with opposite player (shoulder to shoulder).

D = Half pace run back to start and continue.

Source: Jürgen Klopp's Liverpool pre-season training session in Salzburg, Austria - July 2022

Jürgen Klopp Practices: Warm-up Exercises WITHOUT a Ball

5. Coordination Warm-up with Dynamic Jumps and Movements

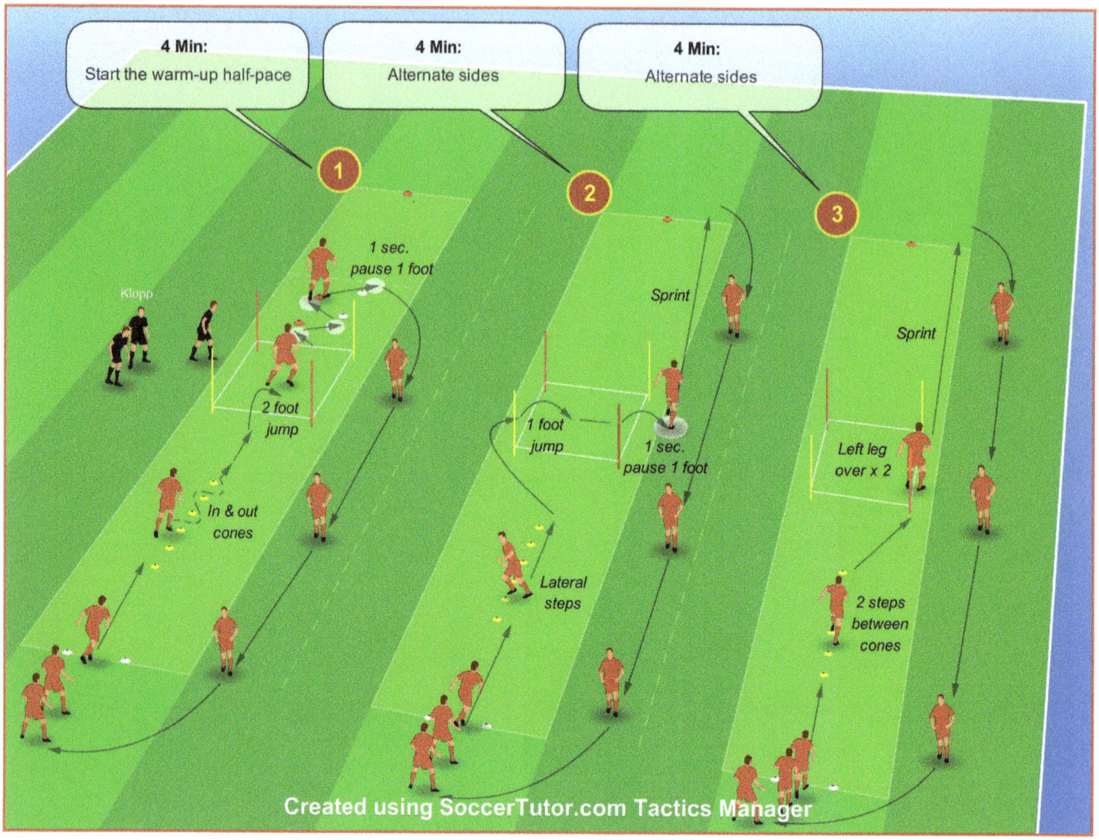

The 4 pole square has rope all around which is 5-8 cm off the ground.

Practice Description

1-4 min. The players use short quick steps in and out of 6 cones. They then make a 2-footed jump into the middle square and complete the sequence with 1 second pauses on alternate feet through the 4 cones + walk back to the start.

5-8 min. Quick lateral steps through the 6 cones, move to left side and make a 1-footed jump into the middle square, pause on 1 foot to exit the square + sprint to the end before walking back to the start. Alternate sides (move to right of middle square) on the next repetition.

8-12 min. 2 quick lateral steps between each of the 6 cones, move to left side and touch the left foot down twice in the middle square + sprint to the end before walking back to the start. Alternate sides (move to left of middle square) on the next repetition.

Source: Jürgen Klopp's Liverpool training session at AXA Training Centre, Liverpool - July 2022

Jürgen Klopp Practices: Warm-up Exercises WITHOUT a Ball

6. Dynamic Warm-up Circuit with All Types of Movements & Obstacles

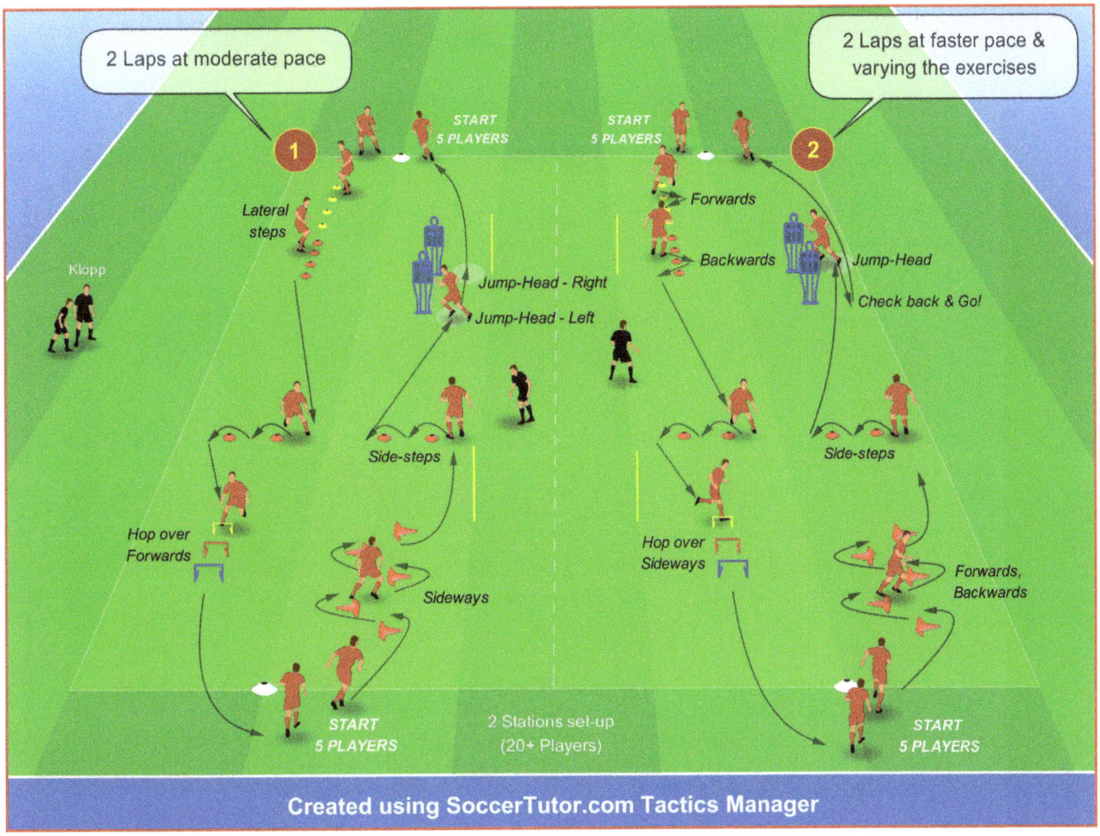

The circuit is exactly duplicated on both sides and the players all start at the same time divided into 4 groups in each corner.

Practice Description

1. Move sideways through the large cones, which are on their side.
2. Side-steps over the 2 cones.
3. Jump up and gesture to head towards the left at the first mannequin.
4. Repeat towards the right.
5. Run to opposite starting point.
6. Lateral steps through the cones.
7. Run forward + side-steps over the 2 cones.
8. Hop over the 3 hurdles forward, which increase in size (smallest to largest).
9. Repeat so that 2 laps have been completed.
10. 2 more laps with varied exercises described in the diagram.

Source: Jürgen Klopp's Liverpool training session at AXA Training Centre, Liverpool - July 2022

Warm-up Exercises WITH a Ball

Direct from
Jürgen Klopp's
Training Sessions

Jürgen Klopp Practices: Warm-up Exercises WITH a Ball

1. Technical Ball Control Warm-up with Various Stations

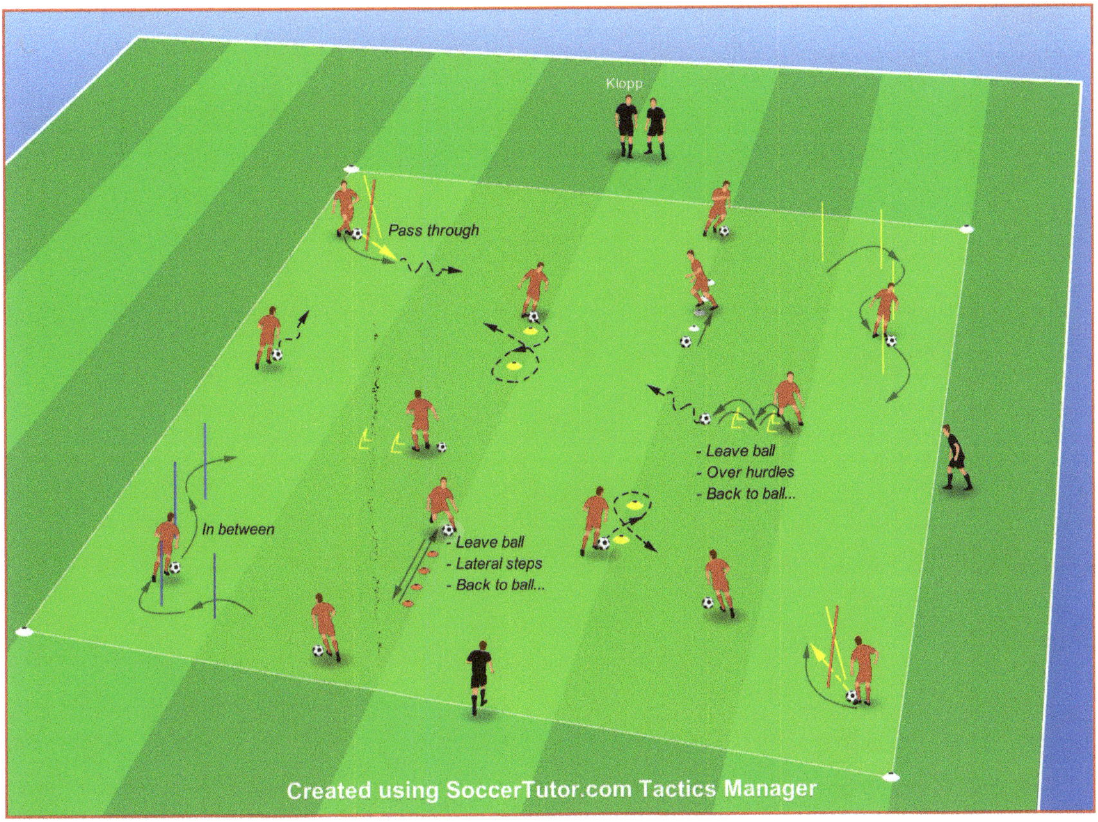

Practice Description

- The players all have a ball and move freely around the area. They perform different types of technical and speed/agility actions for this warm-up.
- **4 Poles** = Dribble in between them.
- **4 Small Cones** = Leave the ball, use lateral steps one way and then back to the ball.
- **2 Large Cones** = Dribble in between and back through.
- **2 Crossed Poles** = Pass in between the poles and move around them to collect the ball.
- **2 Hurdles** = Leave the ball, lateral jumps over hurdles and lateral jumps back to the ball.

Source: Jürgen Klopp's Liverpool training session at AXA Training Centre, Liverpool - December 2021

Jürgen Klopp Practices: Warm-up Exercises WITH a Ball

2. Speed of Movement Warm-up with Volleys and Headers

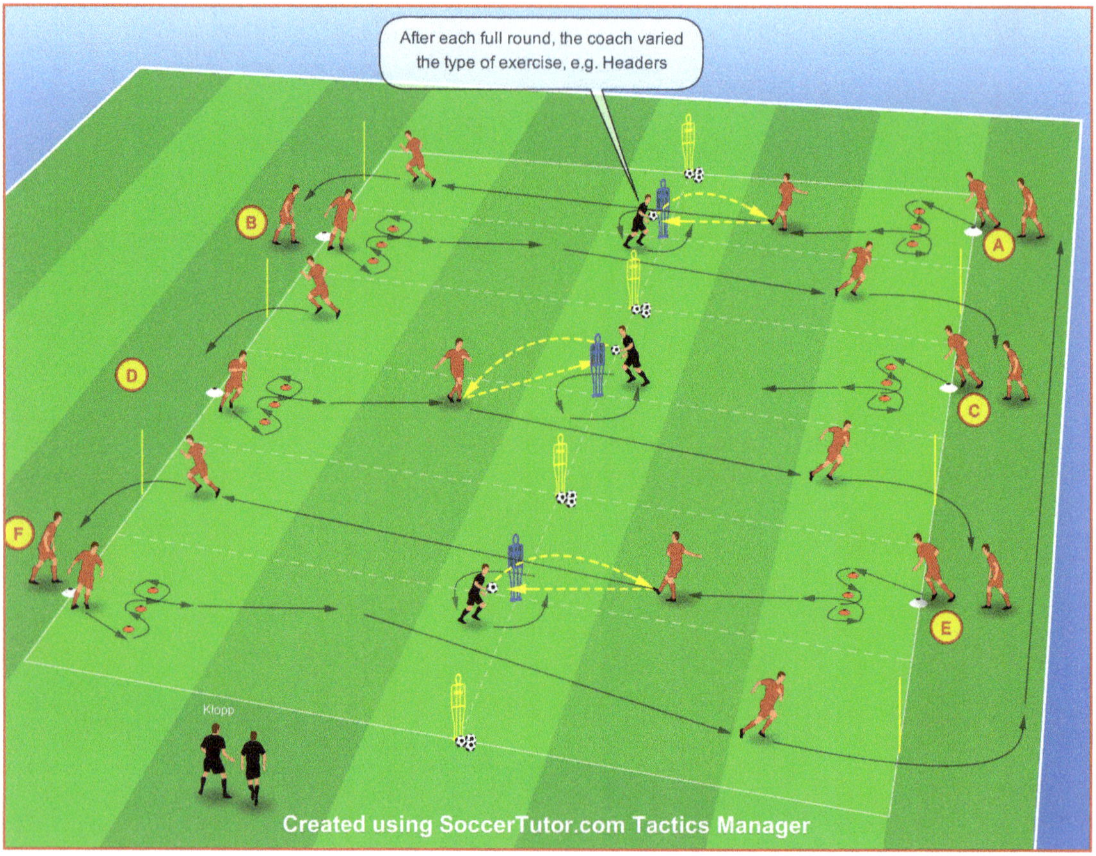

After each full round, the coach varied the type of exercise, e.g. Headers

The players work in groups and start from both ends, as shown. The coach in the middle serves players coming from both sides.

Practice Description

1. Perform quick forward and backward steps through the 3 cones.

2. Move forward and the Coach in the middle throws the ball for the players to volley back first time into his hands.

3. Complete the sequence by running around the pole at the end and joining the opposite group e.g. **A → B**.

4. The next step is to repeat the same sequence in the opposite direction.

5. The players move to the next group after each repetition:

   A → B → C → D → E → F → A

Source: Jürgen Klopp's Liverpool training session at AXA Training Centre, Liverpool - May 2022

Jürgen Klopp Practices: Warm-up Exercises WITH a Ball

3. Dynamic Movements, Speed and Quick One-Twos Warm-up Circuit

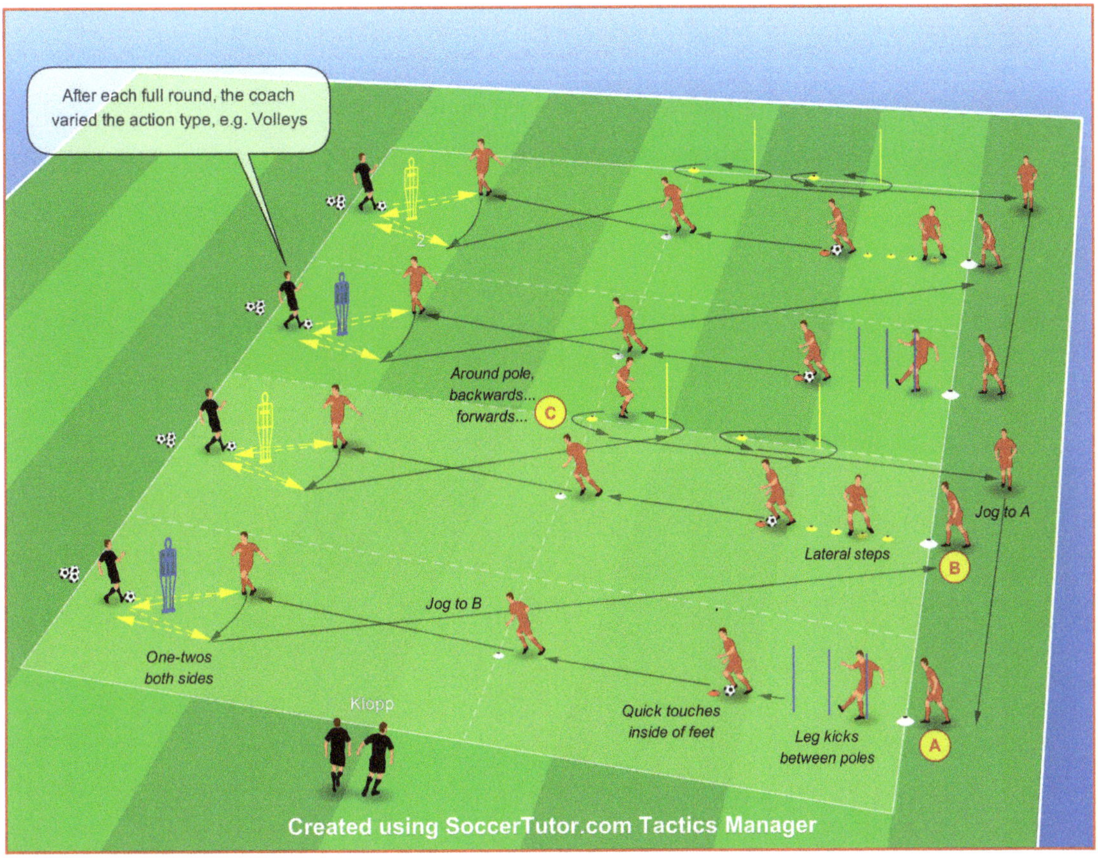

Practice Description

1. From Point A, perform leg kicks through the 3 poles.
2. Quick touches of the ball with the inside or soles of the feet (side-to-side).
3. Jog to the mannequin.
4. The coach feeds the ball on the ground on one side of the mannequin for a pass back, and then repeats to the other side (2 x one-twos).
5. The players jog to Point B.
6. Lateral steps through the 4 cones.
7-9. Repeat steps 2, 3, and 4.
10. Jog to the pole.
11. Run around the pole, move backwards to cone and then forwards. Repeat with the next pole.
12. Leave the area and jog to Point A to continue the circuit.

Source: Jürgen Klopp's Liverpool training session at AXA Training Centre, Liverpool - December 2021

Jürgen Klopp Practices: Warm-up Exercises WITH a Ball

4. Warm-up Competition Game with Speed, Pass, Receive + Shoot

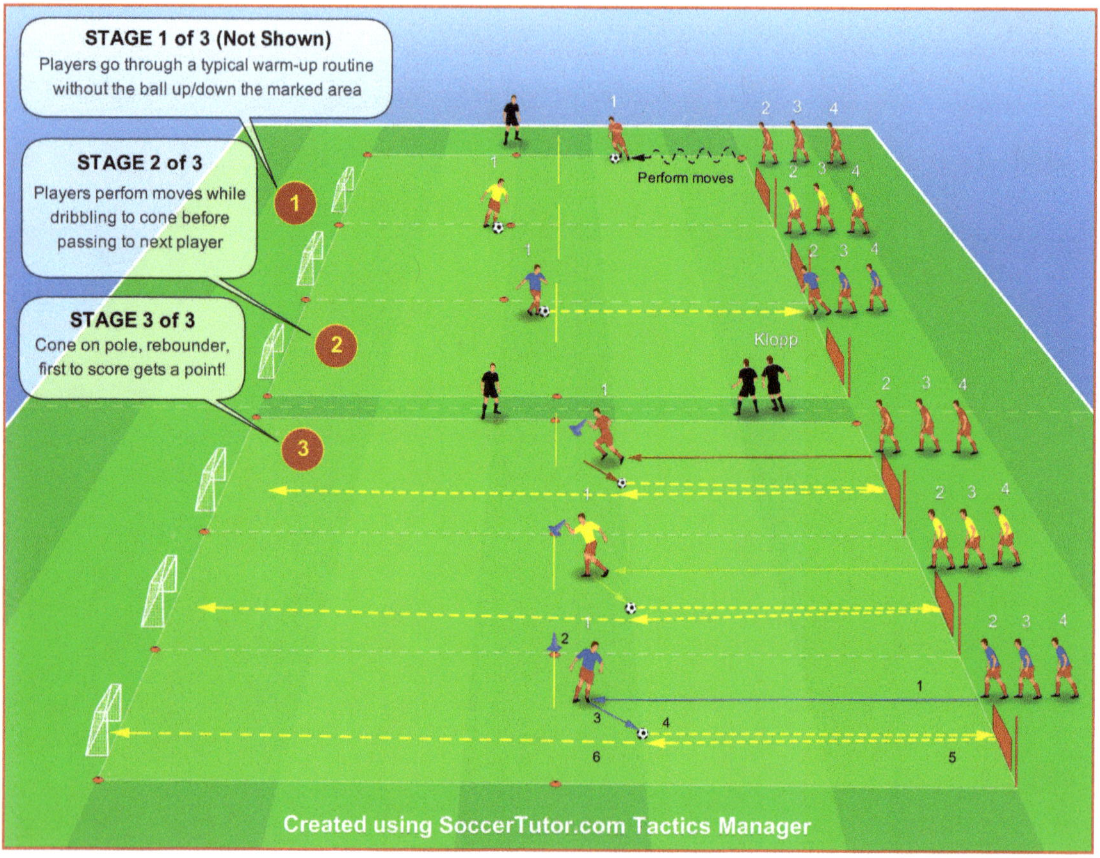

STAGE 1 of 3 (Not Shown)
Players go through a typical warm-up routine without the ball up/down the marked area

STAGE 2 of 3
Players perform moves while dribbling to cone before passing to next player

STAGE 3 of 3
Cone on pole, rebounder, first to score gets a point!

Stage 1/3 (Not shown in diagram)

- The players are in 3 groups and go through a typical warm-up routine without the ball up and down the area including side-steps, high knees while twisting shoulders, pausing on alternate feet, etc.

Stage 2/3

1. Perform technical moves with the ball dribbling forward to the cone.

2. Turn and pass back to the next player waiting. Each player performs 2 reps.

Stage 3/3

1. The coach shouts "Go!" and the first player in each group sprints to put the cone on top of the pole.

2. They then run to the ball, kick it at the rebounder, receive, and turn.

3. The first to score in the mini goal gets a point for their team!

Source: Jürgen Klopp's Liverpool training session at AXA Training Centre, Liverpool - October 2021

Jürgen Klopp Practices: Warm-up Exercises WITH a Ball

5. Juggling Challenger 3-Round Relay Game (Individual, Pairs and Fours)

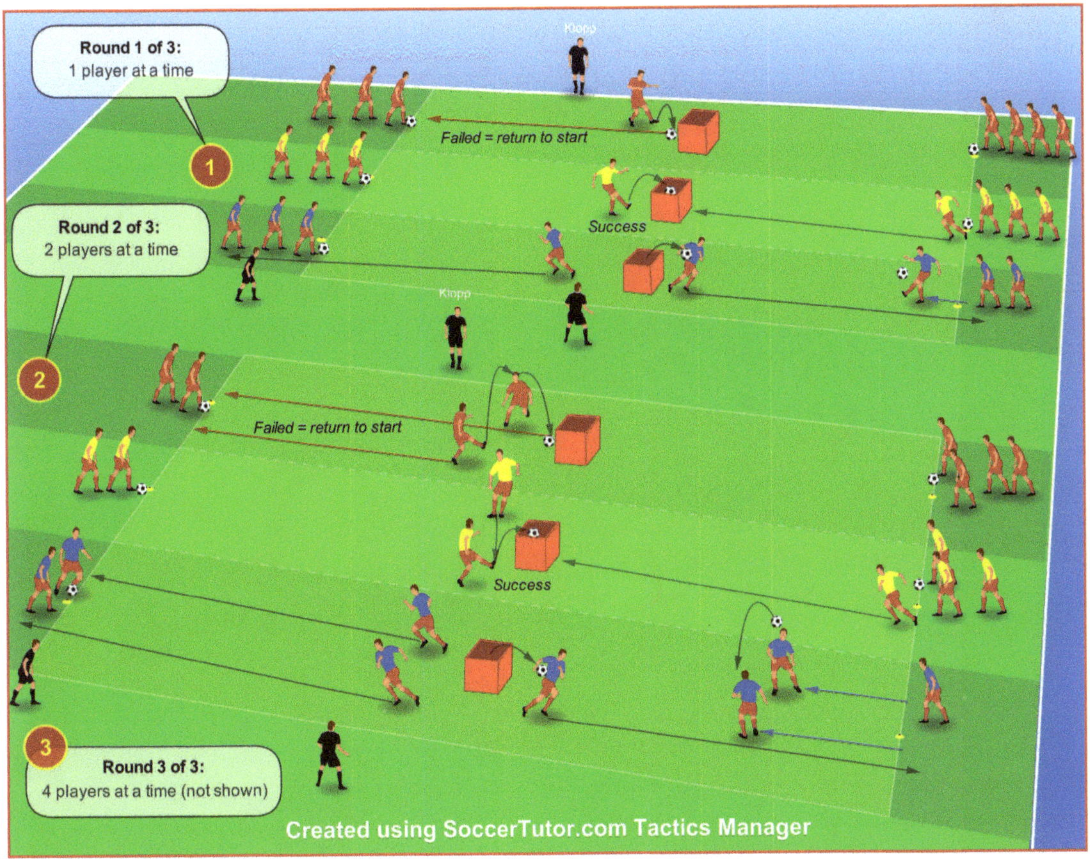

Round 1/3 (1 player at a time)

- The players are in teams of 8. The first round is individual players juggling the ball and trying to score in the bin. If the ball hits the ground, the player must run back to the starting point and try again.

- When a player scores, the next player starts from the opposite end. The team with all 8 players scoring first wins and the losing team do push-ups.

Round 2/3 (2 players at a time)

- Exactly the same but the players juggle in pairs, limited to 1 touch at a time each. The team with all 4 pairs scoring first wins and the losing team do push-ups.

Round 3/3 (4 players at a time)

- The players work in groups of 4, limited to 1 touch at a time each. The team with both (2) groups scoring first wins and the losing team do push-ups.

Source: Jürgen Klopp's Liverpool training session at Melwood Training Ground, Liverpool - March 2019

Jürgen Klopp Practices: Warm-up Exercises WITH a Ball

6. Football Tennis Game with Maximum of 3 Touches and 1 Bounce

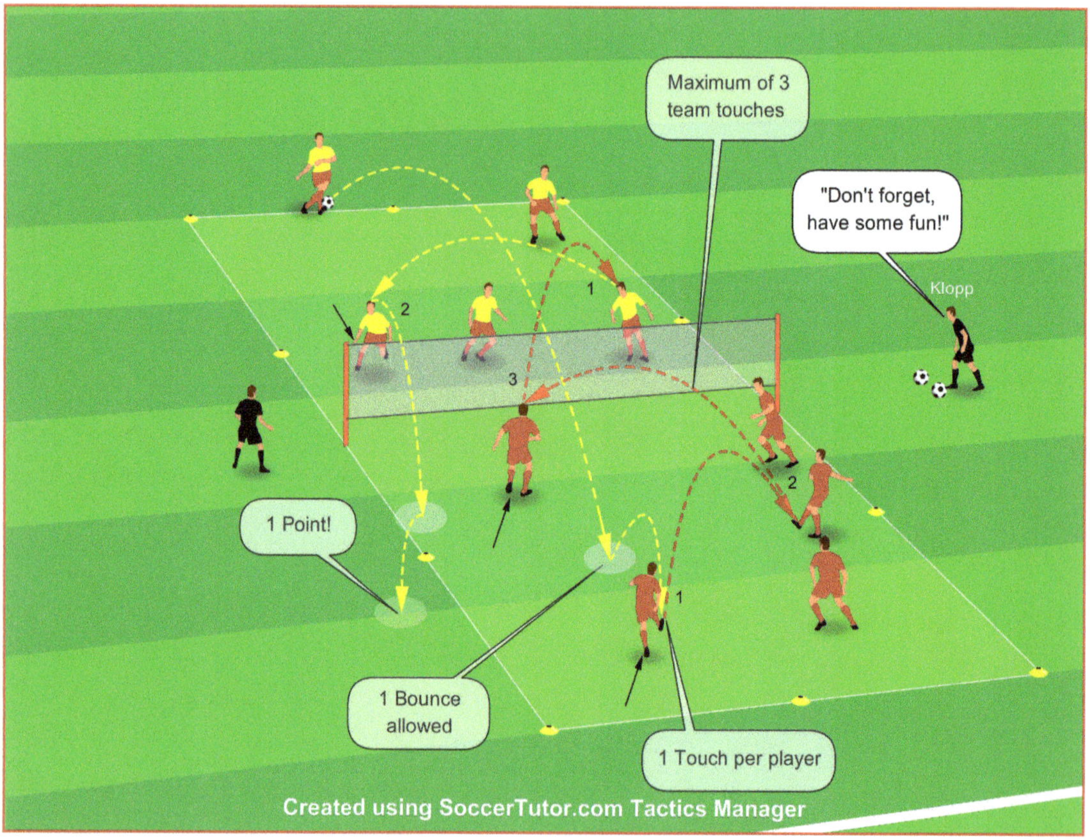

The focus is on fun and the players enjoy competing against each other in this game, celebrating every single point they win.

Practice Description

- In a total area approximately 5 x 15 yards, there are 5 players on each team for this football tennis game.

- The game starts with 1 player on the base line who drops the ball from his hands and volleys (or half-volleys) the ball over the net.

- The team on the other side are allowed a **total of 3 touches but only 1 touch at a time per player**, and the ball can bounce only once before returning it over the net back to their opponents.

- **How to win a point: 1.** The opponents let the ball bounce twice on their side of the net. **2.** The opponents take too many touches, or the ball goes into the net. **3.** The opponent's kick/head the ball outside of the area.

Source: Jürgen Klopp's Liverpool training session at AXA Training Centre, Liverpool - March 2022

Jürgen Klopp Practices: Warm-up Exercises WITH a Ball

7. Double Triangle 2-Touch Passing Warm-up

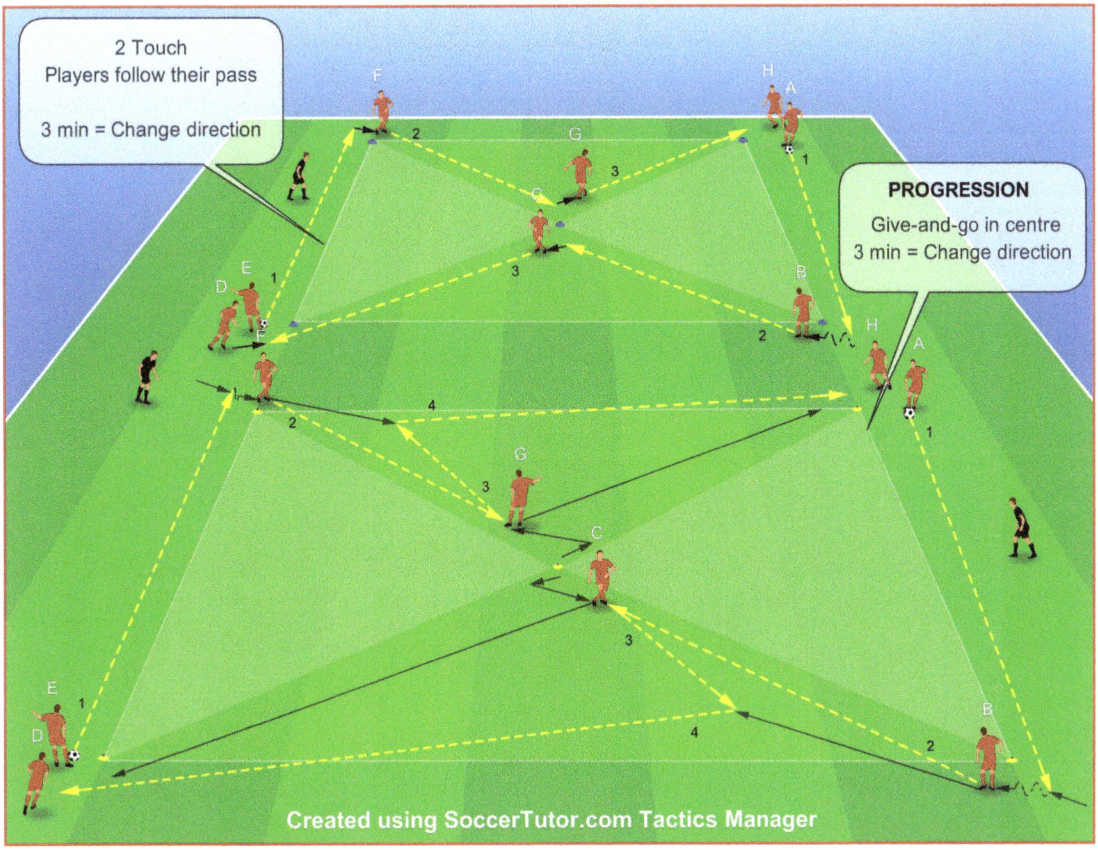

Start with 2 balls simultaneously from Players A and E in a connected circuit. After 3 minutes, the direction changes from clockwise to anti-clockwise.

First Phase (2-Touch)

1. **A/E** pass to **B/F**.
2. **B/F** pass diagonally to the middle players **C/G**, who check away before moving towards the ball to receive.
3. **C/G** pass diagonally to **B/F**.
4. The sequence continues clockwise.

Progression

1-2. Same as first phase.

3. **C/G** set the ball back for the run of **B/F** to complete a one-two.
4. **B/F** pass to **D/H**, who are waiting.
5. The practice continues clockwise.

Source: Jürgen Klopp's Liverpool training session at Melwood Training Ground, Liverpool - April 2019

Speed & Agility

Direct from
Jürgen Klopp's
Training Sessions

Jürgen Klopp Practices: Speed & Agility

1. Fast Reactions to Coach's Signal in a Quick Feet + Sprint Race

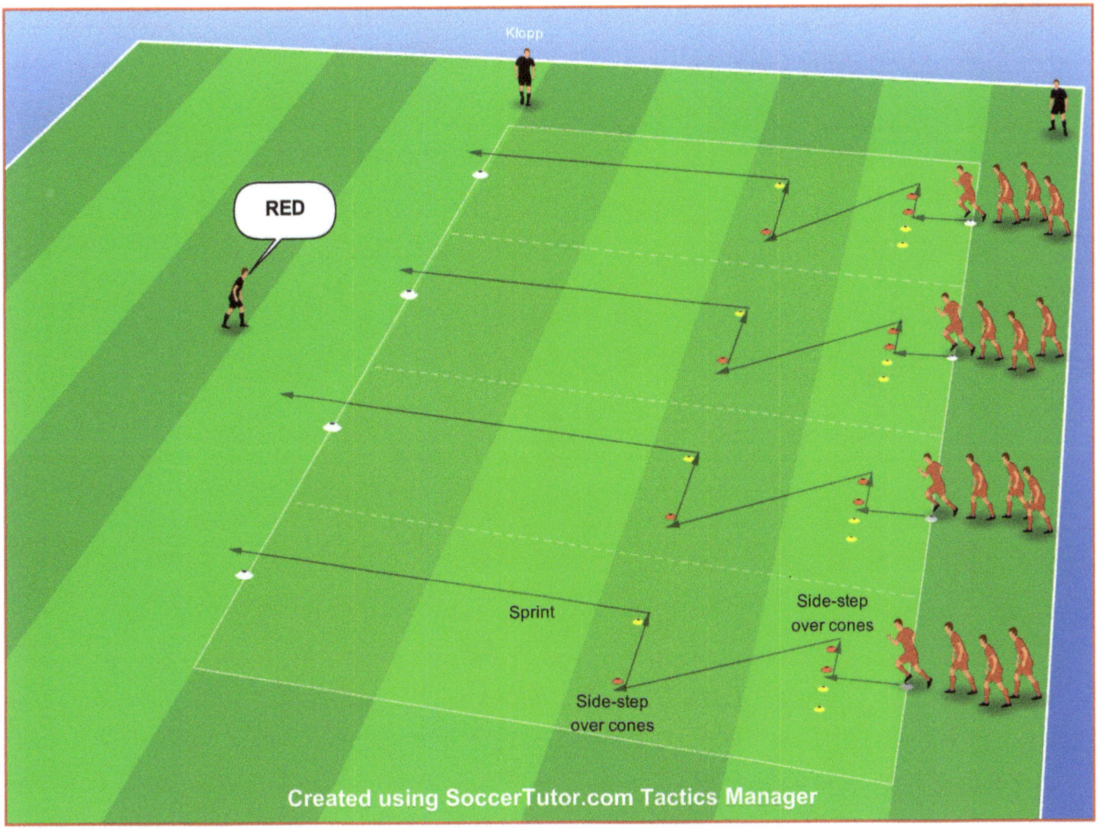

[Diagram: Practice setup showing Klopp as coach, players lined up in groups performing side-steps over cones and sprinting, with "RED" signal being called out]

Practice Description

1. The players line up one behind the other in groups and get ready to compete against each other in sprint races.

2. The first players get ready for the Coach's signal.

3. The Coach calls out "Red" or "Yellow."

4. In this example, the Coach calls out "Red," so the players have to perform quick side-steps over the 2 red cones, then sprint to the red cone and side-step over that and the adjacent yellow cone. It would be vice versa if the Coach called out "Yellow."

5. The sequence is completed by sprinting past the white cone at the end. The fastest wins.

6. The Coach calls out "Red" or "Yellow" again and the next players waiting compete against each other.

Source: Jürgen Klopp's Liverpool training session at AXA Training Centre, Liverpool - August 2021

Jürgen Klopp Practices: Speed & Agility

2. Fast Reactions to "Left or Right" Signal to Drop Back + Sprint Race

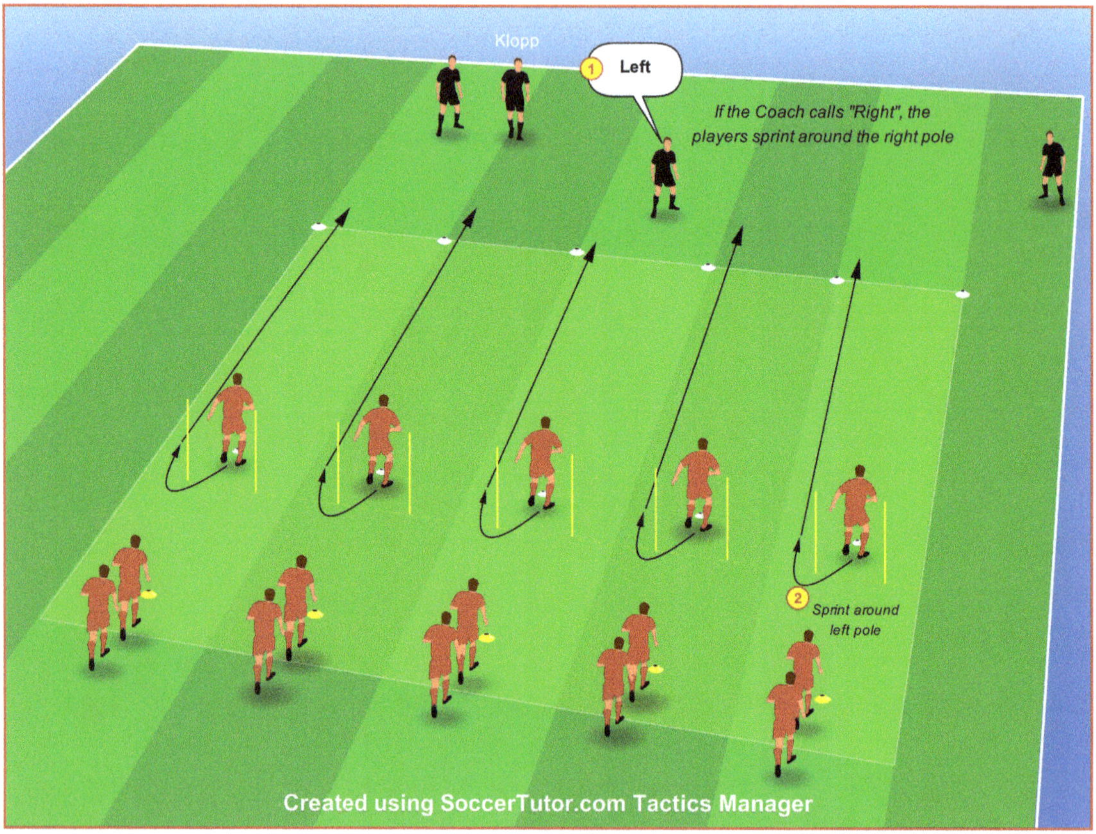

Practice Description

- The players line up in groups and 1 player from each group starts on the white cone waiting for the Coach's signal.
- The players wait bouncing on the balls of their feet, so they are well prepared to make fast reactions (movements).

1. The Coach calls out "Left" or "Right" to act as a signal for the players. In the diagram example, he calls out "Left."
2. The players move backwards through the 2 poles and around the "Left" pole.
3. To complete the race (fastest wins), they sprint forwards past the white cone at the end.
4. The next players waiting move forward to the white cone and the Coach calls out "Left" or "Right" again.

Source: Jürgen Klopp's Liverpool training session at AXA Training Centre, Liverpool - August 2022

Jürgen Klopp Practices: Speed & Agility

3. Fast Reactions to Multiple Signals in a Speed of Movement Race

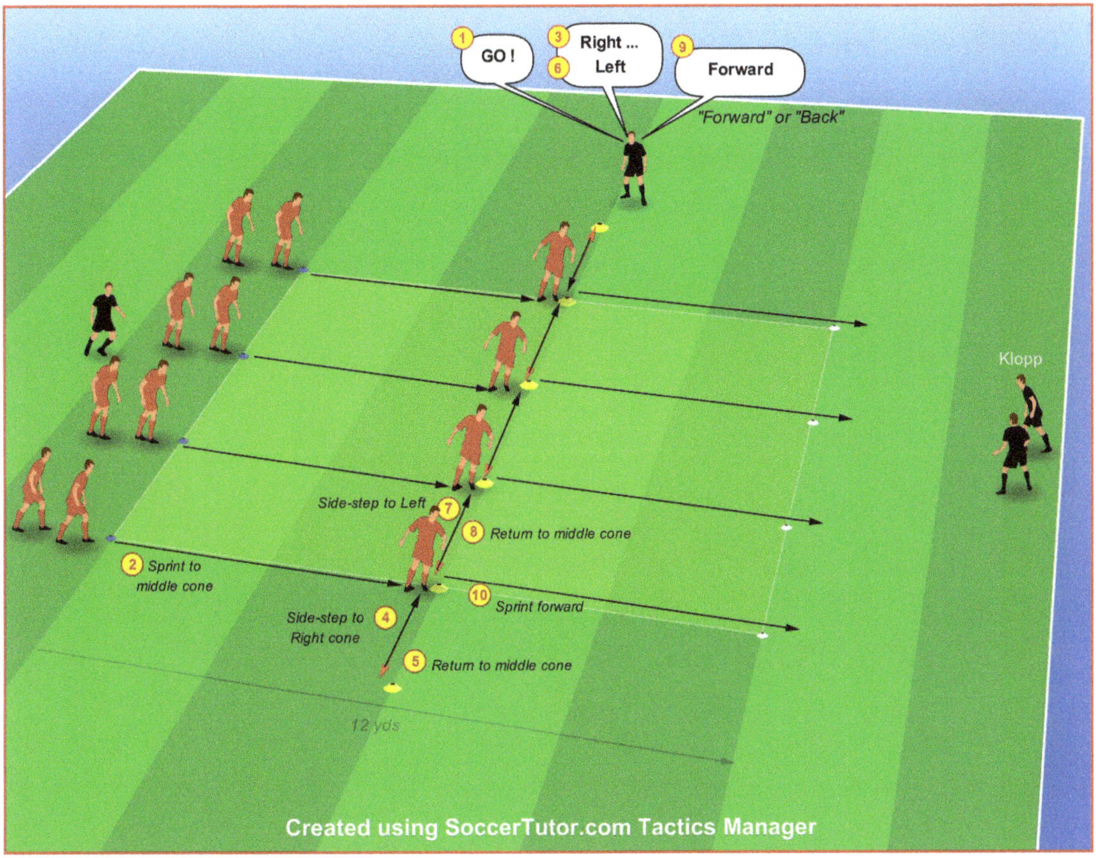

Practice Description

1. The players line up one behind the other in groups and the Coach calls out "<u>Go</u>!"
2. The first players sprint to the middle cone in front of them.
3. The Coach calls out "<u>Right</u>" or "<u>Left</u>."
4. The players side-step to that side.
5. Return back to the middle cone.
6. The Coach calls out "<u>Right</u>" or "<u>Left</u>."
7. The players side-step to that side.
8. Return back to the middle cone.
9. The Coach calls out "<u>Forward</u>" or "<u>Back</u>."
10. The players sprint to the white cone if "<u>Forward</u>" is called out and turn and sprint back to the blue cone if "<u>Back</u>" is called.

Source: Jürgen Klopp's Liverpool training session at Melwood Training Ground, Liverpool - January 2019

Jürgen Klopp Practices: Speed & Agility

4. Fast Side-to-Side Reactions with Mannequins, Turn + Sprint Race

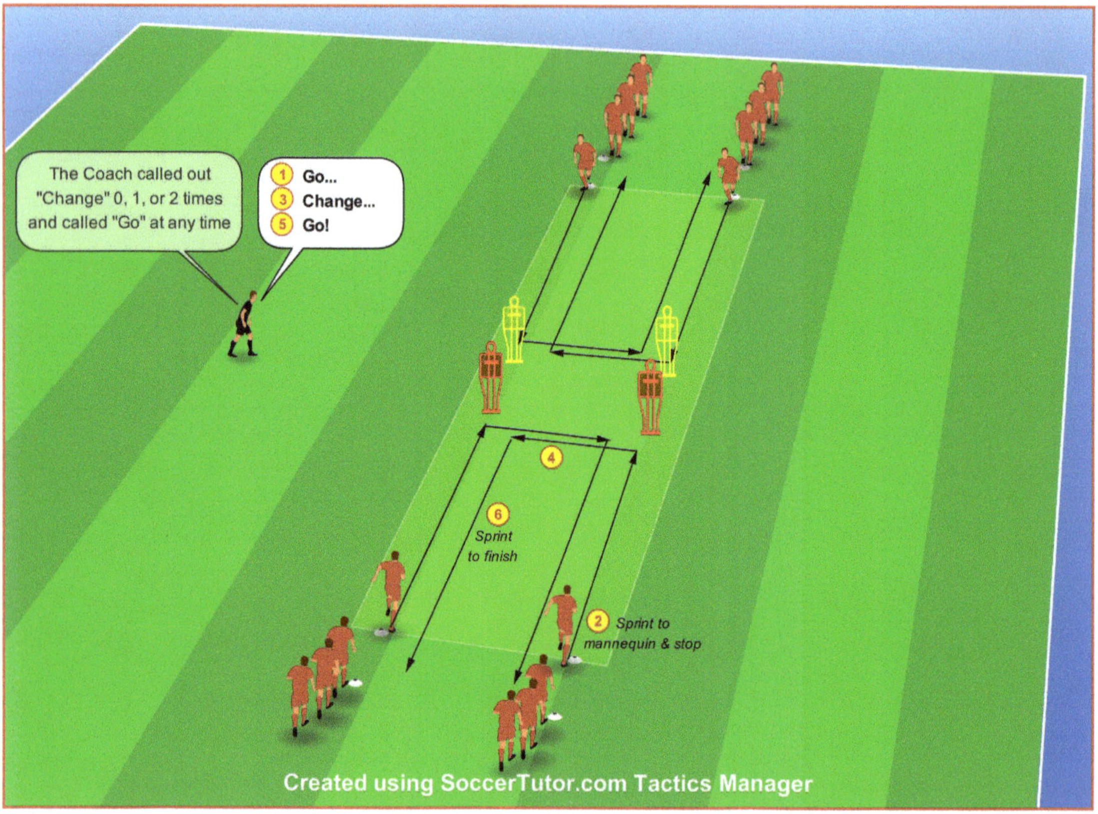

The Coach called out "Change" 0, 1, or 2 times for each repetition - the diagram shows an example where it was called once.

Practice Description

1. The players line up one behind the other in groups and the Coach calls out "Go!"

2. The first players sprint to the mannequin on their side, stop, and bounce on the balls of their feet waiting for a signal.

3-4. The Coach either calls out "Go!" and all 4 players sprint back to the start, or he calls out "Change" and the players switch sides to the other mannequin. He may also call out "Change" twice to switch back to the original mannequin, but in this example, it is just once.

5. The Coach calls out "Go!"

6. The players turn and sprint back to the starting cones, and the fastest wins!

NOTE: The players must avoid each other when switching between the 2 mannequins.

Source: Jürgen Klopp's Liverpool pre-season training session in Evian, France - August 2021

Jürgen Klopp Practices: Speed & Agility

5. Fast Side-to-Side Reactions to Sound & Visual Signals + Sprint Race

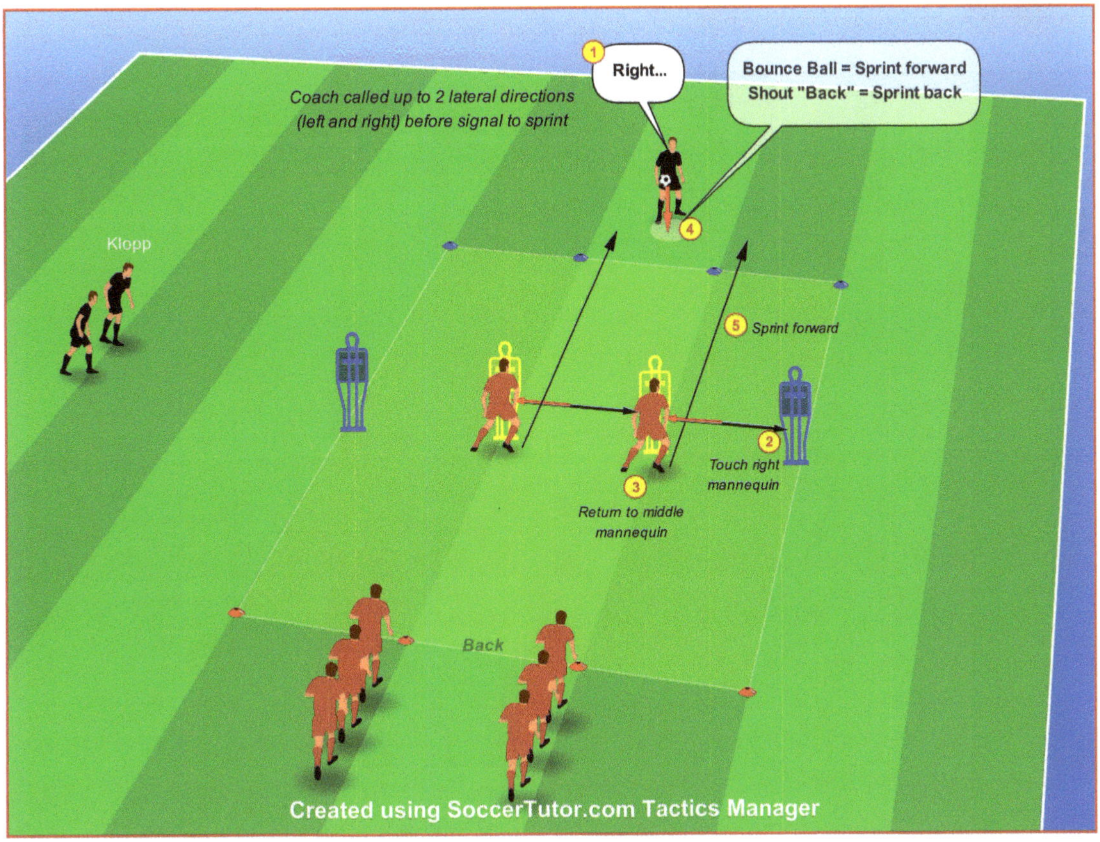

The Coach called out a direction (left or right) once or twice - the diagram shows an example where it was called once.

Practice Description

1. The players line up and the first players position themselves in front of the middle yellow mannequins, bouncing on the balls of their feet waiting for a signal.

2. The Coach calls out "<u>Right</u>" or "<u>Left</u>" and the players move to that side to touch the mannequin (right in diagram).

3. Both players return to the middle yellow mannequins. The Coach may call out "<u>Right</u>" or "<u>Left</u>" twice to switch back, but in this example, it is just once.

4-5. If the Coach calls out "<u>Back</u>," the players turn and sprint back to the red cones. If the Coach <u>bounces the ball</u>, the players sprint forward to the blue cones.

6. The next players waiting move into the middle to repeat the same sequence.

Source: Jürgen Klopp's Liverpool training session at AXA Training Centre, Liverpool - December 2020

Jürgen Klopp Practices: Speed & Agility

6. Fast Turns, Awareness & Changes of Direction + Sprint Race

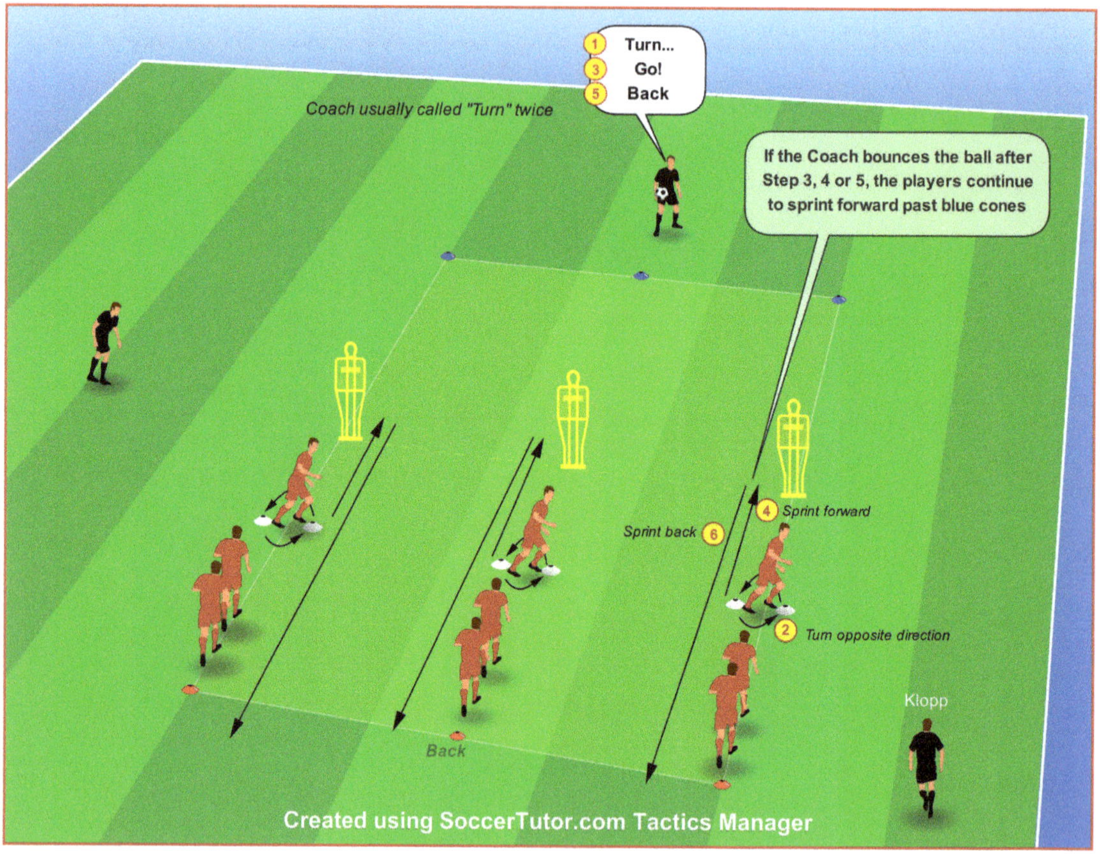

Practice Description

1. One player from each group starts side-on in between 2 large cones (bouncing on balls of feet), waiting for a signal. The Coach calls out "Turn."

2. The players turn 180° each time "Turn" is called out, which is usually twice.

3. The Coach calls out "Go!"

4. The players sprint forward to the mannequin.

5. The Coach calls out "Back."

6. The players turn and sprint back to the red cones, and the fastest wins!

NOTE: If the Coach bounces the ball at any time after step 3, 4, or 5, the players have to be aware and carry on sprinting to the blue cone instead of turning back. This caught out many Liverpool players during this practice.

Source: Jürgen Klopp's Liverpool training session at Melwood Training Ground, Liverpool - September 2020

Jürgen Klopp Practices: Speed & Agility

7. React to Signal + Sprint in 1v1 Duel

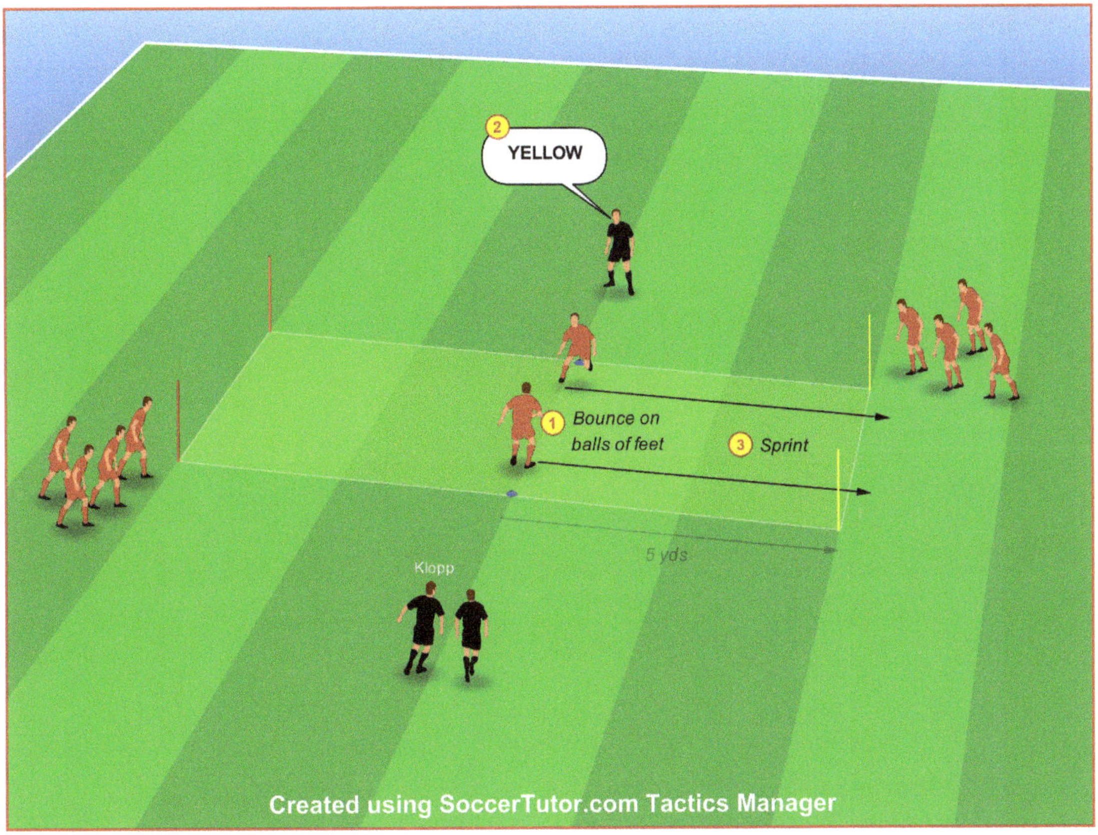

There are 2 red poles at one end and 2 yellow poles at the other end. The players are paired and compete in 1v1 duels.

Practice Description

1. One player from each end jogs into the middle to their respective cone to face their opponent and bounce on the balls of their feet, waiting for a signal.

2. The Coach calls out the colour "<u>Yellow</u>" or "<u>Red</u>."

3. Both players react immediately and sprint towards the poles of the same colour called out. In this example, the Coach calls "<u>Yellow</u>", so the 2 players sprint and race to the end with the yellow poles.

4. The next 2 players enter to duel, and the practice continues.

Source: Jürgen Klopp's Liverpool pre-season training session in Lyon, France - August 2019

Jürgen Klopp Practices: Speed & Agility

8. Physical Duel, React to Signal + Sprint Race

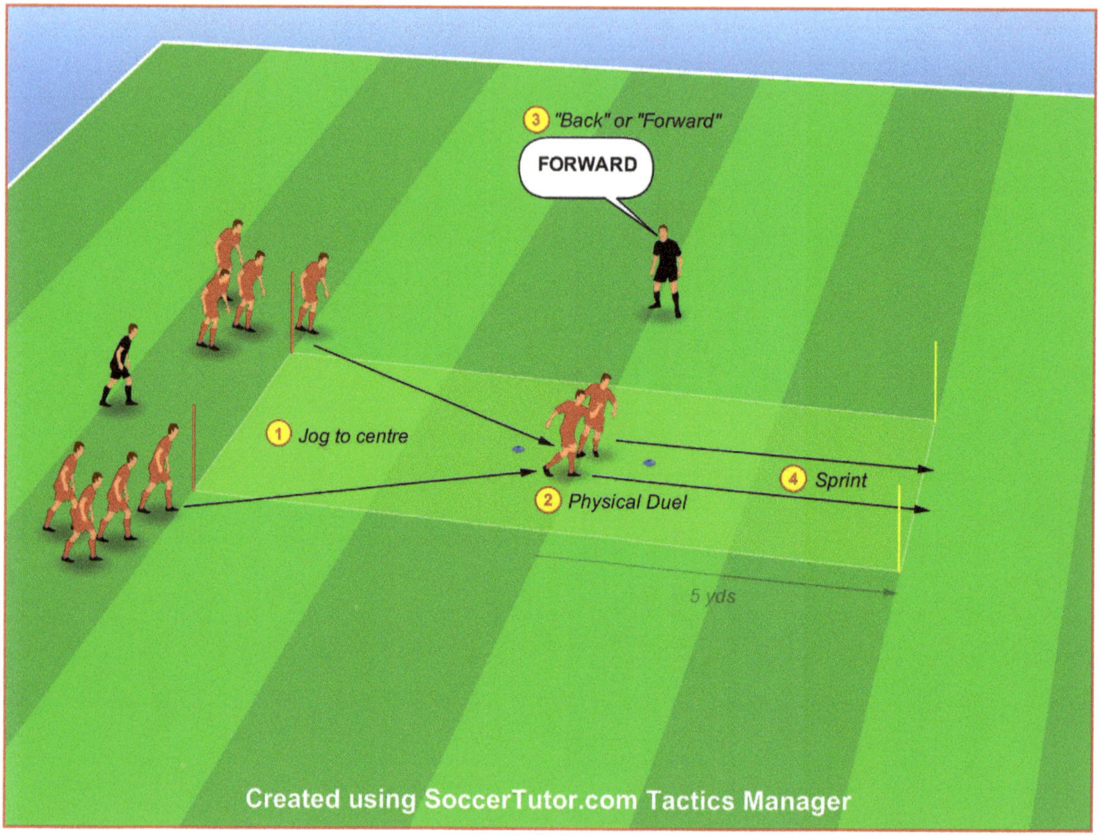

[Diagram showing the practice setup with players, coach calling "FORWARD", and labels: 1. Jog to centre, 2. Physical Duel, 3. "Back" or "Forward", 4. Sprint, 5 yds]

The players line up one behind the other in 2 groups at one end.

Practice Description

1. One player from each group jogs into the centre side-on to their opponent.

2. The players get shoulder to shoulder for a 50% effort physical duel.

3. The Coach calls out "<u>Back</u>" or "<u>Forward</u>" and the players turn and sprint through the correct poles.

4. In this example, "<u>Forward</u>" is called out and the players sprint to the end through the yellow poles, as shown.

5. The next 2 players enter to duel, and the practice continues.

Source: Jürgen Klopp's Liverpool training session at Melwood Training Ground, Liverpool - August 2019

Jürgen Klopp Practices: Speed & Agility

9. Quick Turns, React to Signal + Sprint Race to Finish Line

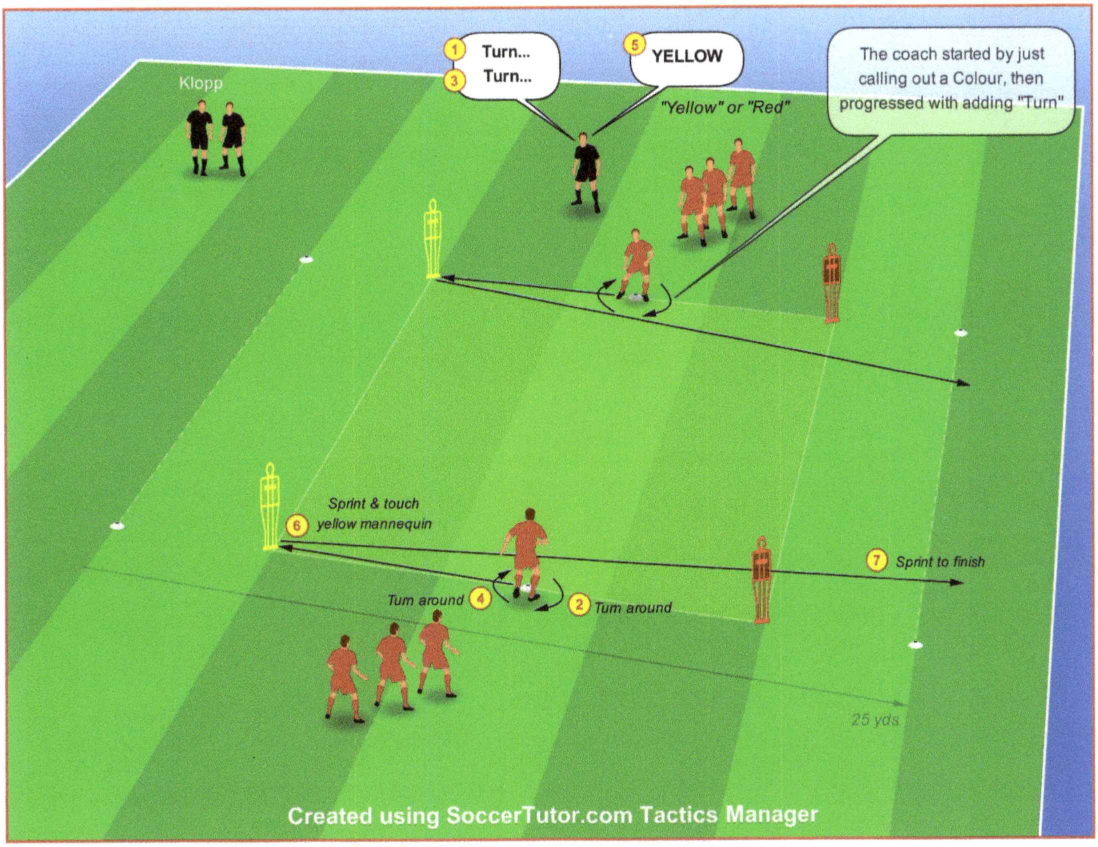

The practice started off simply by sprinting and touching the mannequins + sprint to finish, but progressed to include turns, which is fully described in the description.

Practice Description

1. One player from each group starts on either side of the area facing each other. The Coach calls out "Turn."
2. The players turn around 180°.
3. The Coach calls out "Turn" again.
4. The players turn around 180° again.
5. The Coach calls out "Yellow" or "Red."
6. The players quickly sprint and touch that colour mannequin (yellow in diagram).
7. The 2 players complete the sequence by turning and racing to the opposite finish line - fastest wins!
8. The next 2 players enter to compete against each other, and the practice continues.

Source: Jürgen Klopp's Liverpool training session at AXA Training Centre, Liverpool - September 2021

Jürgen Klopp Practices: Speed & Agility

10. Rotate Position, React to Signal + Sprint Race

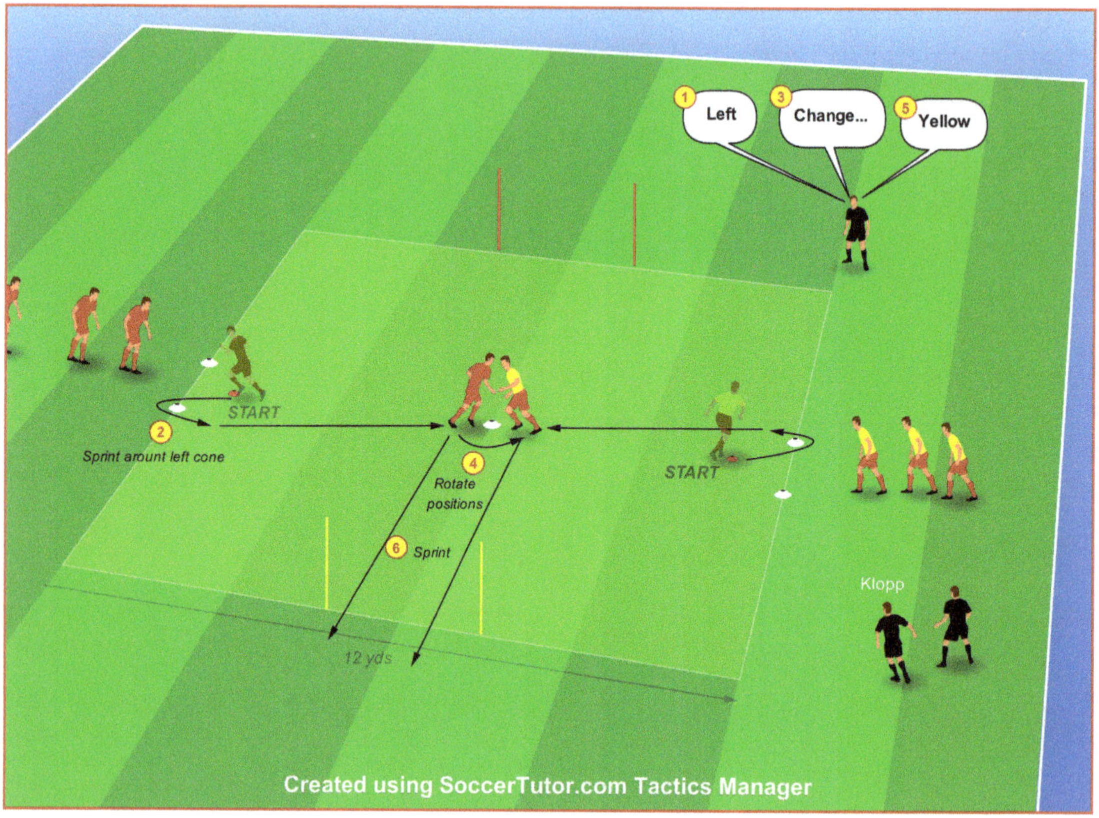

Practice Description

1. One player from each group starts at either side of the area facing away from each other on the red cones. The Coach calls out "<u>Left</u>" or "<u>Right</u>."

2. The players sprint around the respective cone called out, which is the cone to their "<u>Left</u>" in this example.

3. The players move to face each other and lightly hold on to each others' arms. The Coach calls out "<u>Change</u>."

4. The players rotate positions around 180° together.

5. The Coach calls out "<u>Yellow</u>" or "<u>Red</u>."

6. The players react quickly and sprint through the correct poles (yellow poles in diagram). The fastest wins!

7. The next 2 players enter to compete against each other, and the practice continues.

Source: Jürgen Klopp's Liverpool training session at AXA Training Centre, Liverpool - November 2020

Jürgen Klopp Practices: Speed & Agility

11. Spin, React to Signal + Sprint Race to Finish

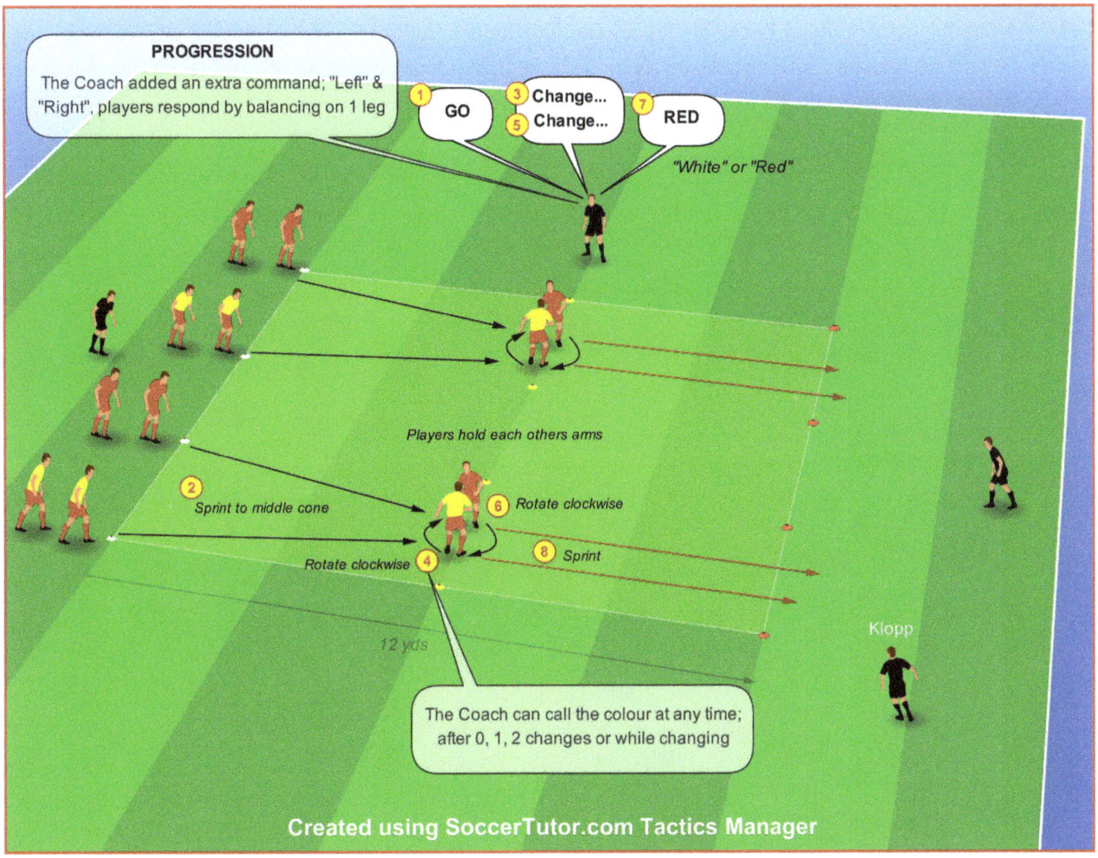

The Coach called out "Change" 0, 1, or 2 times for each repetition - the diagram shows an example where it was called twice.

Practice Description

1. The Coach calls out "Go!"

2. One player from each group sprints to the middle cone to face their opponent. They hold each others' arms.

3. The Coach calls out "Change."

4. The players rotate 180° clockwise still holding on to each others' arms.

5. The Coach calls out "Change" again.

6. The players rotate 180° clockwise.

7. The Coach calls out "White" or "Red," which relate to the cones at each end.

8. The 2 players turn and race past the correct colour cones ("Red" in diagram). The fastest wins!

Source: Jürgen Klopp's Liverpool pre-season training session in Salzburg, Austria - July 2022

Jürgen Klopp Practices: Speed & Agility

12. Speed, Coordination & Agility Race with Signaled Fast Reactions

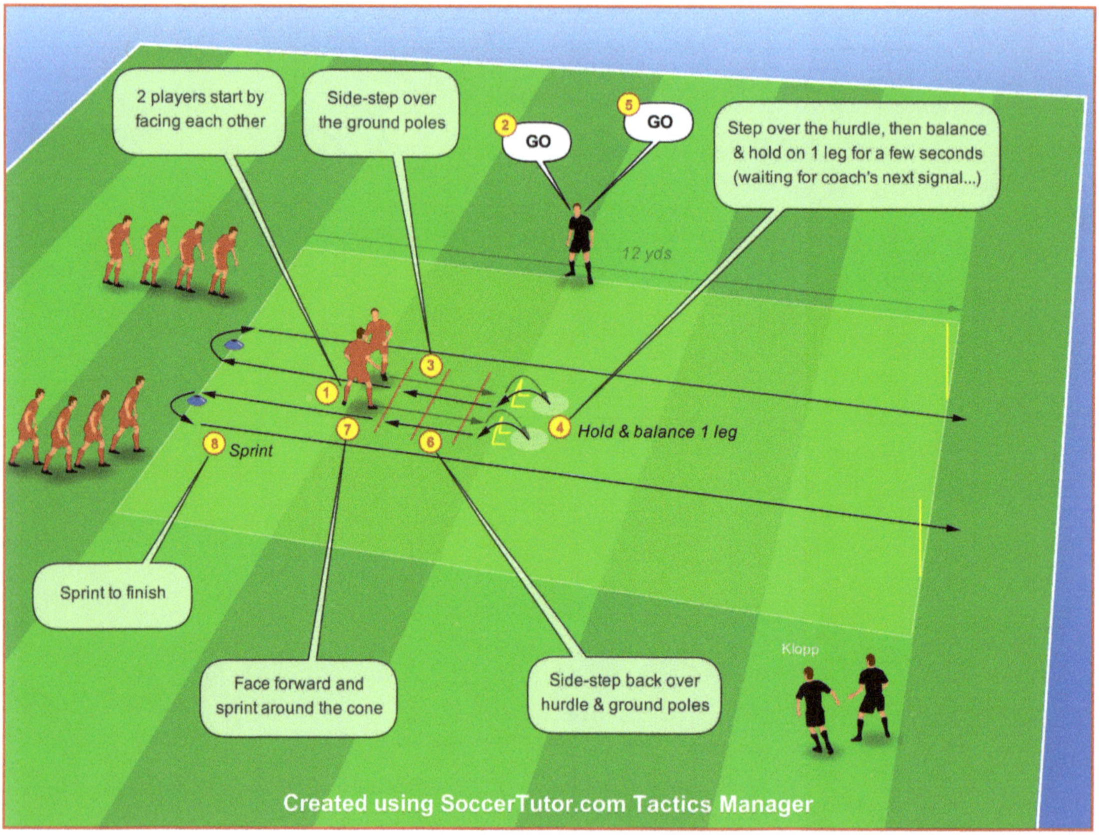

Practice Description

1. One player from each group moves into the area to face their opponent in the position shown.
2. The Coach calls out "Go!"
3. Side-step over the floor poles.
4. Side-step over the hurdle, balance on one leg for a few seconds, and wait for the Coach's next signal.
5. The Coach calls out "Go!"
6. Side-step back over the hurdle and through the ground poles.
7. Turn to face forward and sprint around the blue cone.
8. Sprint all the way to the opposite end of the area. The fastest wins!

Source: Jürgen Klopp's Liverpool training session at Melwood Training Ground, Liverpool - December 2018

Jürgen Klopp Practices: Speed & Agility

13. Speed, Coordination & Agility Circuit with Sprints

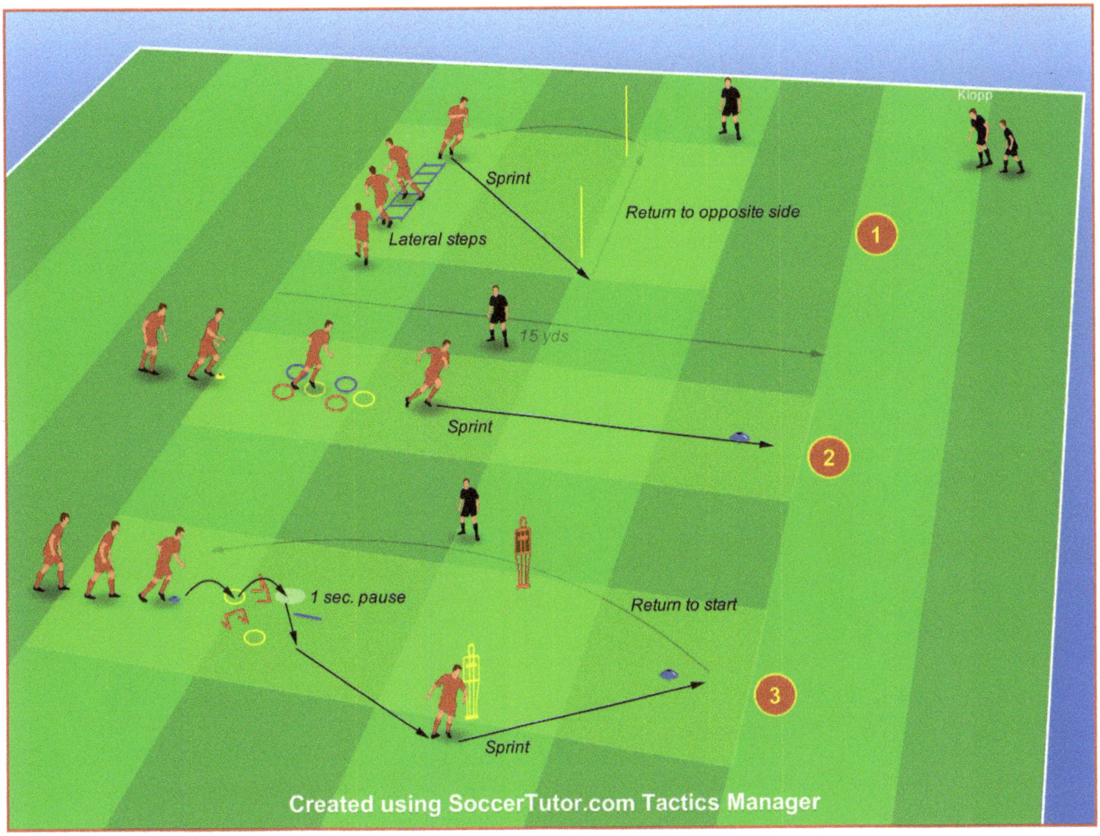

The players form groups and perform the 3 different exercises in turn.

Exercise 1

1. Step one foot in the speed ring and the other foot over the hurdle, both with a 1 second pause.
2. Sprint around one of the mannequins and past the blue cone.
3. Return to start by going around the other mannequin.

Exercise 2

1. Fast one-footed steps through the speed rings.
2. Sprint past the blue cone.

Exercise 3

1. Lateral steps through the speed ladder.
2. Sprint diagonally past one of the poles.
3. Return to opposite side by going around the other pole.

Source: Jürgen Klopp's Liverpool training session at Melwood Training Ground, Liverpool - January 2017

Jürgen Klopp Practices: Speed & Agility

14. Quick Steps, Changes of Direction and Short Sprints

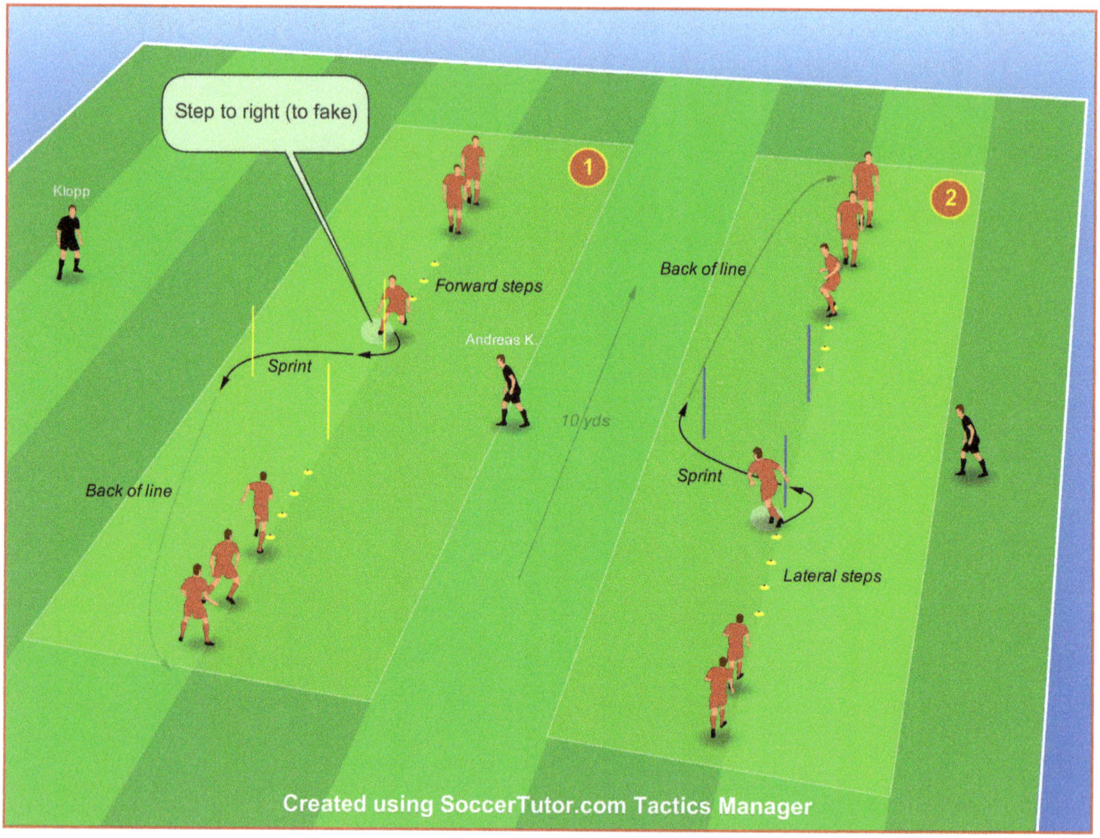

The players form groups and perform the 2 slightly different exercises one after the other.

Exercise 1

1. Quick <u>forward steps</u> through the 4 cones.
2. Sprint around the first pole and change direction to move diagonally and run around the next pole.
3. Run to the back of the line of the opposite group as the next player goes.

Exercise 2

1. Quick <u>lateral steps</u> through the 4 cones.
2. Sprint around the first pole and change direction to move diagonally and run around the next pole.
3. Run to the back of the line of the opposite group as the next player goes.

Source: Jürgen Klopp's Liverpool training session at Melwood Training Ground, Liverpool - February 2019

Jürgen Klopp Practices: Speed & Agility

15. Quick Steps, Slalom, Plyometric Exercises & Agility Circuit

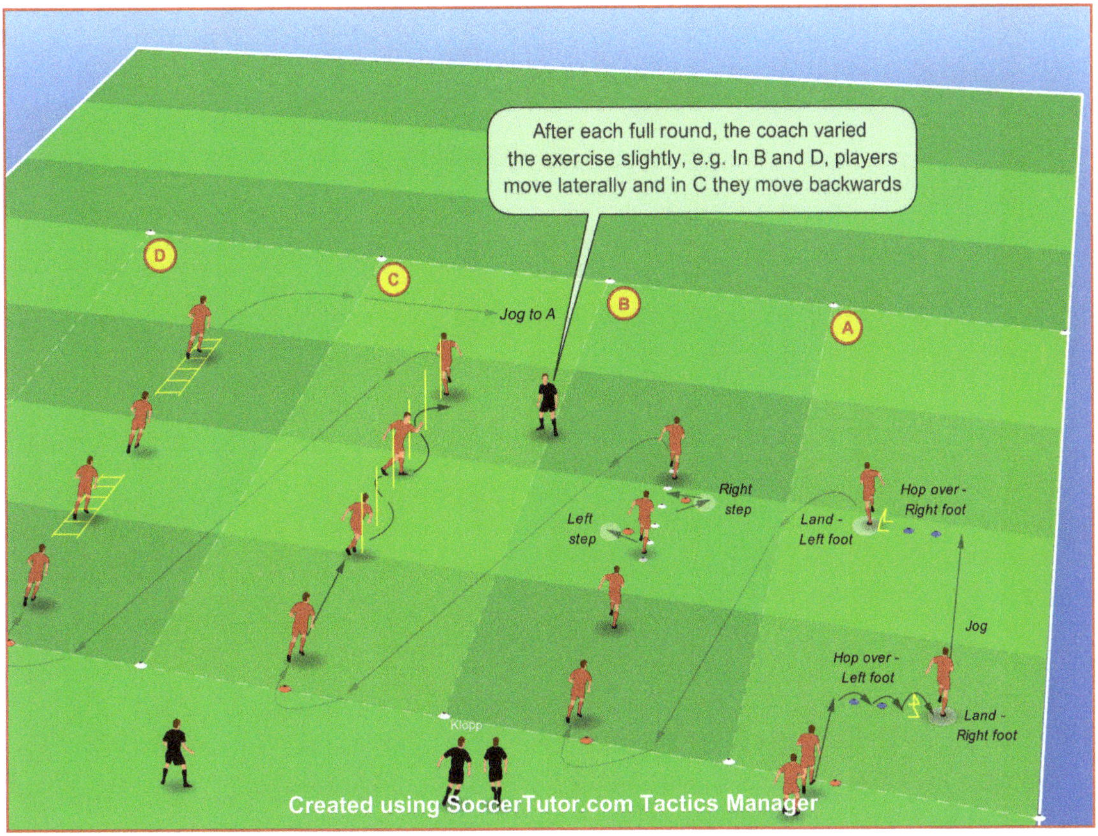

After each full round, the coach varied the exercise slightly, e.g. In B and D, players move laterally and in C they move backwards

This works as a full circuit with the players moving through station A → B → C → D → A.

Practice Description

STATION A. Hop over 2 cones and 1 hurdle with the left foot and land on the right foot. Jog forward. Hop over 2 cones and 1 hurdle with the right foot and land on the left foot.

STATION B. Quick forward steps through the cones with a left step over left red cone + right step over right red cone.

STATION C. Slalom through the 6 poles.

STATION D. Quick steps through both the speed ladders. Jog to the starting position of Station A.

Source: Jürgen Klopp's Liverpool training session at AXA Training Centre, Liverpool - April 2022

Jürgen Klopp Practices: Speed & Agility

16. Agility Circuit with Plyometric Exercises for Speed & Explosiveness

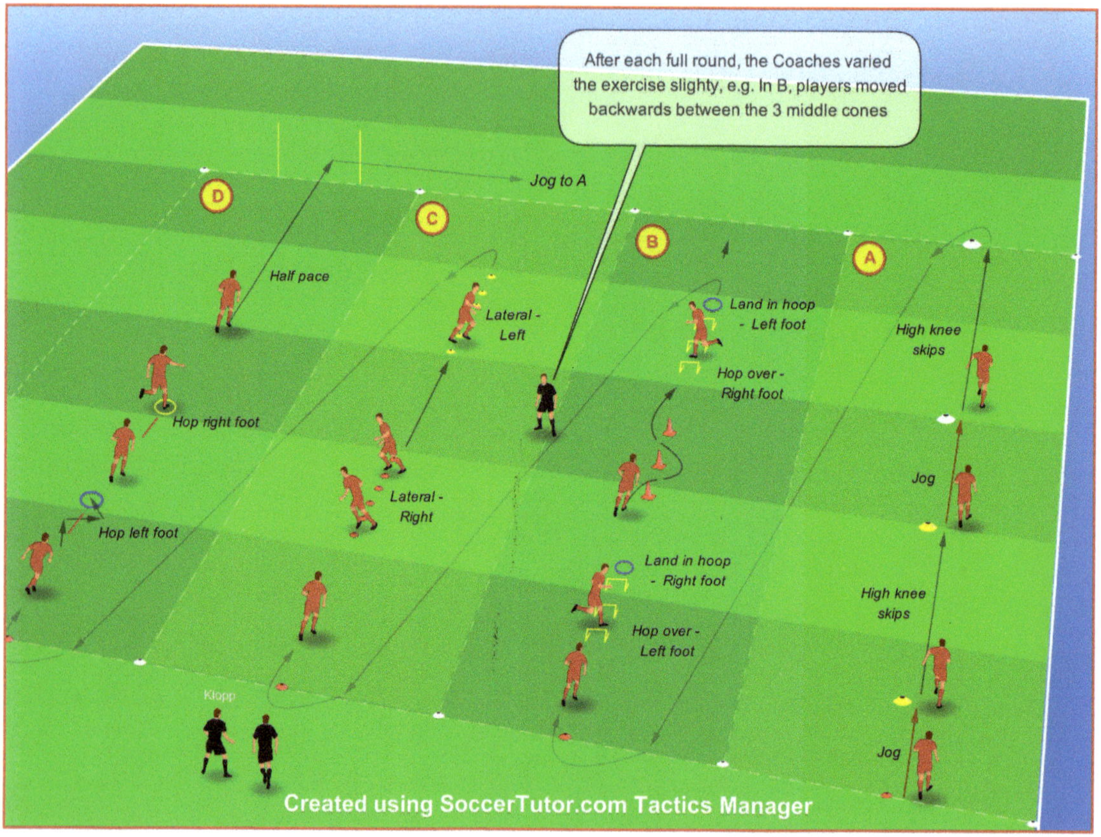

This works as a full circuit with the players moving through station A → B → C → D → A.

Practice Description

STATION A. Jog to 1st cone + high knee skips to 2nd cone. Repeat with 3rd and 4th cones.

STATION B. Hop over 3 hurdles on left foot + land in hoop on right foot. Use side-steps through the 3 large cones. Finish by hopping over 3 hurdles on right foot and land on left foot in hoop.

STATION C. Lateral steps through the 5 cones, leading with the right foot, followed by lateral steps through the next 5 cones leading with the left foot.

STATION D. Hop on left foot to jump over the ground pole 4 times + land in hoop on left foot. Repeat at the next stage hopping on the right foot. Run half pace to the end of the station and jog to the starting position of Station A.

Source: Jürgen Klopp's Liverpool training session at Melwood Training Ground, Liverpool - July 2018

Jürgen Klopp Practices: Speed & Agility

17. Fast Feet, Sprints, Plyometric Exercises & Jumps in a Speed Circuit

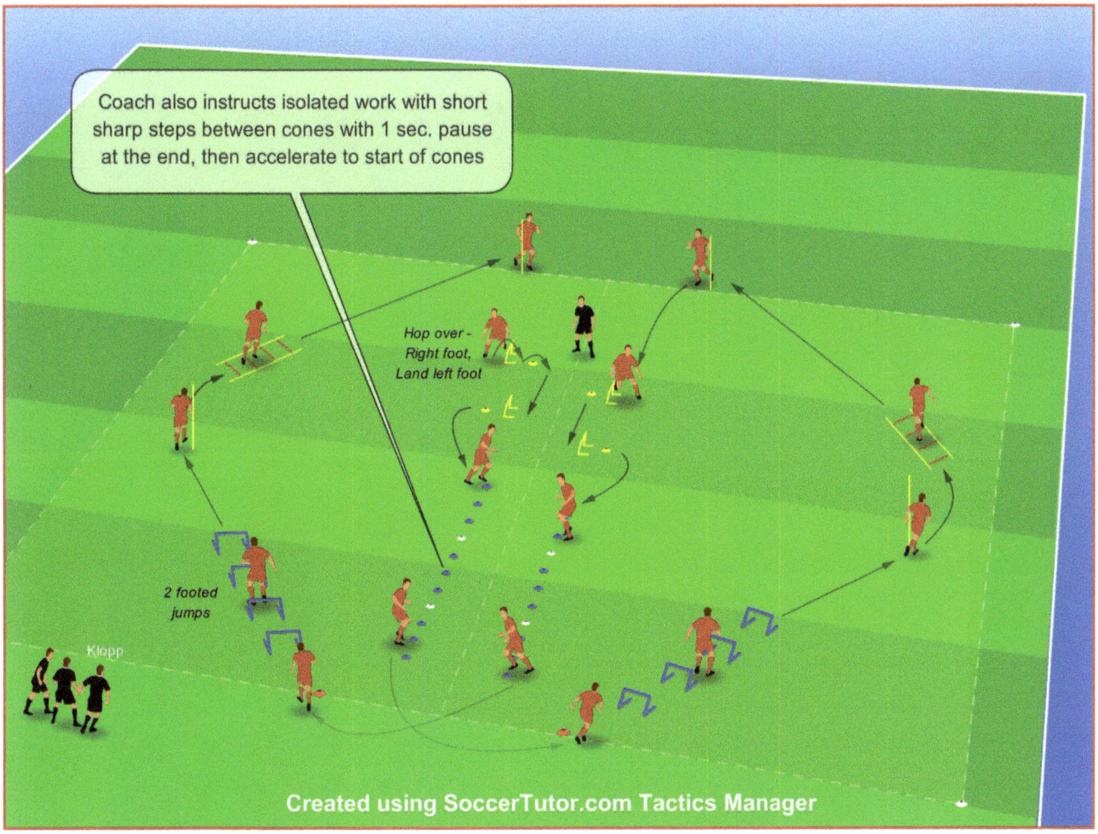

Practice Description

1. Hop over the hurdle and cone with the right foot and land on the left foot.
2. Hop over the hurdle and cone with the left foot and land on the right foot.
3. Quick steps/speed work through the cones with changes of direction.
4. Jog to the hurdles on opposite side.
5. Two-footed jumps over the 4 hurdles.
6. Run around the pole.
7. Quick steps through the speed ladder.
8. Jog back to start and repeat in opposite direction.

Source: Jürgen Klopp's Liverpool training session at AXA Training Centre, Liverpool - August 2022

Passing Combinations

Direct from Jürgen Klopp's Training Sessions

"With a few new movements, with a few new passing options, you can change the whole game."

Jürgen Klopp Practices: Passing Combinations

1. One-Two, Pass and Move 3-Player Support Play Combinations

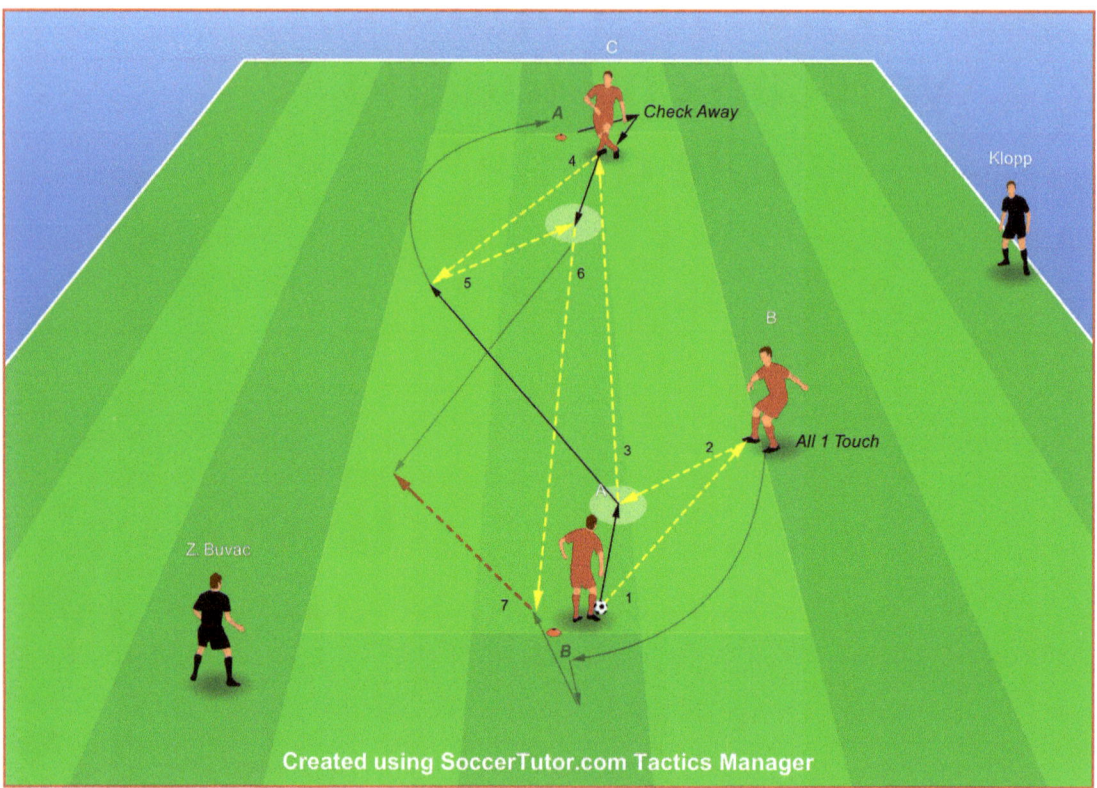

Practice Description

1. **A** passes to **B**.

2. **B** passes back for **A** to move forward onto and completes the one-two. **B** moves to Position A.

3. **B** passes to **C** at the other end, who checks away before moving to receive.

4. **C** passes for **A**, who moves diagonally to provide a good support angle for **C**.

5. **A** sets the ball back for **C** to move forward onto. **A** moves to Position C.

6. **C** passes to the other end, where **B** has moved into Position A. **B** checks away before moving to receive.

7. **B** passes for **C**, who moves diagonally to provide a good support angle for **B** and the practice continues end to end.

Source: Jürgen Klopp's Liverpool training session at Melwood Training Ground, Liverpool - January 2018

Jürgen Klopp Practices: Passing Combinations

2. One-Two, Pass and Move 4-Player Support Play Combinations

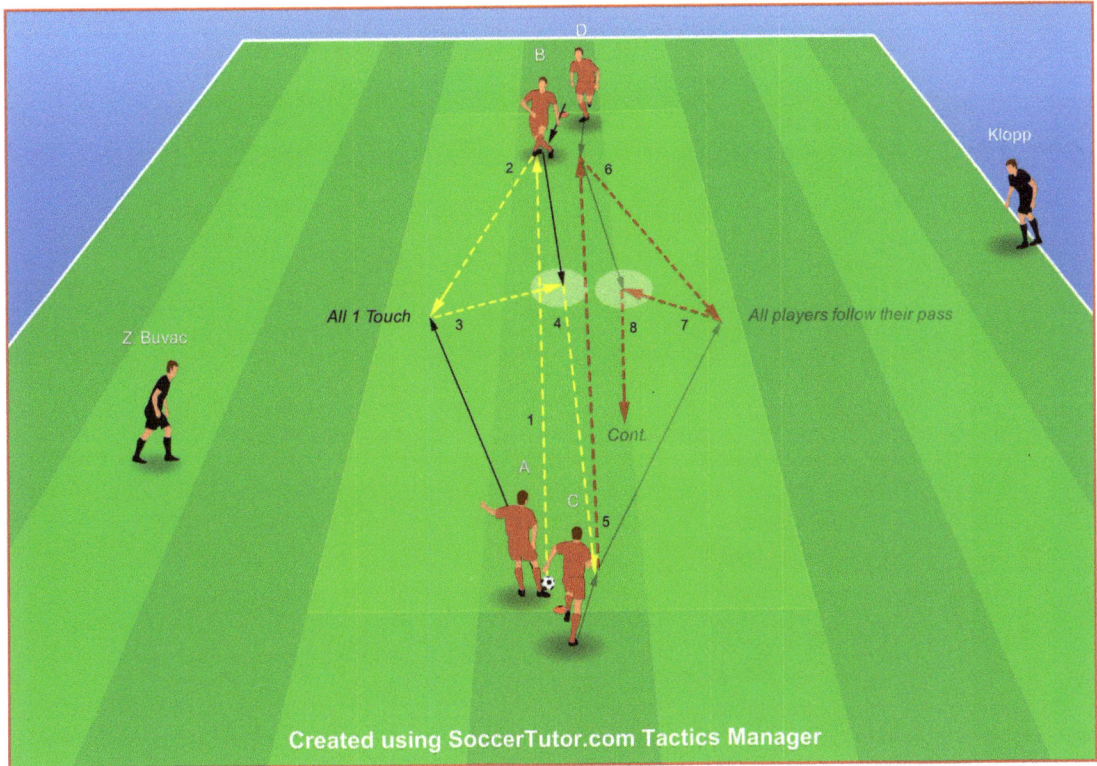

In this practice, all players follow their pass (A → B → C → D).

Practice Description

1. **A** passes to **B**, who moves forward off the cone.
2. **B** passes to the side for **A**, who moves diagonally to provide a good support angle for **B**.
3. **A** passes inside for **B** to move forward onto.
4. **B** passes to **C**, who moves forward off the cone.
5. **C** passes to **D**, who moves forward off the cone.
6. **D** passes to the side for **C**, who moves diagonally to provide a good support angle for **D**.
7. **C** passes inside for **D** to move forward onto.
8. **D** passes to the next player waiting in Position A and the practice continues end to end.

Source: Jürgen Klopp's Liverpool training session at Melwood Training Ground, Liverpool - January 2018

Jürgen Klopp Practices: Passing Combinations

3. Lofted Passing with 2-Pairs (Pass and Receive)

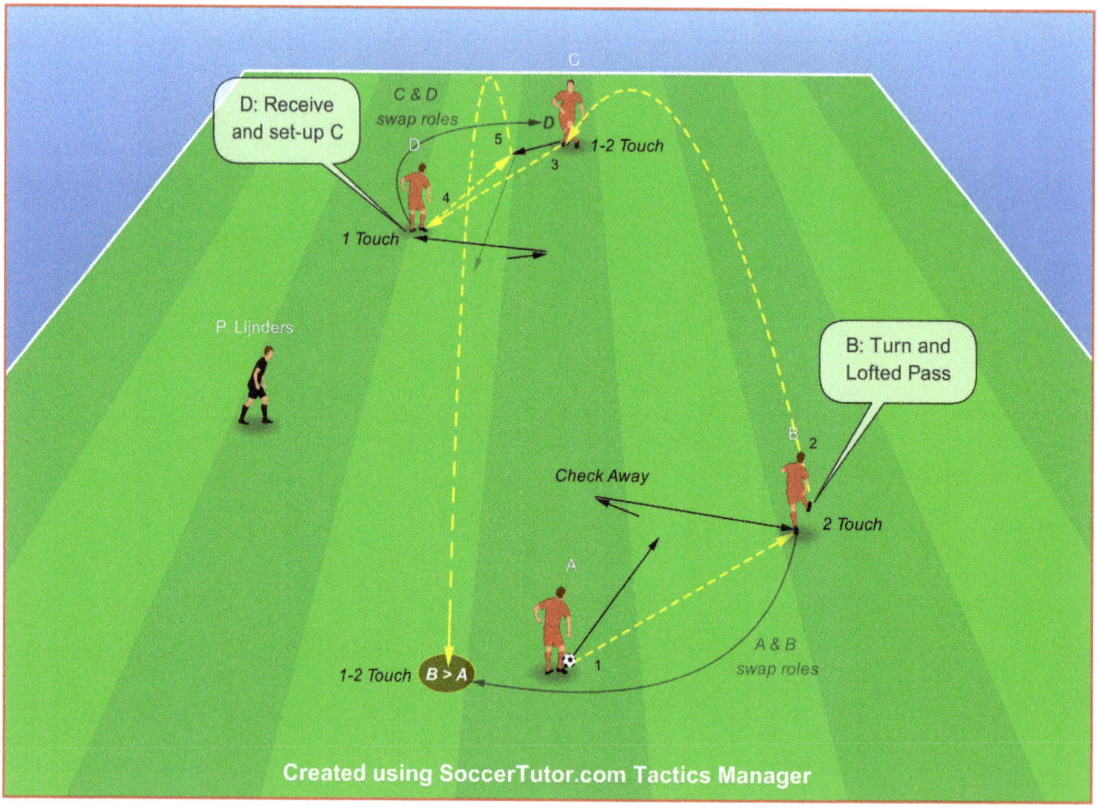

Practice Description

1. **A** passes to **B**, who checks away before moving to a wide angle to receive on the half-turn.

2. **B** plays a lofted pass to **C**.

   * A and B switch positions/roles.

3. **C** either passes first time or receives and passes (2 touches) to **D**.

4. **D** passes the ball back (lay-off) to set up **C** to play the next lofted pass.

5. **C** plays a lofted pass to **B**.

   * C and D switch positions/roles.

6. **B** either passes first time or receives and passes (2 touches) to **A**, and the practice continues with **A's** lofted pass to **D**.

Source: Jürgen Klopp's Liverpool training session at Melwood Training Ground, Liverpool - May 2020

Jürgen Klopp Practices: Passing Combinations

4. Passing in Fours + Quick Change of Direction to Go in Behind

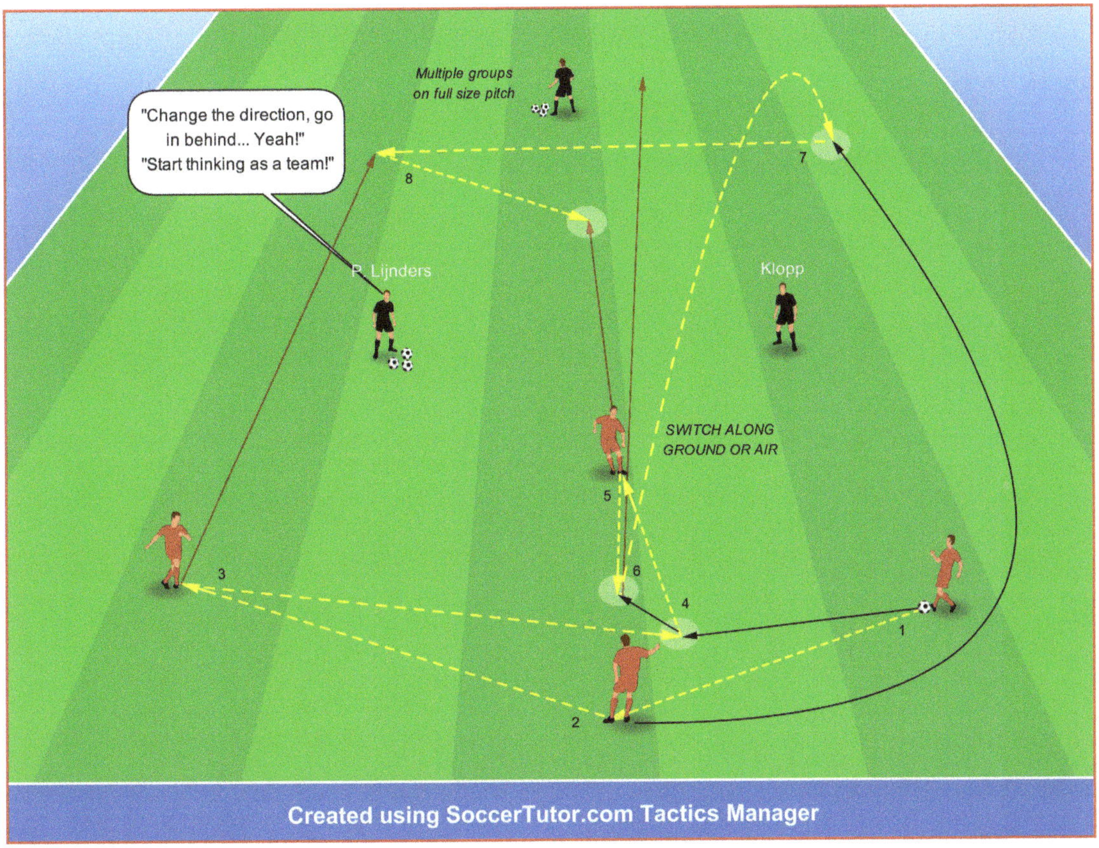

There are multiple groups performing the same practice on a full size pitch.

Practice Description

1-5. The practice starts with the 4 players passing between each other.

Players occasionally switch positions after their pass (not shown in diagram).

Trigger. One player makes a forward run, which acts as the "trigger." In the diagram, this is the deepest player.

6. The ball is set back for a teammate to play a forward (ground or lofted) pass for the run of the teammate that "triggered" the change of direction.

* All players "break" forward to the opposite end, as shown.

7-8... The practice continues with the 4 players passing between each other until the trigger for a change of direction to the opposite end again.

Source: Jürgen Klopp's Liverpool training session at AXA Training Centre, Liverpool - November 2020

Jürgen Klopp Practices: Passing Combinations

5. Two-Touch (Pass and Receive) Triangle

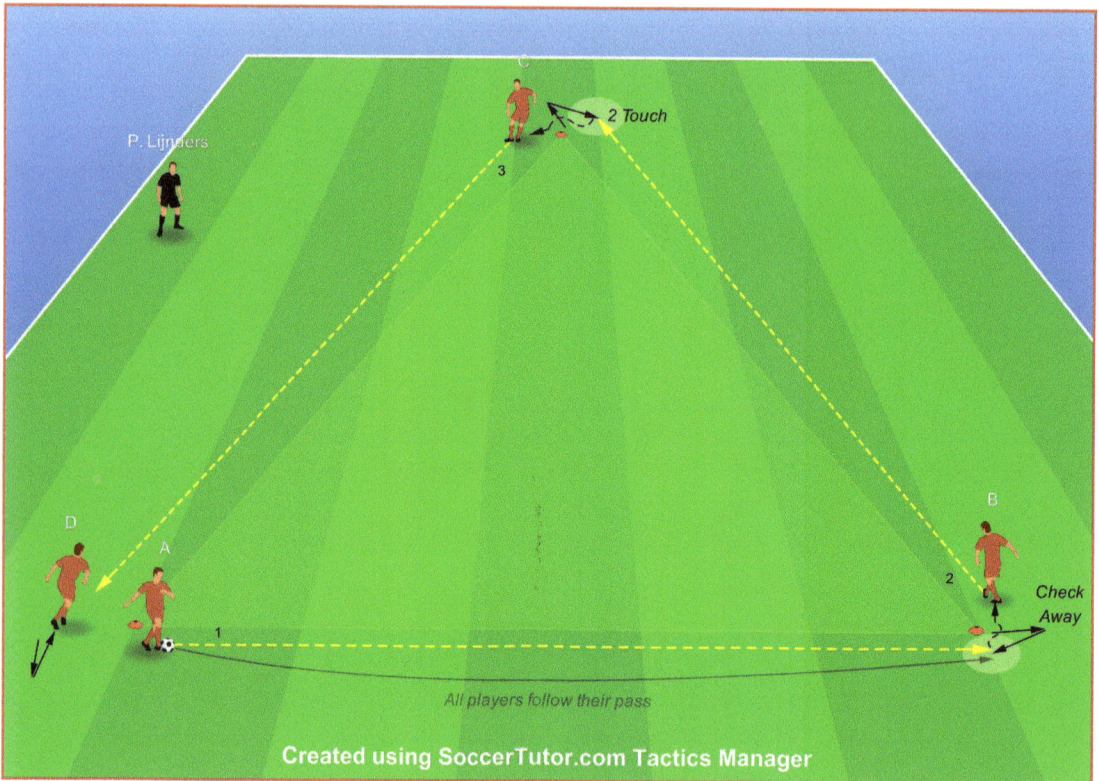

In this practice, all players use 2 touches to receive and pass outside the cones, and then follow their pass (**A → B → C → D**).

Practice Description

1. **A** passes to **B**, who checks away before moving to receive and then opens up to receive outside of the cone.

2. **B** passes to **C**, who does the same - checks away and opens up to receive.

3. **C** passes to **D**, who does the same - checks away and opens up to receive.

4. The sequence is repeated with **D** playing the next pass to **A**, as the practice continues in an anti-clockwise direction.

Source: Jürgen Klopp's Liverpool training session at Melwood Training Ground, Liverpool - July 2018

Jürgen Klopp Practices: Passing Combinations

6. Support Play and Timing of Movement Triangle with One-Twos

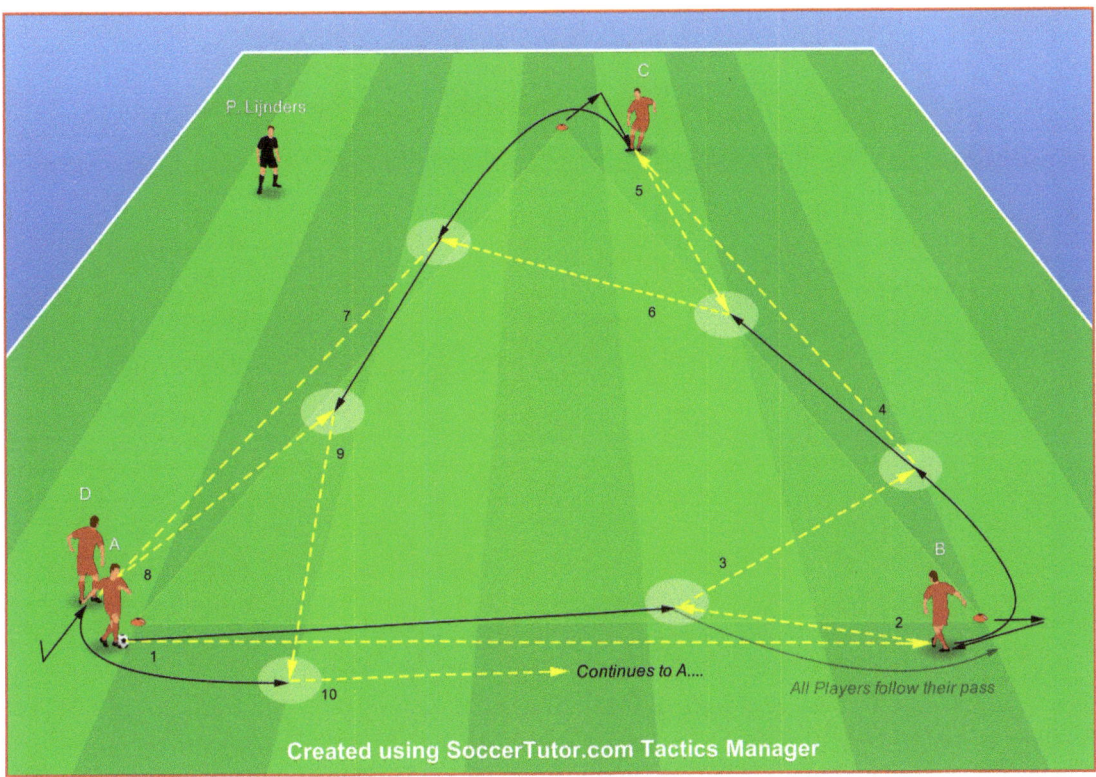

In this practice, all players follow their pass (A → B → C → D).

Practice Description

1. **A** passes to **B**, who checks away before moving towards **A** to receive.

2. **B** passes back for **A** to run onto.

3. **A** passes for **B** to move around the cone and receive.

4. **B** passes to **C**, who checks away before moving towards **B** to receive.

5. **C** passes back for **B** to run onto.

6. **B** passes for **C** to move around the cone and receive.

7. **C** passes to **D**, who checks away before moving towards **C** to receive.

8. **D** passes back for **C** to run onto.

9. **C** passes for **D** to move around the cone and receive.

10. The sequence is repeated with **D** playing the next pass as the practice continues in an anti-clockwise direction.

Source: Jürgen Klopp's Liverpool training session at Melwood Training Ground, Liverpool - July 2018

Jürgen Klopp Practices: Passing Combinations

7. Central Support, Diagonal Pass, Receive and Dribble in a Triangle

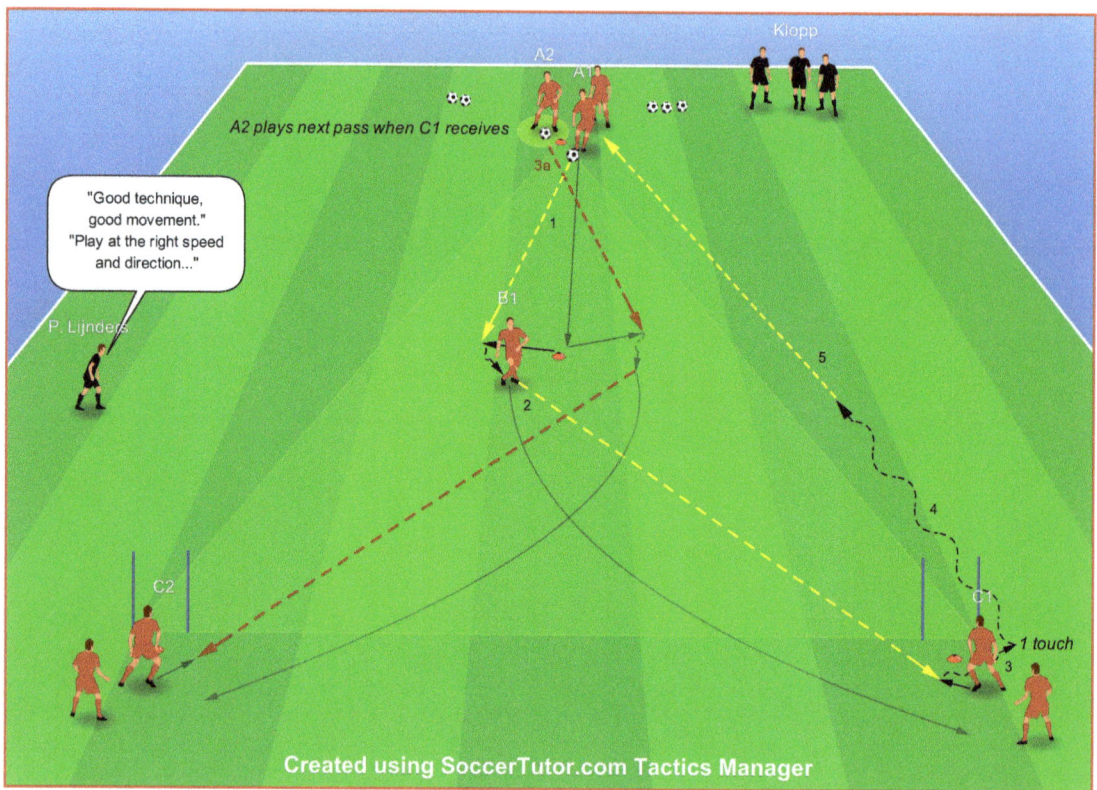

In this practice, the players follow their pass (A1 → B1 → C1 → A + A2 → A1 → C2 → A).

Practice Description

1. **A1** passes to **B1**, who moves off the cone and receives on the half-turn.

2. **B1** passes to **C1**.

3. **C1** opens up to receive behind the cone and around the 2 poles.

4. **C1** dribbles the ball towards the start.

5. **C1** passes to the next player waiting at the start position.

3a. As soon as **C1** receives from **B1**, **A2** passes a <u>second ball</u> to **A1**, who moves off the cone and receives on the half-turn.

... **A1** passes to **C2**, who opens up to receive behind the cone and around the 2 poles.

... **C2** also dribbles and passes back to the start.

... The next player waiting at <u>Position A</u>, who receives from **C1**, starts the exact same sequence to continue the practice.

Source: Jürgen Klopp's Liverpool training session at Ramon Sanchez-Pizjuan Stadium, Seville - July 2017

JÜRGEN KLOPP: PRACTICES FROM KLOPP'S SESSIONS

Jürgen Klopp Practices: Passing Combinations

8. Double Triangle Link Support Play in a "Passing Y"

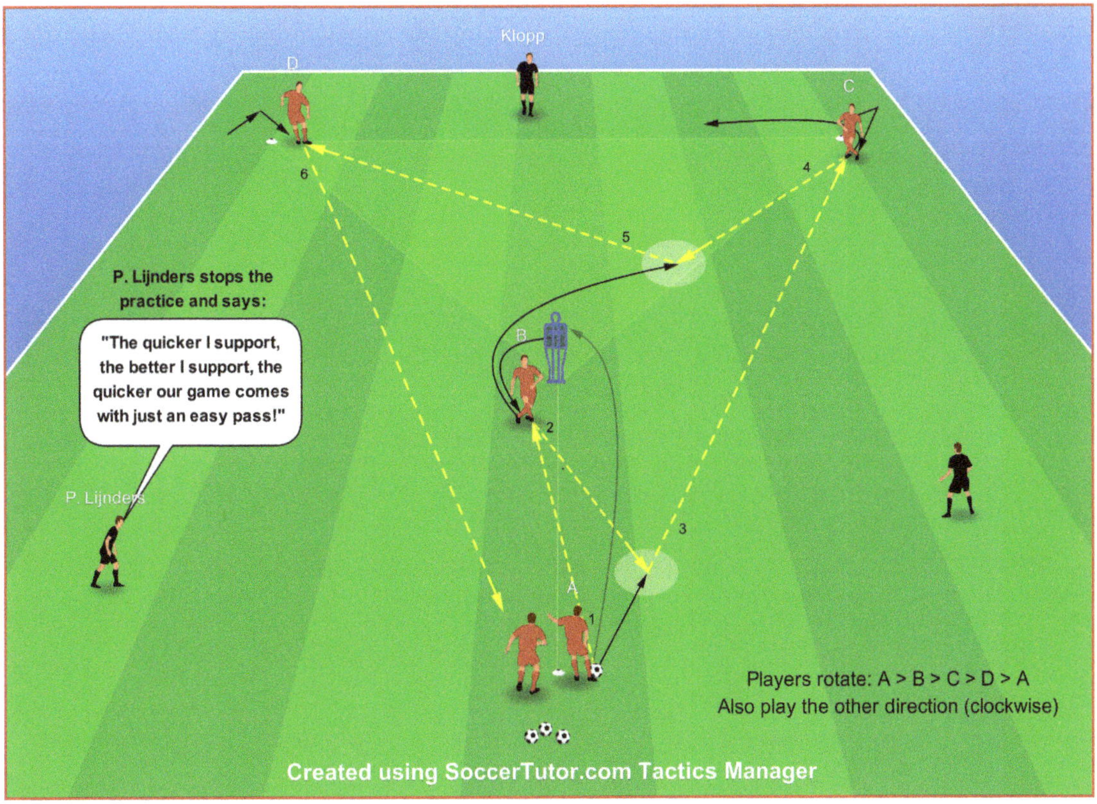

This practice is played in a clockwise and anti-clockwise direction and all players rotate their positions (A → B → C → D → A).

Practice Description

1. **A** passes to **B**, who drops back around the mannequin to receive.
2. **B** passes back to **A**, who moves at an angle to receive the return.
3. **A** passes diagonally to **C**, who checks off the cone before moving to receive.
4. **C** passes to **B**, who makes a well-timed movement around the mannequin to receive.
5. **B** passes diagonally to **D**, who checks off the cone before moving to receive.
6. **D** passes to the next player waiting at Position A and the same sequence is repeated as the practice continues.

Source: Jürgen Klopp's Liverpool training session at AXA Training Centre, Liverpool - March 2021

Jürgen Klopp Practices: Passing Combinations

9. Pass, Press, and Rotate in a 2-Ball Passing Diamond

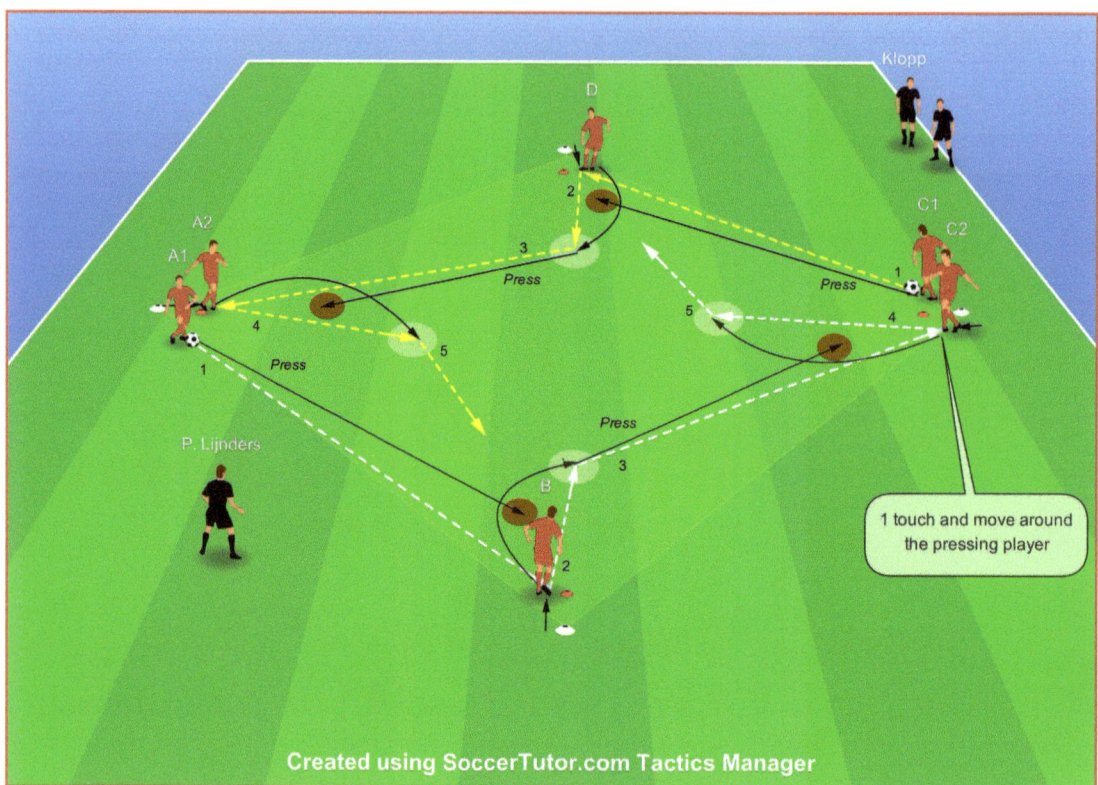

*The practice starts with **2 balls simultaneously from Players A1 and C1**, the players all use 1 touch only, and the players rotate A → B → C2 → C1 → D → A2 → A1.*

Practice Description

1. **A1/C1** pass to **B/D** and then move to press them, as shown.
2. **B/D** touch the ball forwards and run around the left side of the pressing player **A1/C1** to receive.
3. **B/D** pass to **C2/A2** and then move to press them.
4. **B/D** touch the ball forwards and run around the left side of the pressing player **C2/A2** to receive.
5. **C2/A2** pass to the next players waiting at <u>Positions B & D</u> and the practice continues in an anti-clockwise direction.

Source: Jürgen Klopp's Liverpool training session at AXA Training Centre, Liverpool - November 2020

Jürgen Klopp Practices: Passing Combinations

10. One-Twos and Third Man Run Combinations with Switch of Play

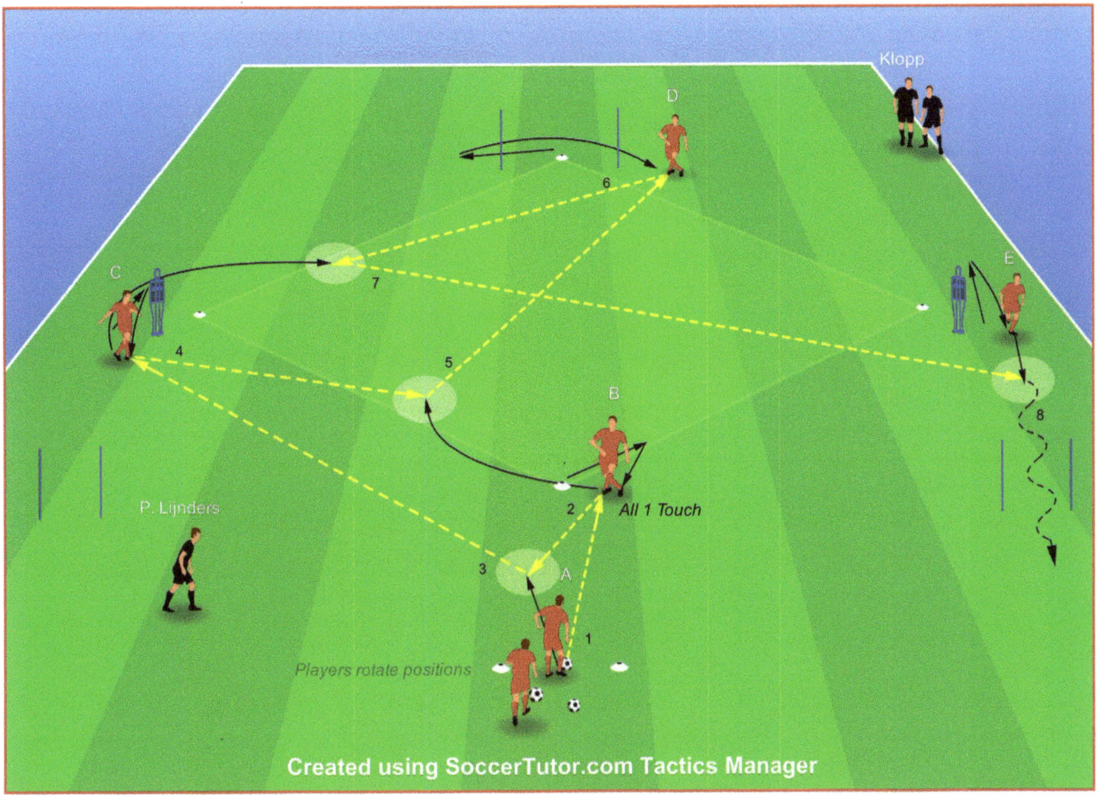

In this practice, the players use **1 touch** throughout and always rotate their positions (A → B → C → D → E → A).

Practice Description

1. **A** passes to **B**, who checks off the cone before dropping back to receive.
2. **B** plays the ball back (lay-off) for **A**.
3. **A** passes to **C**, who checks and drops back to receive in front of the mannequin.
4. **C** passes inside for **B's** movement.
5. **B** passes to **D**, who checks away and then moves all the way across around the 2 poles to receive.
6. **D** lays the ball off for **C**, who runs around the mannequin to receive.
7. **C** plays the final pass of the sequence for **E**, who first checks and then runs to receive beyond the mannequin.
8. **E** dribbles through the pole gate and back to the start. The practice continues with the next player at Position A.

Source: Jürgen Klopp's Liverpool training session at Melwood Training Ground, Liverpool - May 2017

Jürgen Klopp Practices: Passing Combinations

11. Third Man Run Combinations + Give & Go Passing Circuit

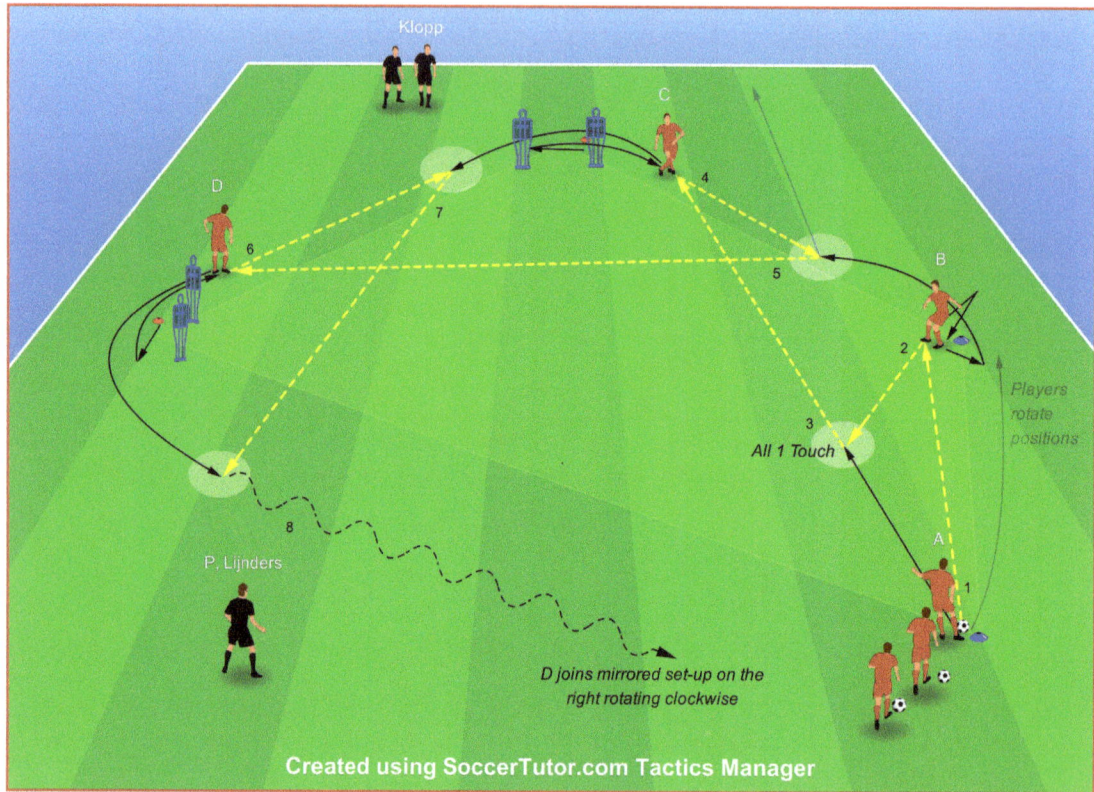

In this practice, the players use **1 touch** throughout and always rotate their positions (A → B → C → D → **Mirrored Group**).

Practice Description

1. **A** passes to **B**, who checks off the cone before moving to receive.
2. **B** plays the ball back (lay-off) for the forward run of **A**.
3. **A** passes to **C**, who checks and moves to receive in front of the mannequin.
4. **C** lays the ball off for **B**, who drops and then runs around the cone to receive.
5. **B** passes across to **D**, who checks and moves to receive in front of the mannequin.
6. **D** lays the ball off for **C**, who runs around the 2 mannequins to receive.
7. **C** plays the final pass of the sequence for **D's** run around the 2 mannequins.
8. **D** dribbles to the mirrored set up to the right of this one, which rotates in a clockwise direction.

Source: Jürgen Klopp's Liverpool training session at Melwood Training Ground, Liverpool - May 2019

Jürgen Klopp Practices: Passing Combinations

12. Two-Touch "Double Triangle" Passing Circuit

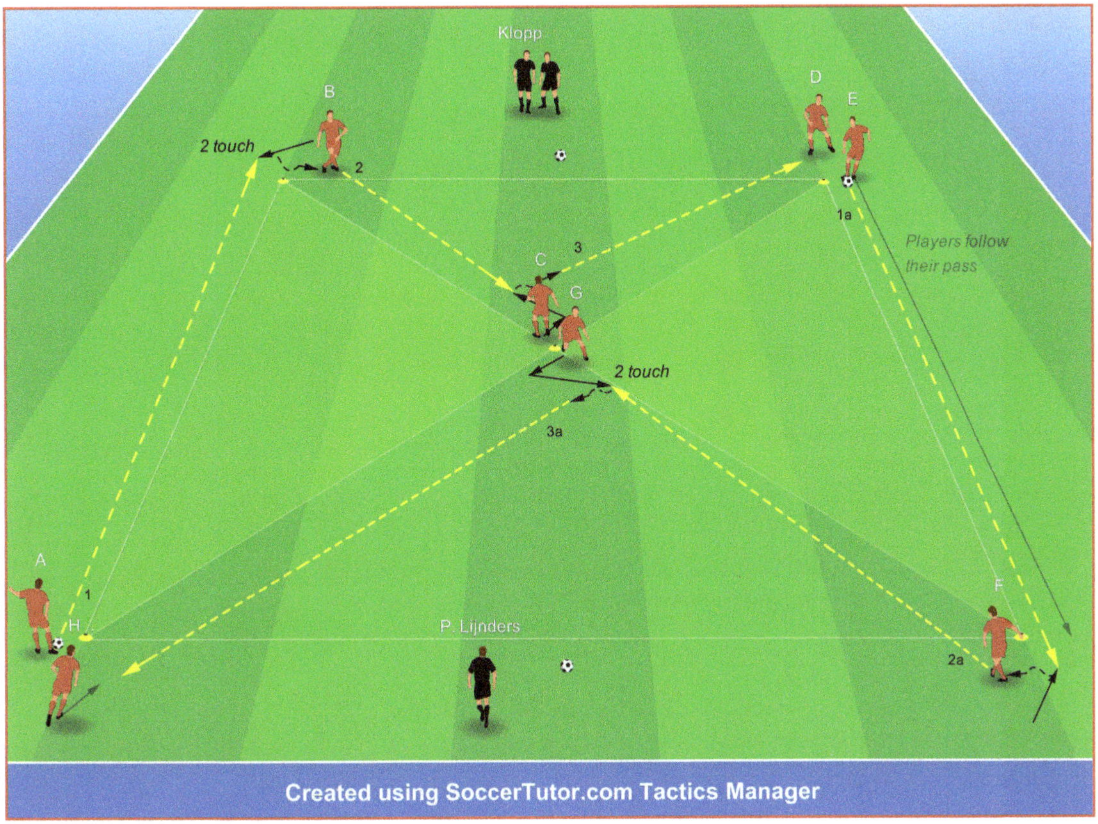

*Practice starts with **2 balls simultaneously from Players A and E** and the players rotate A → B → C → D → E → F → G → H → A).*

Practice Description

1. **A/E** pass to **B/F**, who open up and receive with their first touch.

2. **B/F** use their second touch to pass diagonally to **C/G**, who check, open up and receive with their first touch.

3. **C/G** use their second touch to pass to **D/H**, which completes the sequence.

... The practice continues with the exact same sequence.

Source: Jürgen Klopp's Liverpool training session at Melwood Training Ground, Liverpool - April 2019

13. Two-Touch "Double Triangle" Passing Circuit with One-Two

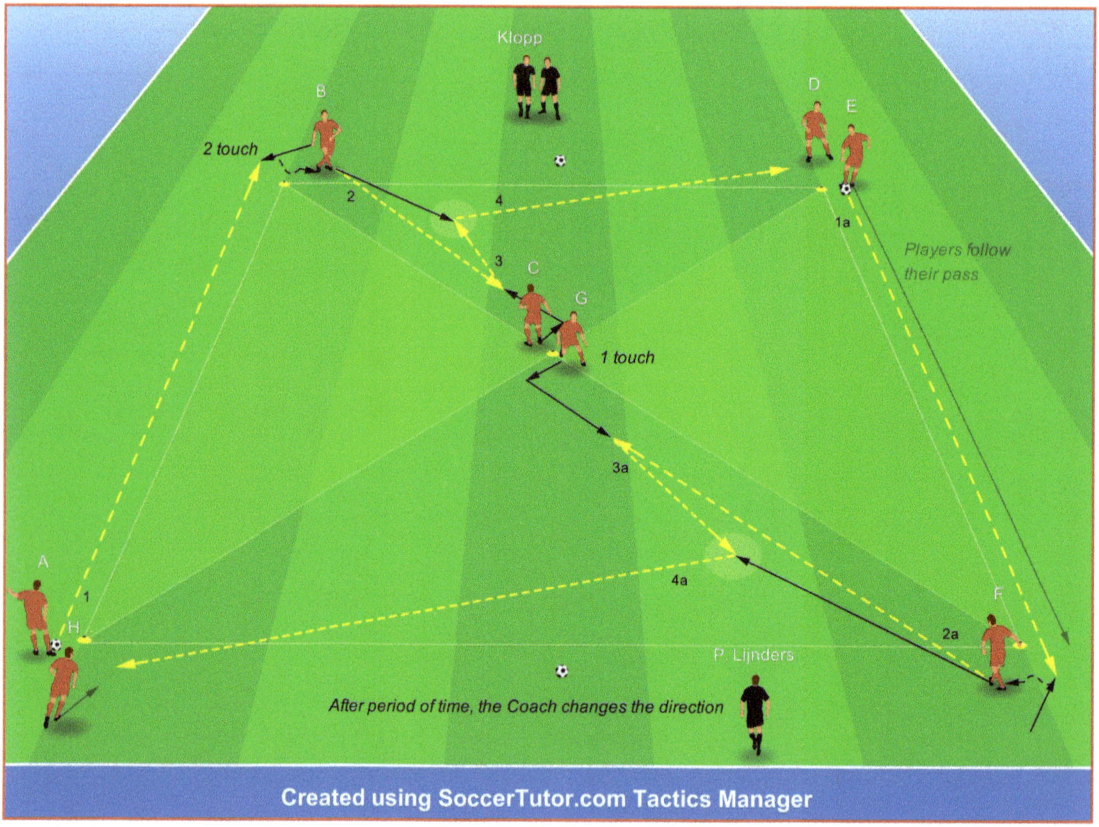

Practice starts with **2 balls simultaneously from Players A and E** and the players rotate A → B → C → D → E → F → G → H → A).

Practice Description

1. **A/E** pass to **B/F**, who open up and receive with their first touch.

2. **B/F** use their second touch to pass diagonally to **C/G**, who check and drop back to receive.

3. **C/G** pass the ball back for **B/F** (1 touch).

4. **B/F** move to meet the return and pass to **D/H**, which completes the sequence.

... The practice continues with the exact same sequence.

Source: Jürgen Klopp's Liverpool training session at Melwood Training Ground, Liverpool - April 2019

Jürgen Klopp Practices: Passing Combinations

14. Open Up to Support in a Multi-Direction Passing Square

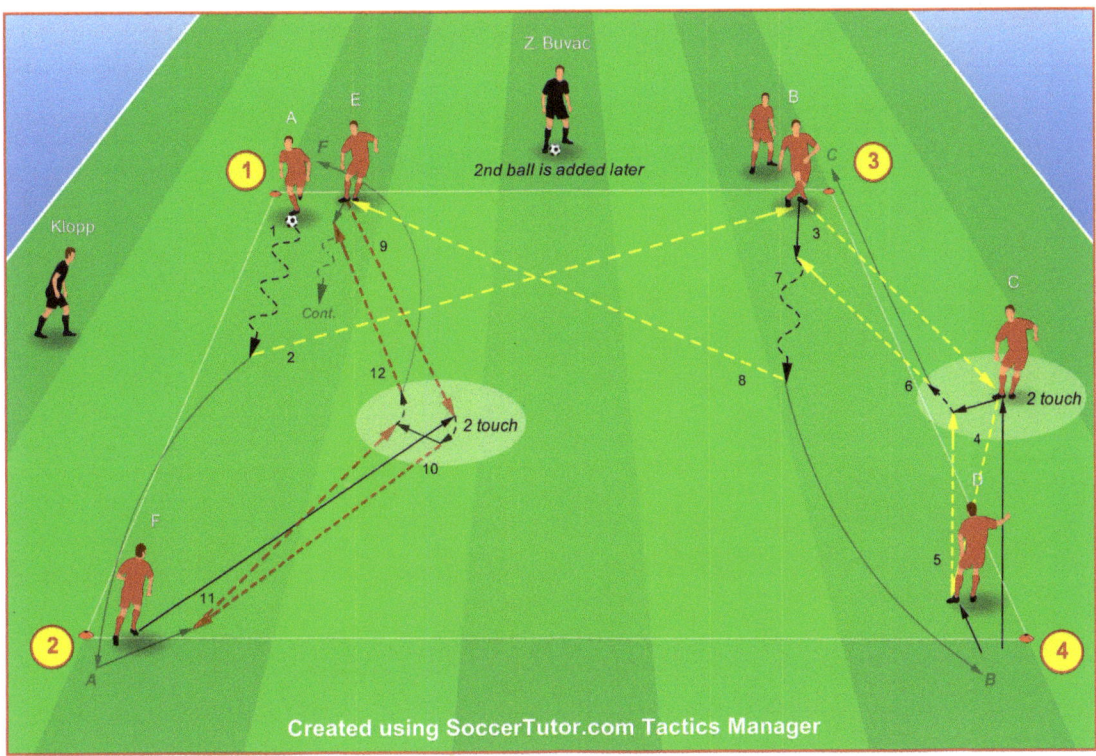

Practice Description

1. **A** carries the ball forward into the area.
2. **A** passes diagonally across to **B** and moves to Position 2.
3. **B** passes outside to **C**, who moves off the cone to receive.
4. **C** uses 2 touches to receive on the half-turn and pass to **D**.
5. **D** passes back to **C**.
6. **C** uses 2 touches to receive on the half-turn and pass to **B**, and then moves to Position 3.
7. **B** carries the ball forward into the area.
8. **B** passes diagonally across to **E** and moves to Position 4.
9. **E** passes to **F**, who moves inside the area to receive.
10. **F** uses 2 touches to receive on the half-turn and pass to **A**.
11. **A** passes back to **C**.
12. **F** uses 2 touches to receive on the half-turn and pass to **E**, and then moves to Position 1.
13. The practice sequence restarts from **E**.

Source: Jürgen Klopp's Liverpool training session at Melwood Training Ground, Liverpool - January 2018

Jürgen Klopp Practices: Passing Combinations

15. Diagonal Passes and Support Play Movements to Left and Right

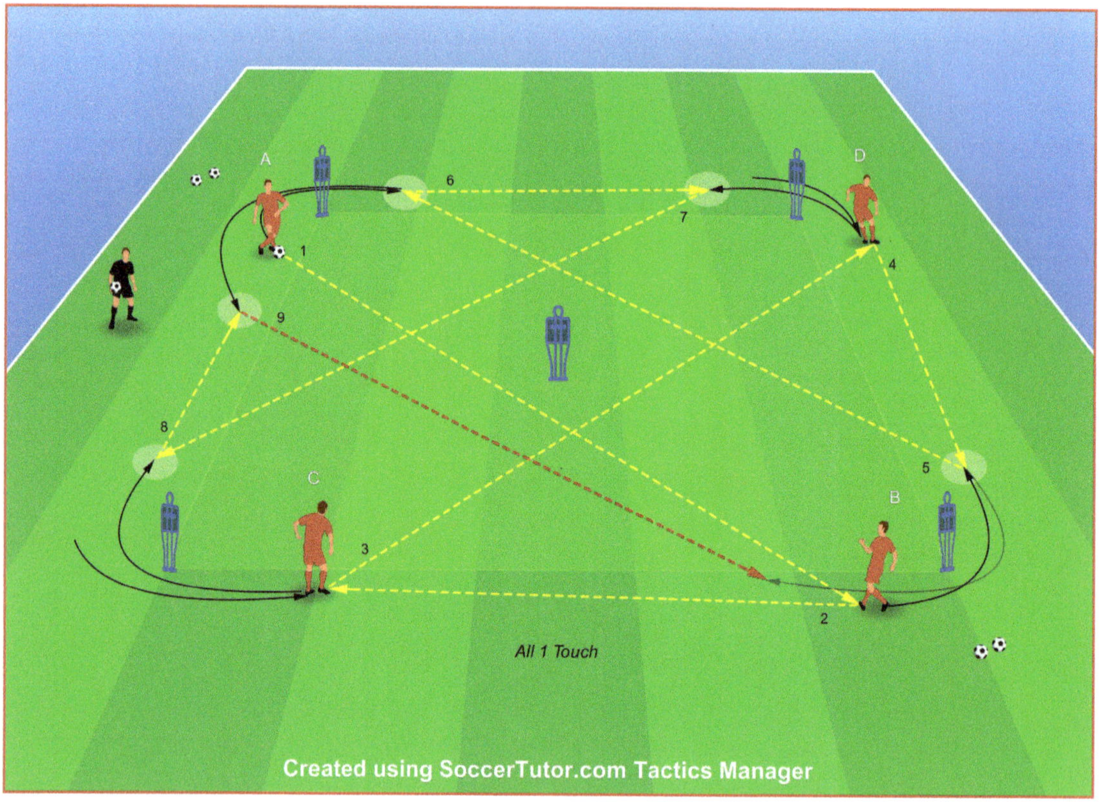

In this practice, the 4 players stay in their corners and do not rotate positions. They **continuously move from one side of the mannequin to the other to provide passing angles to receive** *(left, right, left, etc).*

Practice Description

1. **A** passes diagonally to **B's** left side.
2. **B** passes straight to **C's** right side.
3. **C** passes diagonally to **D's** left side.
4. **D** passes straight to **B's** right side.
5. **B** passes diagonally to **A's** left side.
6. **A** passes straight to **D's** right side.
7. **D** passes diagonally to **C's** left side.
8. **C** passes straight to **A's** right side.
9. The sequence is repeated starting with **A** passing diagonally to **B's** left side again (as in step 1).

Source: Jürgen Klopp's Liverpool training session at Melwood Training Ground, Liverpool - May 2020

Jürgen Klopp Practices: Passing Combinations

16. Receive on Half-Turn + Diagonal Pass

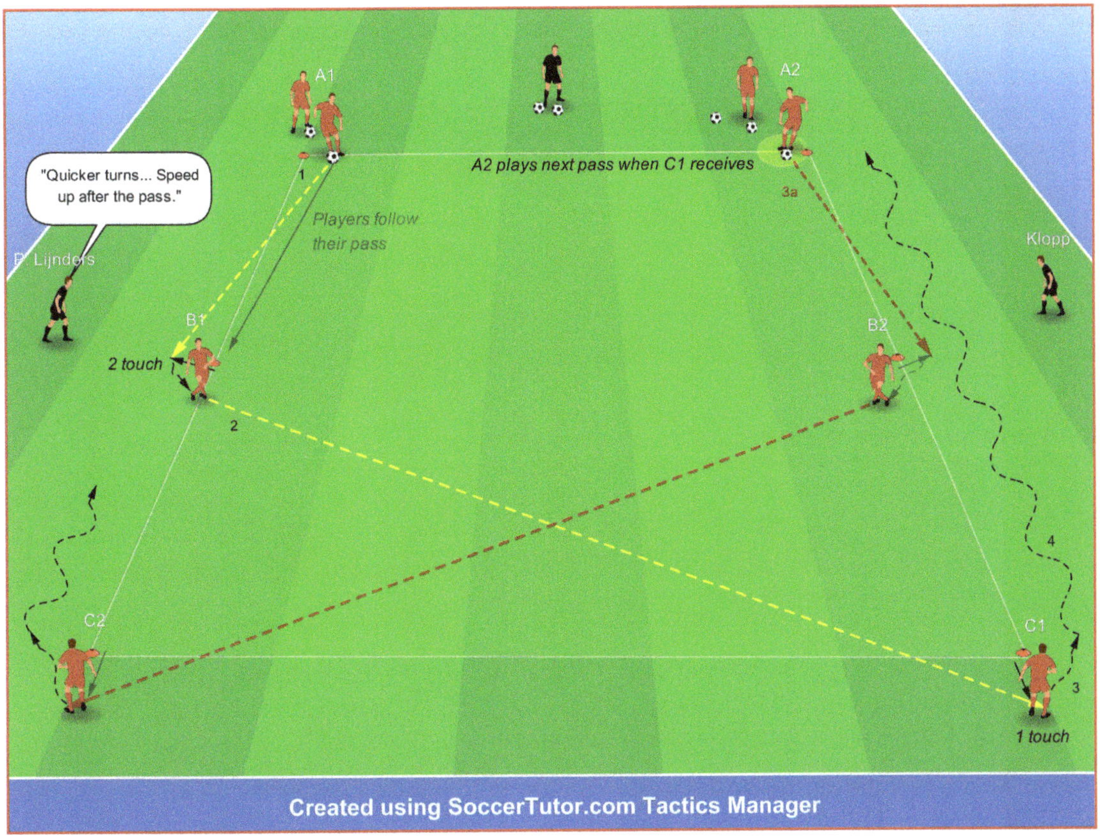

In this practice, the players follow their pass (A1 → B1 → C1 → A2 / A2 → B2 → C2 → A1).

Practice Description

1. **A1** passes to **B1**, who checks off the cone, opens up and receives with first touch.

2. **B1** uses his second touch to pass diagonally to **C1**.

3. **C1** opens up to receive behind the cone with his first touch.

4. **C1** dribbles to Position A2, as shown.

3a. As soon as **C1** receives from **B1**, **A2** passes a second ball to **B2**, who opens up and receives with his first touch.

... **B2** uses his second touch to pass diagonally to **C2**.

... **C2** also opens up to receive and dribbles to Position A1.

... The next player waiting at Position A1 starts the exact same sequence to continue the practice with a new ball.

Source: Jürgen Klopp's Liverpool training session at Melwood Training Ground, Liverpool - September 2019

Jürgen Klopp Practices: Passing Combinations

17. Receive on Half-Turn, Diagonal Pass + One-Two

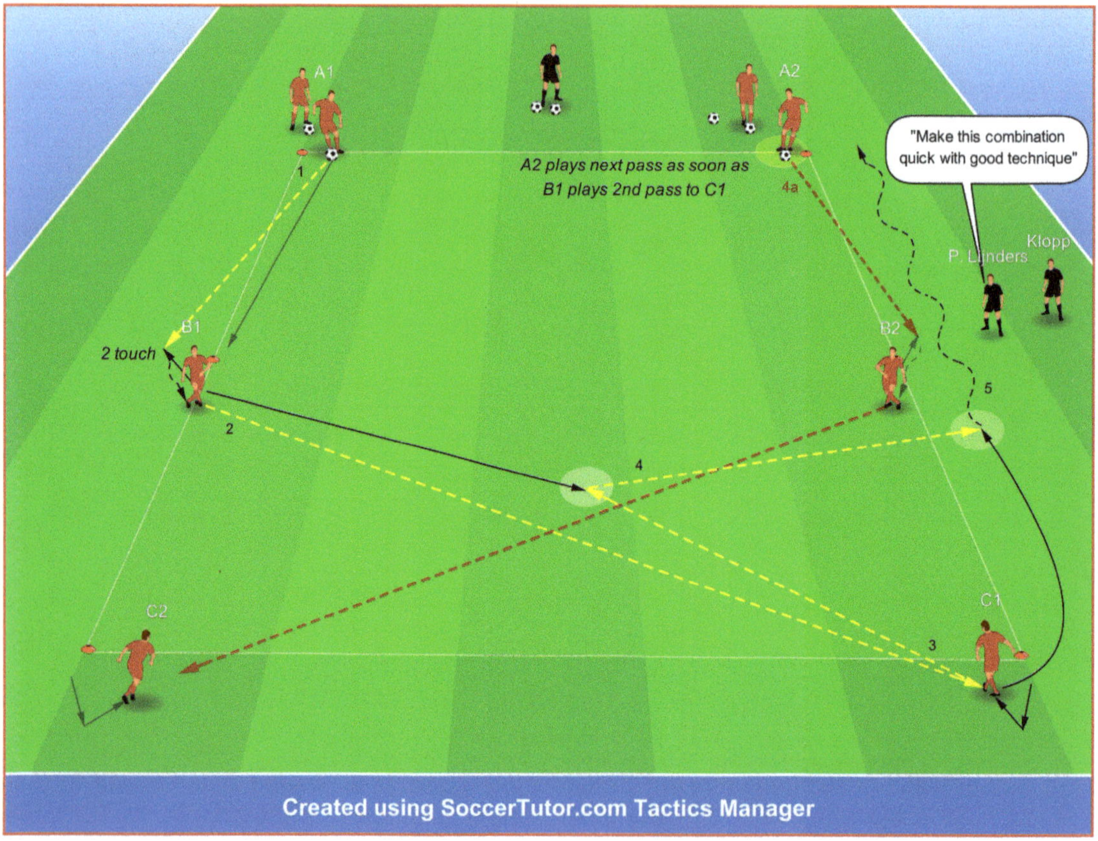

In this practice, the players follow their pass (A1 → B1 → C1 → A2 / A2 → B2 → C2 → A1).

Practice Description

1. **A1** passes to **B1**, who checks off the cone, opens up and receives with first touch.

2. **B1** uses his second touch to pass diagonally to **C1**.

3. **C1** checks off the cone, moves to receive and passes into the area for the diagonal movement of **B1**.

4. **B1** makes a well-weighted pass for the run of **C1** around the cone.

5. **C1** dribbles to <u>Position A2</u>, as shown.

4a. As soon as **B1** plays his second pass to **C1**, **A2** passes a <u>second ball</u> to **B2**, who opens up and receives with his first touch.

... The same sequence is repeated as a mirror image: **A2 → B2 → C2 → B2 → C2 → A1 → Next player at Position A1 goes.**

Source: Jürgen Klopp's Liverpool training session at Melwood Training Ground, Liverpool - September 2019

Jürgen Klopp Practices: Passing Combinations

18. Double One-Two + Pass in Mini Goal

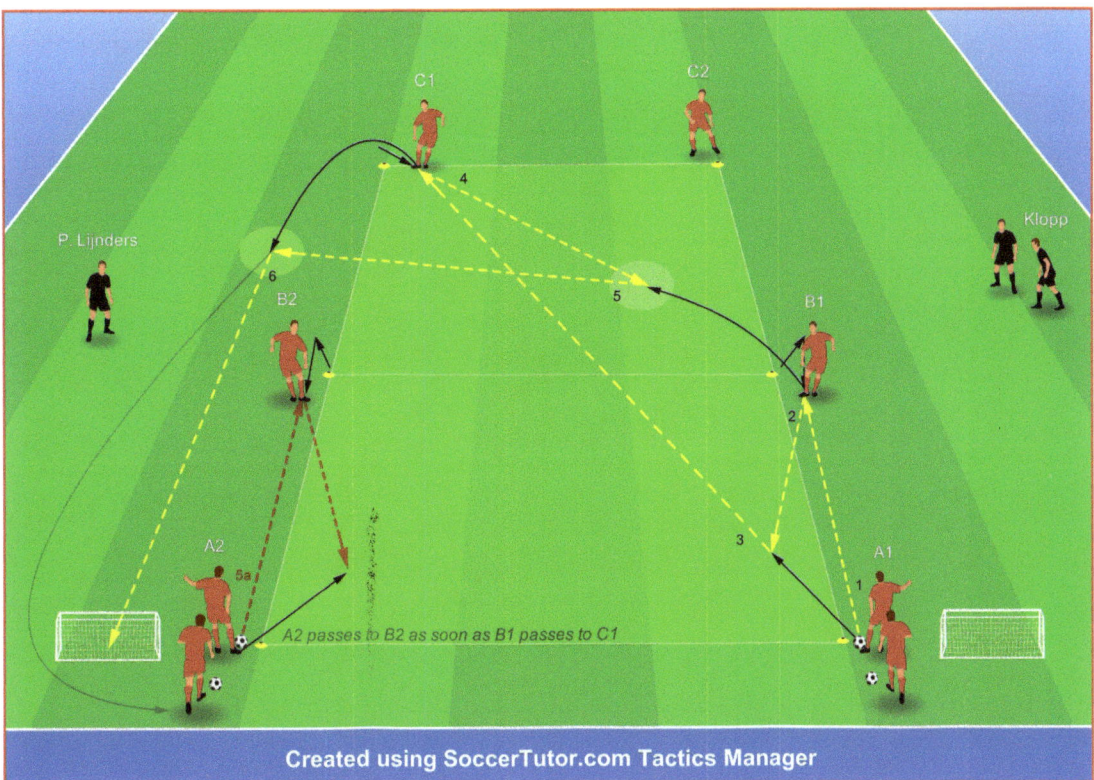

In this practice, the players follow their pass (A1 → B1 → C1 → A2 / A2 → B2 → C2 → A1).

Practice Description

1. **A1** passes to **B1**, who checks off the cone and drops back to receive.
2. **B1** passes back to **A1**.
3. **A1** plays a diagonal pass to **C1**.
4. **C1** lays the ball off for **B1's** movement around the cone.
5. **B1** passes across for the well-timed run of **C1** around the cone.
6. **C1** passes into the mini goal and moves to Position A2.

5a. As soon as **B1** passes to **C1**, **A2** passes a second ball to **B2**, who checks off the cone and drops back to receive.

... The same sequence is repeated as a mirror image:

A2 → B2 → C2 → B2 → C2 → Mini Goal.

Source: Jürgen Klopp's Liverpool training session at Melwood Training Ground, Liverpool - August 2019

Jürgen Klopp Practices: Passing Combinations

19. Quick One-Twos and Timing of Support + Switch of Pass

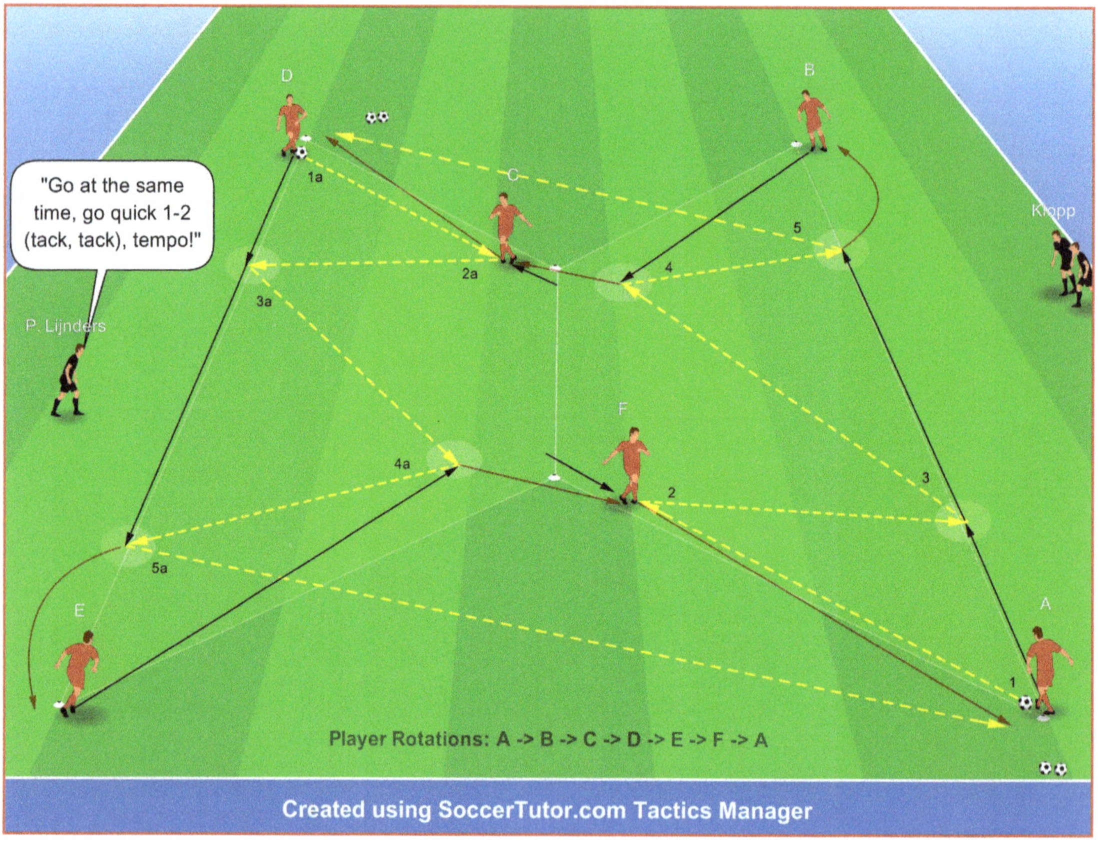

Practice starts with **2 balls simultaneously from Players A and D** *and the players rotate* A → B → C → D → E → F → A).

Practice Description

1. **A/D** pass to **C/F**, who move off their middle cones.

2. **C/F** pass in front of **A/D** to run onto.

3. **A** passes to **C** and **D** passes to **F**. **C** and **F** both move across to the other side to receive (red arrows in diagram).

4. **C/F** pass in front of **D/A** to run onto.

5. **A** passes across to **C**, who has already moved to Position D.

   D passes across to **F**, who has already moved to Position A.

   ... The practice continues with the exact same sequence.

Source: Jürgen Klopp's Liverpool training session at AXA Training Centre, Liverpool - February 2021

Jürgen Klopp Practices: Passing Combinations

20. Give & Go + Switch in Two Connected Passing Squares

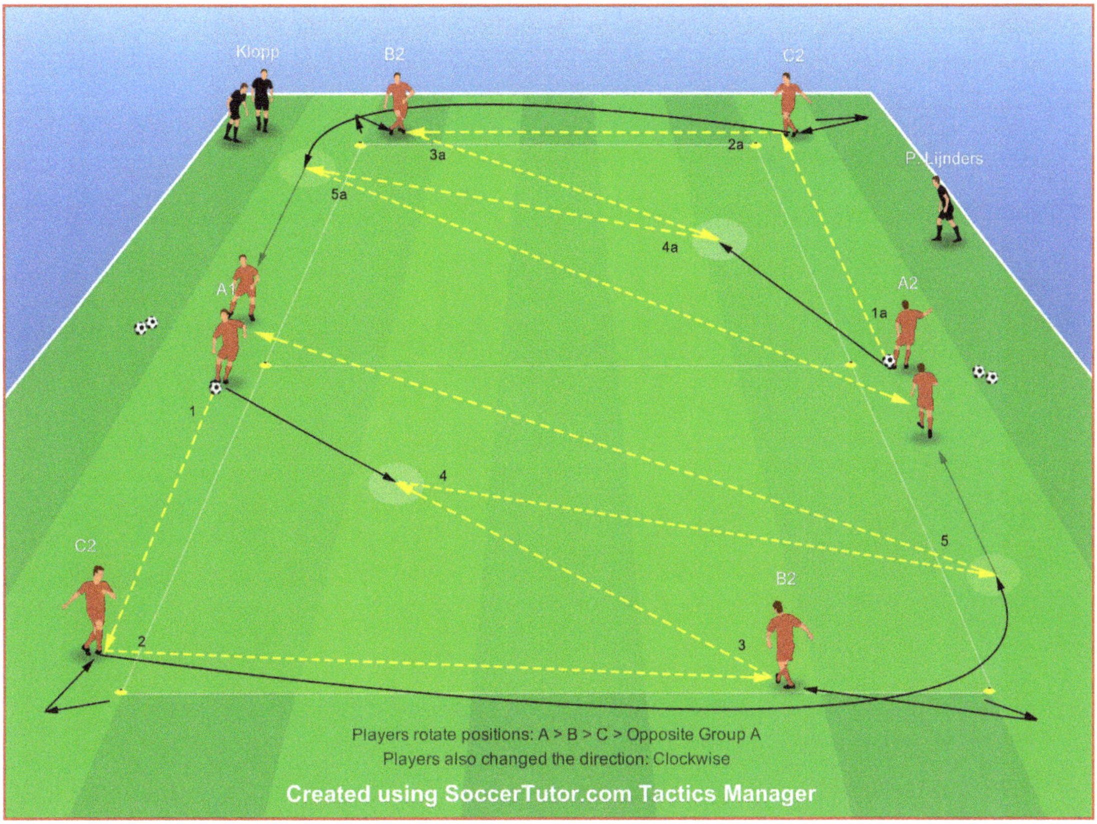

[Diagram of practice setup]

The practice starts with **2 balls simultaneously from Players A1 and A2**, is played in a clockwise and anti-clockwise direction + all players rotate their positions: A → B → C → Opposite Group A.

Practice Description

1. **A1/A2** pass to **C1/C2**, who check off their cones before moving to receive.

2. **C1/C2** pass to **B1/B2**, who check off their cones before moving to receive.

3. **B1/B2** pass into the area for the movement of **A1/A2**.

4. **A1/A2** play well-weighted passes for the long runs of **C1/C2** to receive.

5. **C1/C2** pass to Position A. They then move to the start of the opposite group.

... The same sequence is repeated, and the practice is continuous.

Source: Jürgen Klopp's Liverpool training session at Melwood Training Ground, Liverpool - June 2020

Jürgen Klopp Practices: Passing Combinations

21. Short One-Twos in a "Double Square" with Central Support Play

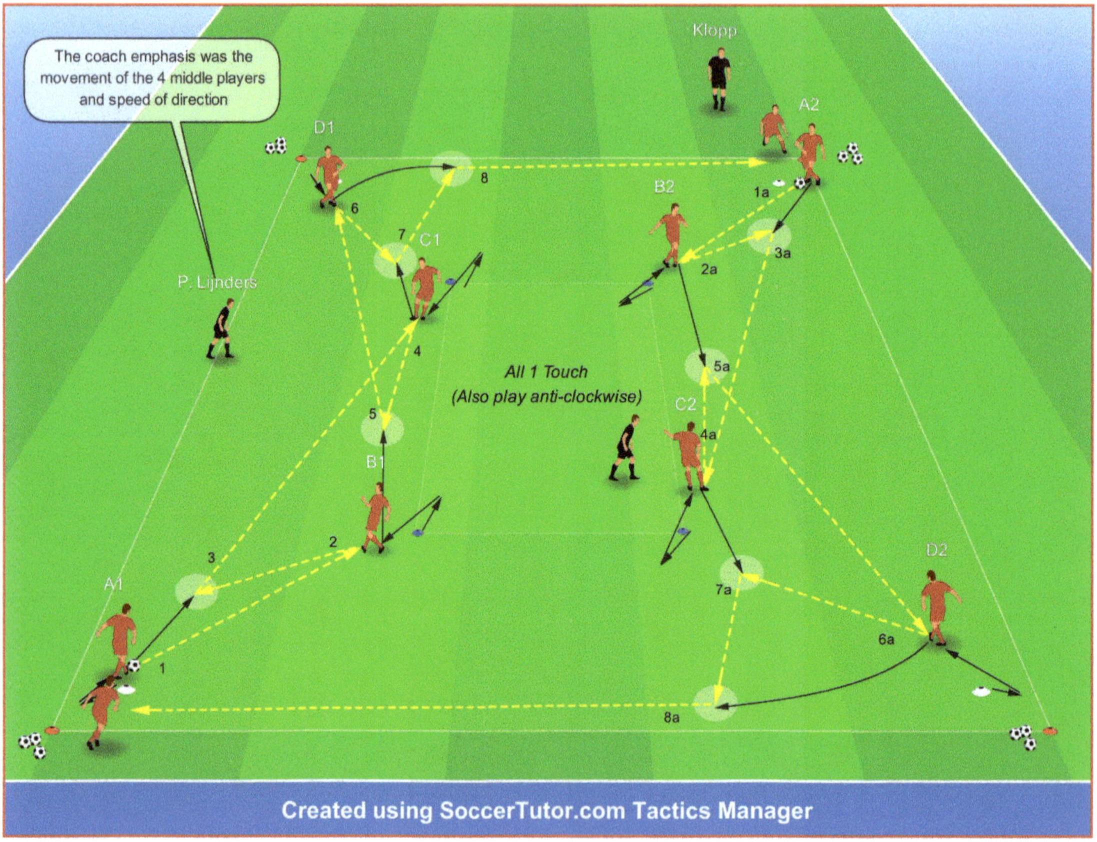

The practice starts with **2 balls simultaneously from Players A1 and A2** and all players rotate their positions:
A → B → C → D → Opposite Group A.

Practice Description

* The 4 middle players all check off their cones before moving to receive

1. **A1/A2** pass to **B1/B2**.
2. **B1/B2** pass back to **A1/A2**.
3. **A1/A2** pass to **C1/C2**.
4. **C1/C2** lay the ball back for **B1/B2**.
5. **B1/B2** pass to **D1/D2**.
6. **D1/D2** lay the ball back for **C1/C2**.
7. **C1/C2** pass in front of **D1/D2** for them to move onto.
8. **D1** passes to Position A2 and **D2** passes to Position A1, and the same sequence starts from the next players waiting.

Source: Jürgen Klopp's Liverpool training session at Melwood Training Ground, Liverpool - October 2020

Jürgen Klopp Practices: Passing Combinations

22. Breaking the Lines with Angled Support, Lay-offs and Forward Runs

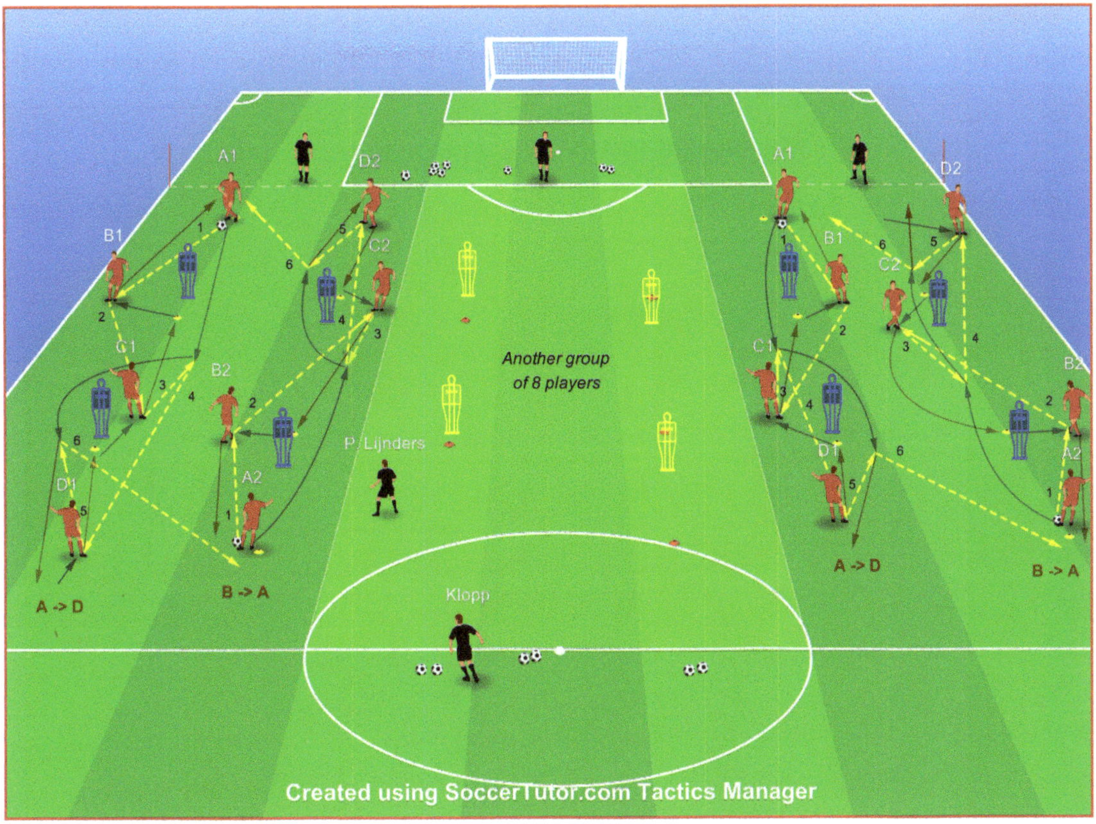

*The practice starts with **2 balls simultaneously from Players A1 and A2** and all players create good angles to receive.*

Practice Description

1. **A** passes to **B**.
2. **B** passes to **C** and moves back to Position A.
3. **C** sets the ball back for **A**, who has moved forward past the first mannequin. **C** moves back to Position B.
4. **A** passes to **D**.
5. **D** sets the ball back for **A**, who makes a curved run around the second mannequin. **D** moves back to Position C.
6. **A** passes to Position A of the other group next to them and moves to Position D.

... The same sequence is repeated in this continuous practice.

Source: Jürgen Klopp's Liverpool pre-season training session in Charlotte, NC, United States - July 2018

Jürgen Klopp Practices: Passing Combinations

23. Breaking the Lines with Angled Support, Lay-offs + Third Man Run

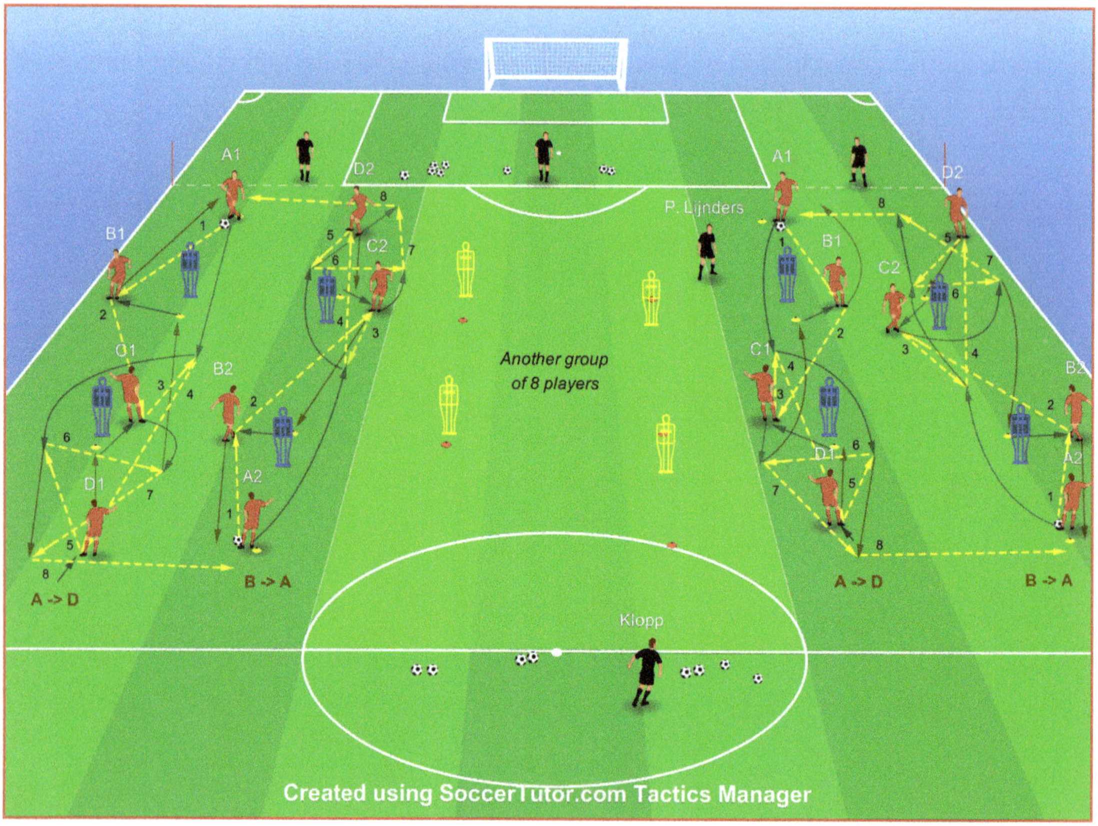

The practice starts with **2 balls simultaneously from Players A1 and A2** and all players create good angles to receive.

Practice Description

1. **A** passes to **B**.
2. **B** passes to **C** and moves back to Position A.
3. **C** sets the ball back for **A**, who has moved forward past the first mannequin.
4. **A** passes to **D**.
5. **D** sets the ball back for **A**, who makes a curved run around the second mannequin. **D** moves back to Position C.
6. **A** passes across to **C**, who turns to receive.
7. **C** plays the return for **A** on the run. **C** moves back to Position B.
8. **A** passes to Position A of the other group next to them and moves to Position D. The same sequence is then repeated in this continuous practice.

Source: Jürgen Klopp's Liverpool pre-season training session in Charlotte, NC, United States - July 2018

Jürgen Klopp Practices: Passing Combinations

24. Passing and Support Play with Quick Rotations and Movements

Pattern Example 1: Receive <u>OUTSIDE</u> 4 Box Mannequins First

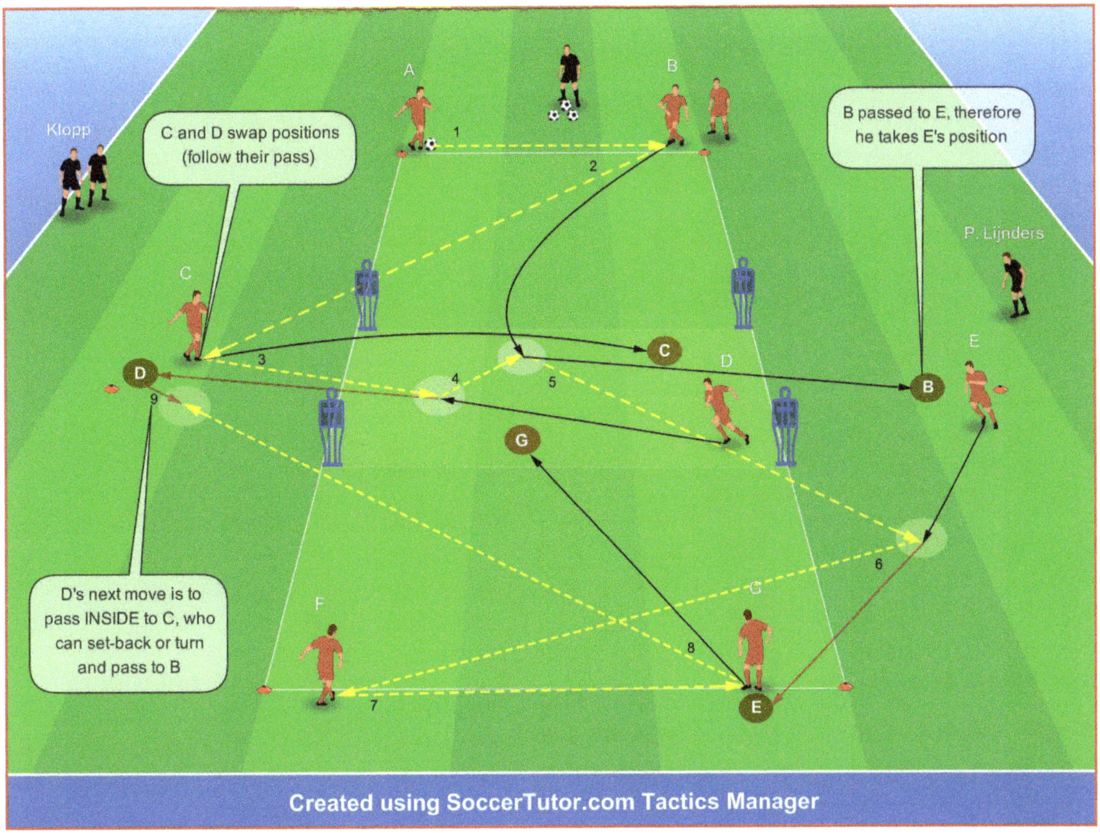

Practice Description

1. **A** passes to **B**.
2. **B** passes to **C**, who is positioned <u>OUTSIDE</u> of the 4 box mannequins by the wide cone. He can choose to receive <u>INSIDE</u> too (see next page).
3. **C** passes to **D**, who moves across from the other side to provide support.
4. **D** sets the ball back for the advancing **B**.
5. **B** passes out wide and in front of the mannequin for the forward run of **E**.
6. **E** passes diagonally to **F**.
7. **F** passes across to **G**.
8. **G** passes to **D**, who is now positioned <u>OUTSIDE</u> of the 4 box mannequins.
9-10. **D** passes inside to **C**, and **C** sets the ball back for **G** or turns and passes to **B**.

Source: Jürgen Klopp's Liverpool training session at AXA Training Centre, Liverpool - July 2022

Jürgen Klopp Practices: Passing Combinations

Pattern Example 2: Receive INSIDE 4 Box Mannequins First

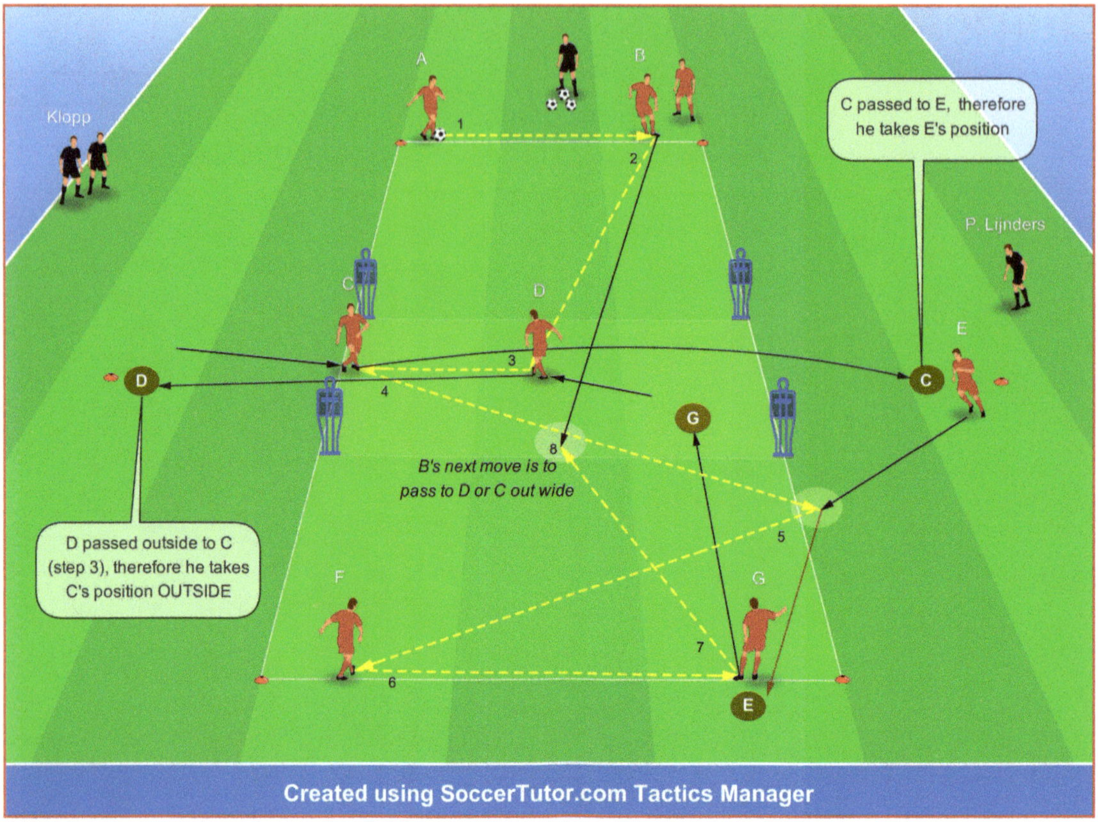

Practice Description

1. **A** passes to **B**.
2. **B** passes to **D**, who is positioned INSIDE in the middle of the 4 box mannequins. He can choose to receive OUTSIDE too (see previous page).
3. **D** passes to **C**, who moves inside from outside to provide support.
4. **C** passes out wide and in front of the mannequin for the forward run of **E**.
5. **E** passes diagonally to **F**.
6. **F** passes across to **G**.
7. **G** passes to **B**, who has moved INSIDE of the 4 box mannequins.
8. **B** decides to pass out wide and in front of the mannequin for the forward run of either **D** or **C**.

Player Movements

- The players are able to choose whether they move INSIDE or OUTSIDE first (to receive pass from Player B).
- The players' movements after their passes are clearly displayed in both diagrams.

Variation

- Coach P. Lijnders adds one-two combinations.

Source: Jürgen Klopp's Liverpool training session at AXA Training Centre, Liverpool - July 2022

Jürgen Klopp Practices: Passing Combinations

25. Short Possession Play + Change Direction with Sprints to Support

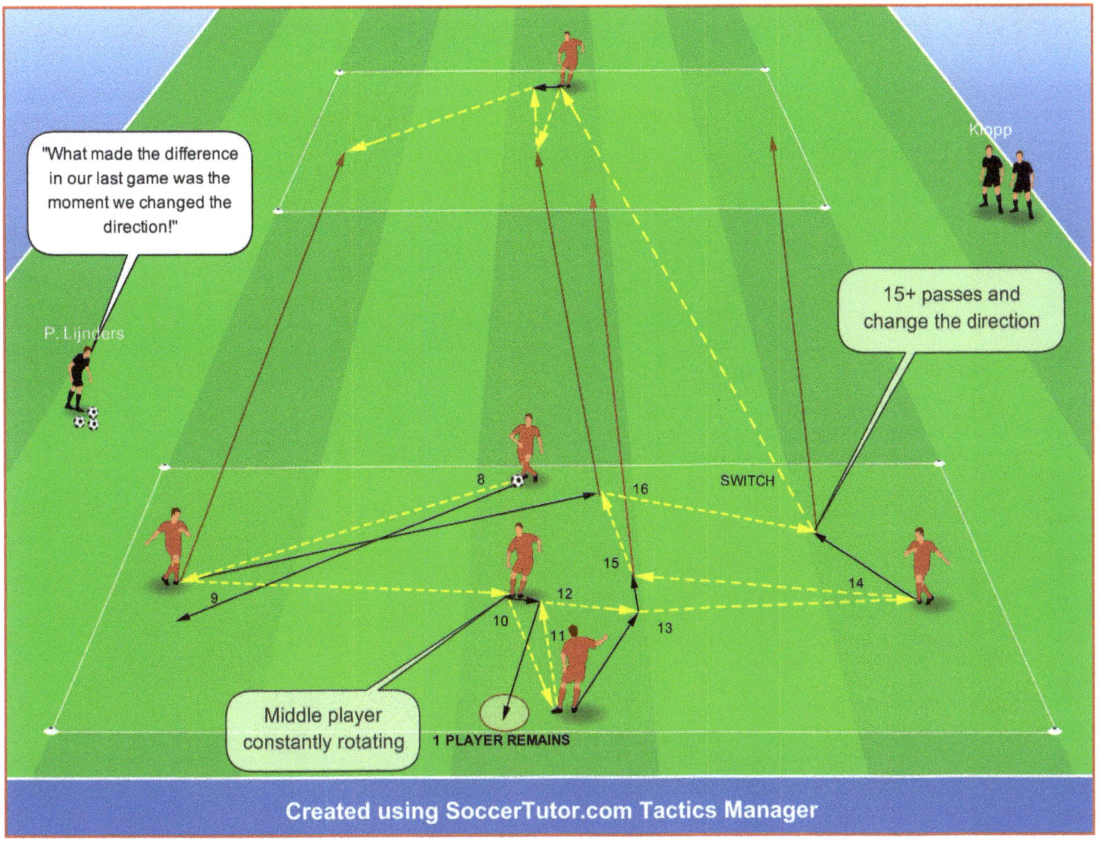

Practice Description

- There are 5 players with a ball in one end zone and 1 player without a ball in the opposite end zone.
- The 5 players pass the ball between each other by playing through the rotating middle player.
- The middle player constantly changes, as he switches positions with an outside player after exchanging passes.
- After 15+ passes, one player passes the ball to the free player in the opposite end zone.
- All the players except one (who remains) sprint across to provide support and continue the practice.
- The 5 players repeat the same aim to complete 15+ passes with a rotating middle player, and then move the ball to the opposite end zone + provide quick support.

Source: Jürgen Klopp's Liverpool training session at AXA Training Centre, Liverpool - August 2022

Jürgen Klopp Practices: Passing Combinations

26. Possession Play + Quick Transition to Score with New Ball

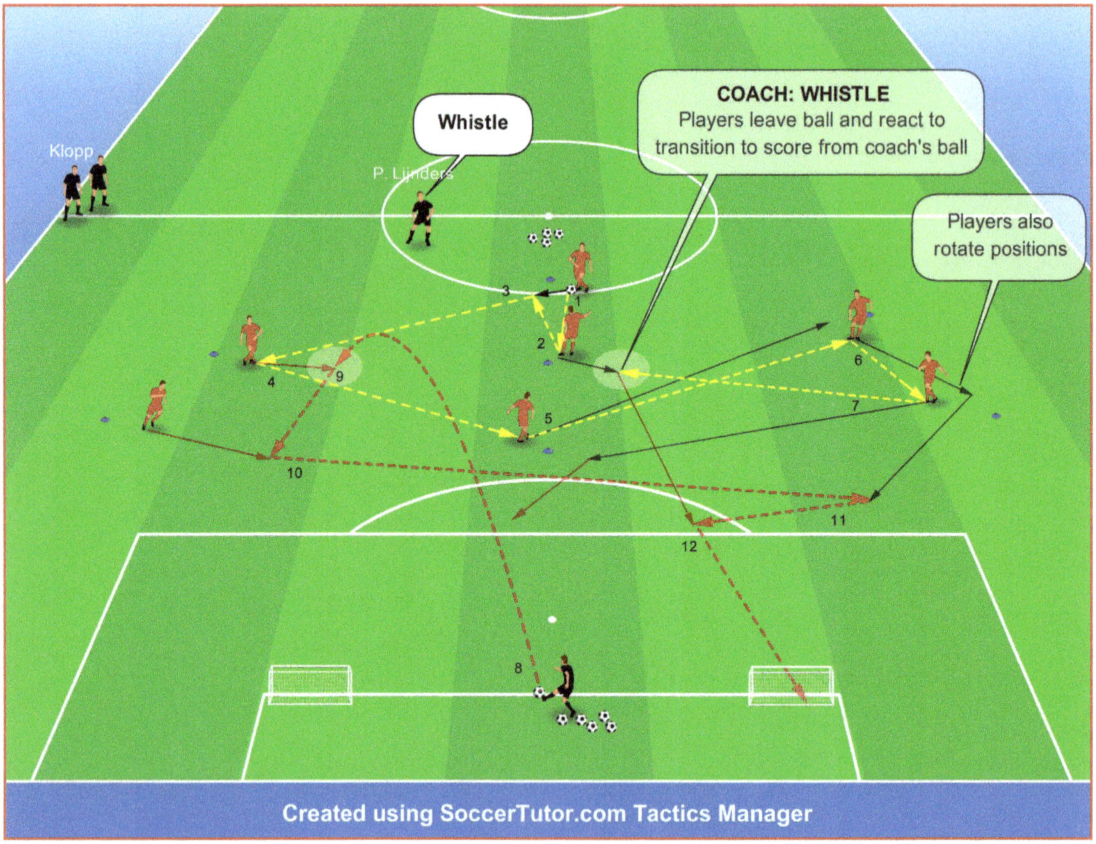

Practice Description

- There are 7 cones marked out as shown, each with a player positioned there.
- The players pass the ball between each other and also sometimes rotate positions.
- They are waiting for the Coach's whistle to be blown.
- When the Coach P. Lijnders blows the whistle, it triggers a transition.
- The players leave the ball they have been using and the other Coach plays a new ball in from the end.
- The players make a fast break attack with the new ball, which is displayed with the red arrows, to score in one of the mini goals.
- The Liverpool players used many different combinations (free decision making). The diagram example displays one combination which was observed.

Source: Jürgen Klopp's Liverpool training session at AXA Training Centre, Liverpool - November 2021

Jürgen Klopp Practices: Passing Combinations

27. Possession Play + Quick Transition to Score in Target Goals

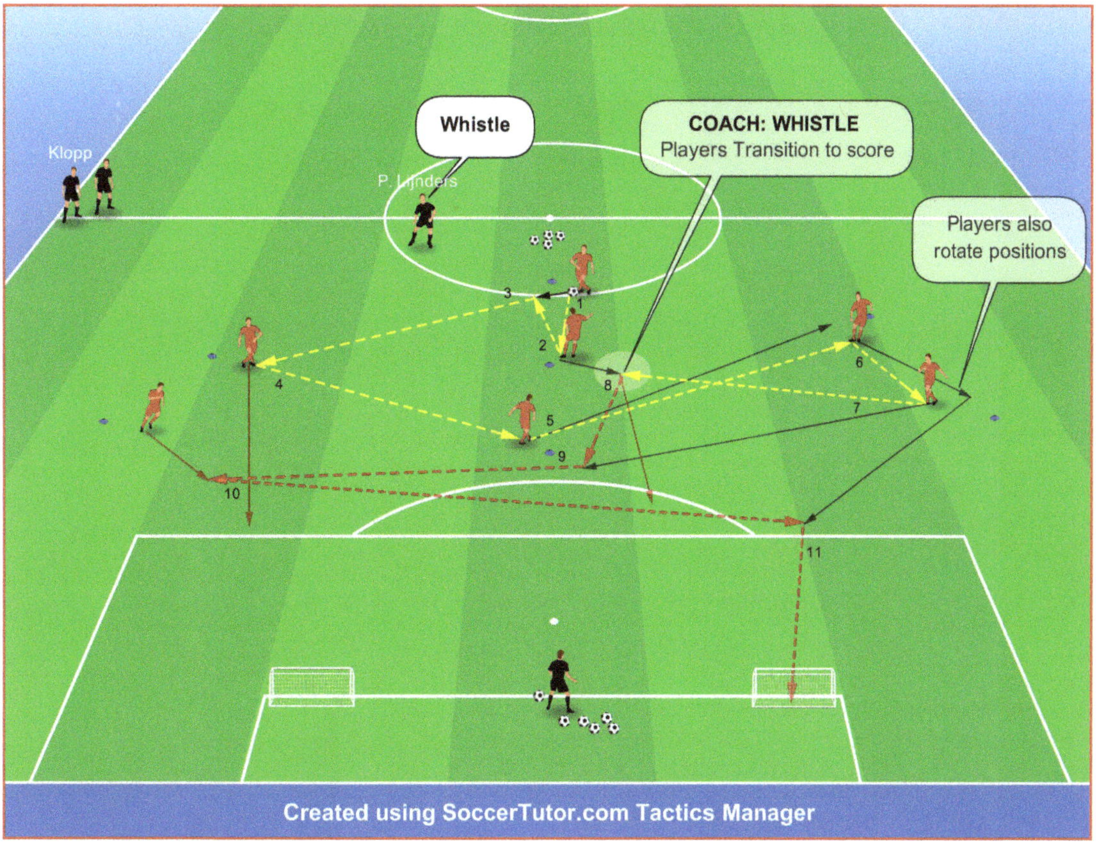

Practice Description

- There are 7 cones marked out as shown, each with a player positioned there.
- The players pass the ball between each other and also sometimes rotate positions.
- They are waiting for the Coach's whistle to be blown.
- When the Coach P. Lijnders blows the whistle, it triggers a transition.
- The players make a fast break attack with the same ball, which is displayed with the red arrows, to score in one of the mini goals.
- The Liverpool players used many different combinations (free decision making). The diagram example displays one combination which was observed.

Source: Jürgen Klopp's Liverpool training session at AXA Training Centre, Liverpool - November 2021

Diamond Passing Combinations

Direct from
Jürgen Klopp's
Training Sessions

©SOCCERTUTOR.COM

JÜRGEN KLOPP: PRACTICES FROM KLOPP'S SESSIONS

Jürgen Klopp Practices: Diamond Passing Combinations

1. Diamond with Give & Go, Switch, One-Two + Through Pass

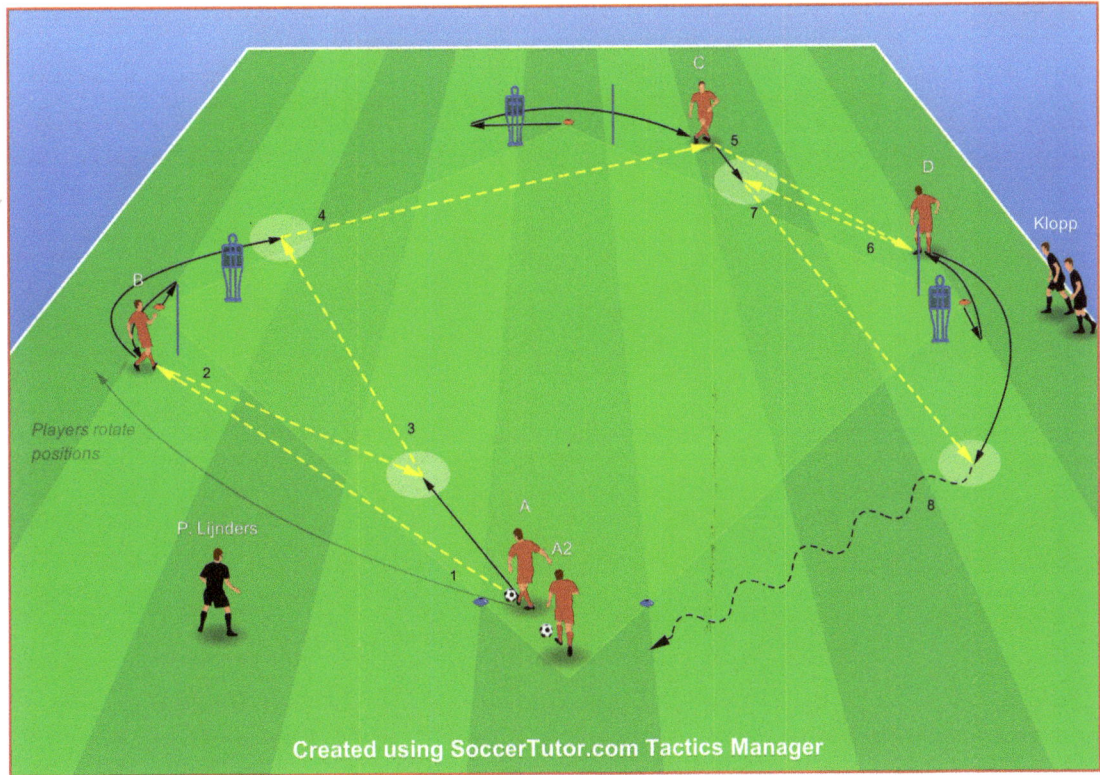

All players check off their cone before moving to receive and rotate their positions:
A → B → C → D → A2.

Practice Description

1. **A** passes to **B**.
2. **B** passes back to **A**.
3. **A** passes for the run of **B** around the mannequin.
4. **B** passes across for **C**, who moves around the pole to receive.
5. **C** passes to **D**.
6. **D** passes back to **C**.
7. **C** passes for the run of **D** around the mannequin.
8. **D** dribbles the ball to the start.
... **A2** starts with a new ball and the same sequence is repeated.

Source: Jürgen Klopp's Liverpool training session at Melwood Training Ground, Liverpool - January 2019

Jürgen Klopp Practices: Diamond Passing Combinations

2. Diamond with One-Two, Lay-offs, Give & Go + Through Pass

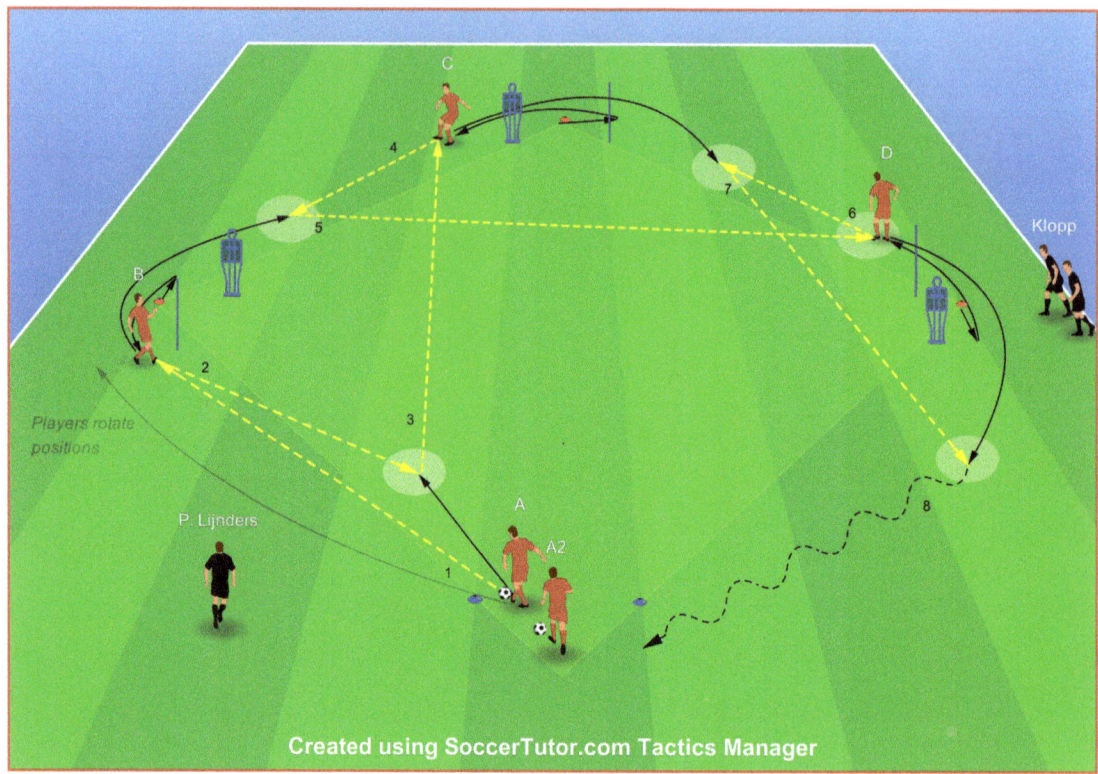

All players check off their cone before moving to receive and rotate their positions:
A → B → C → D → A2.

Practice Description

1. **A** passes to **B**.
2. **B** passes back to **A**.
3. **A** passes to **C**.
4. **C** sets the ball back for **B**, who moves around the mannequin to receive.
5. **B** passes across the diamond to **D**.
6. **D** sets the ball back for **C**, who moves around the mannequin to receive.
7. **C** plays the final pass for the run of **D** around the mannequin.
8. **D** dribbles the ball to the start.
... **A2** starts with a new ball and the same sequence is repeated.

Source: Jürgen Klopp's Liverpool training session at Melwood Training Ground, Liverpool - January 2019

Jürgen Klopp Practices: Diamond Passing Combinations

3. Diamond with One-Two, Lay-off + Final Switch Pass

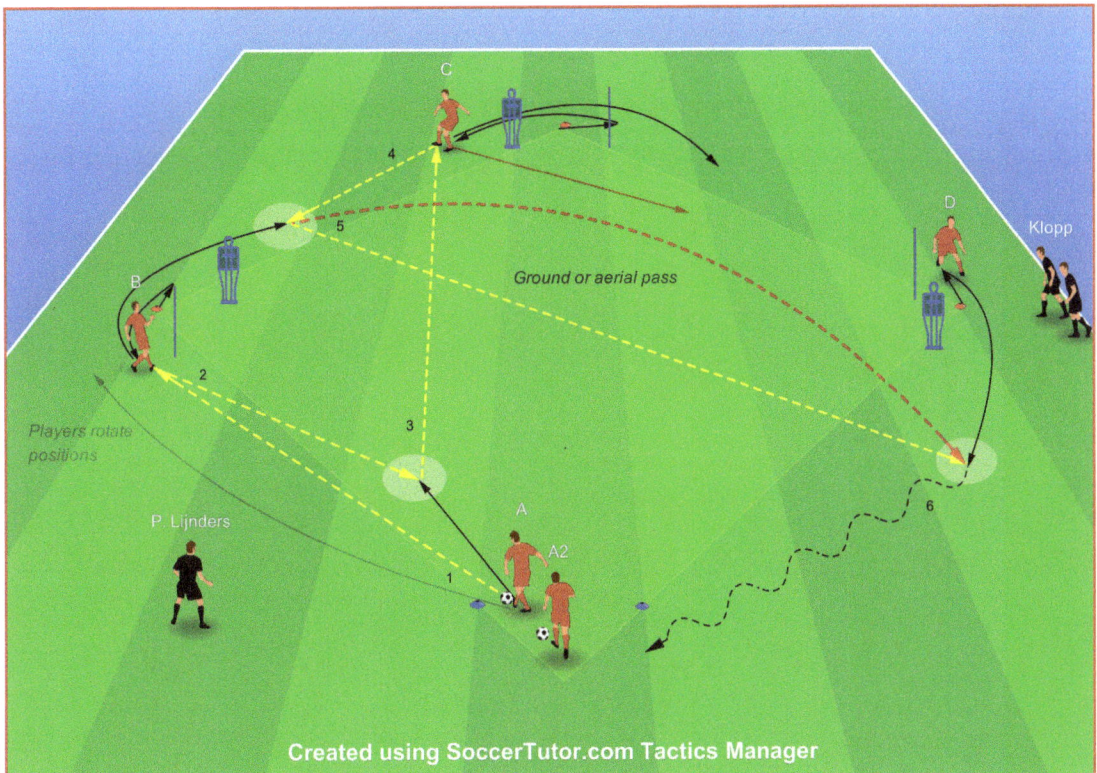

All players check off their cone before moving to receive and rotate their positions: A → B → C → D → A2.

Practice Description

1. **A** passes to **B**.
2. **B** passes back to **A**.
3. **A** passes to **C**.
4. **C** sets the ball back for **B**, who moves around the mannequin to receive.
5. **B** plays the final pass across the diamond diagonally (ground or aerial pass) to **D**, who makes a run around the mannequin to receive.
6. **D** dribbles the ball to the start.
... **A2** starts with a new ball and the same sequence is repeated.

Source: Jürgen Klopp's Liverpool training session at Melwood Training Ground, Liverpool - January 2019

Jürgen Klopp Practices: Diamond Passing Combinations

4. Diamond with Short Combination Play + Final Switch Pass

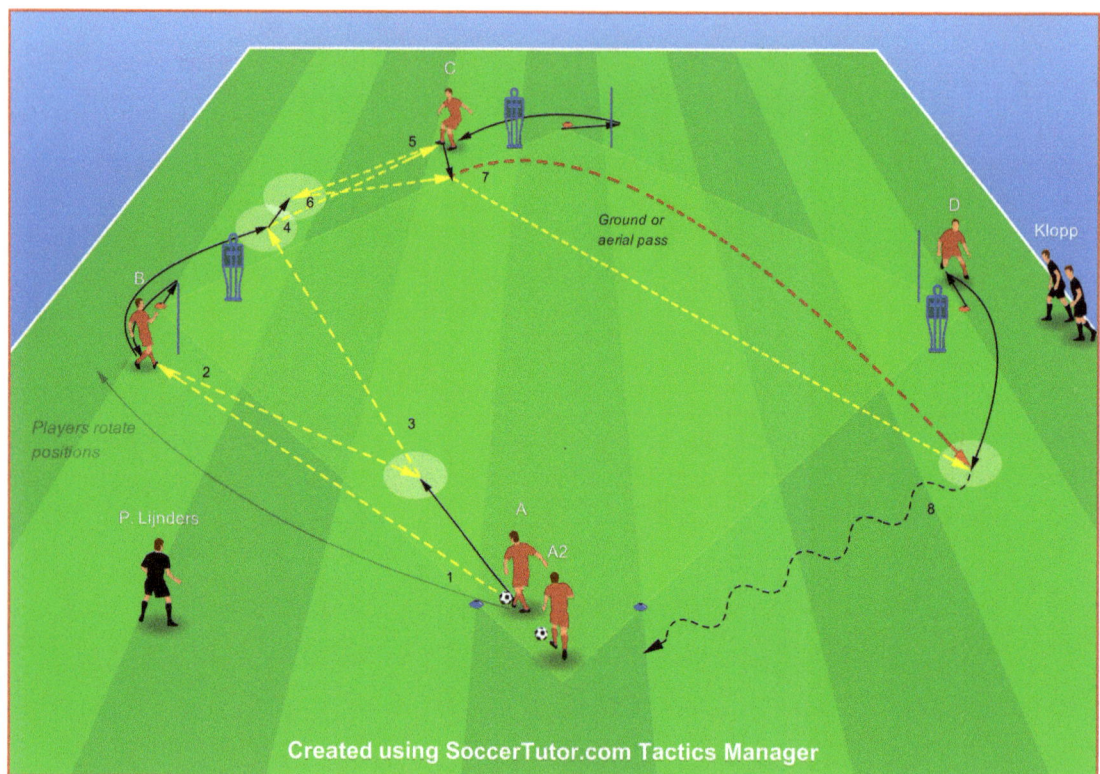

All players check off their cone before moving to receive and rotate their positions: A → B → C → D → A2.

Practice Description

1. **A** passes to **B**.
2. **B** passes back to **A**.
3. **A** passes to **C**, who moves around the mannequin to receive.
4. **B** passes to **C**.
5. **C** passes back to **B**.
6. **B** passes back to **C** again.
7. **C** plays the final pass across the diamond diagonally (ground or aerial pass) to **D**, who makes a run around the mannequin to receive.
8. **D** dribbles the ball to the start.
... **A2** starts with a new ball and the same sequence is repeated.

Source: Jürgen Klopp's Liverpool training session at Melwood Training Ground, Liverpool - January 2019

Jürgen Klopp Practices: Diamond Passing Combinations

5. Diamond with One-Two, Pass, One-Two, Pass

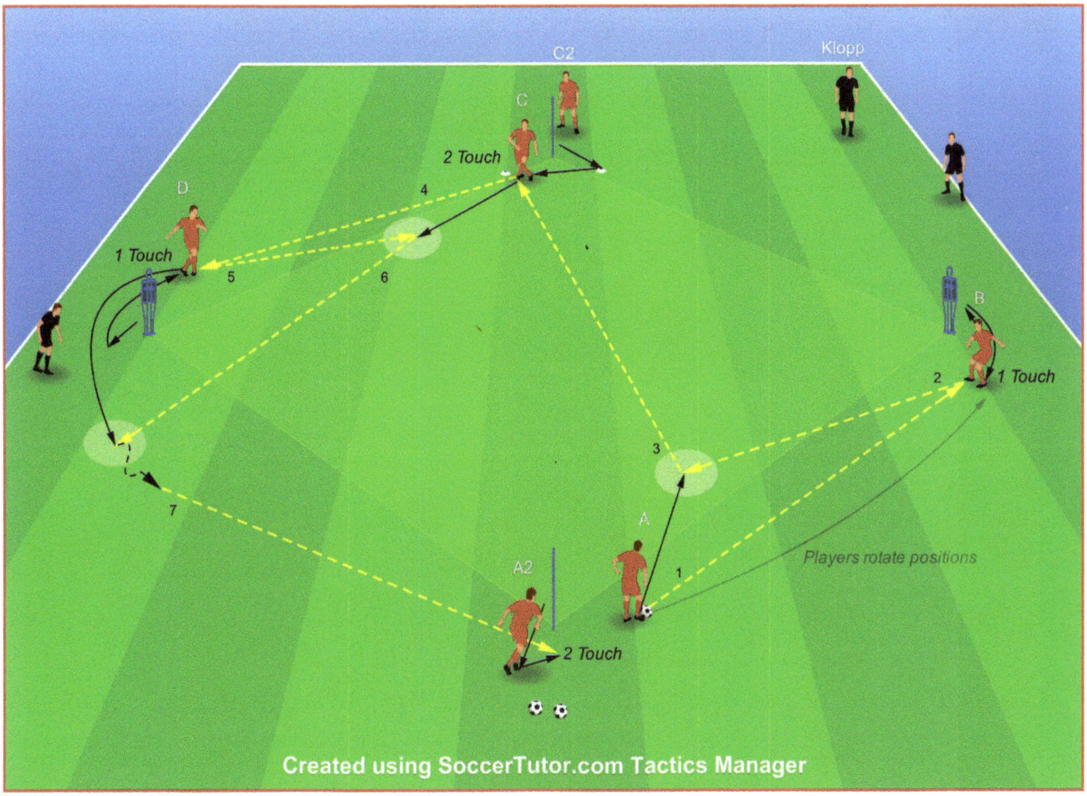

All players check away before moving to receive and rotate their positions:
A → B → C2 → C → D → A2.

Practice Description

1. **A** passes to **B**.
2. **B** passes back to **A**.
3. **A** passes to **C**, who checks off the cone before moving to receive.
4. **C** passes to **D**.
5. **D** passes back to **C**.
6. **C** passes to **D** again, who moves around the mannequin to receive.
7. **D** receives and passes to **A2**, who starts the next repetition of the same sequence.

Source: Jürgen Klopp's Liverpool training session at Anfield, Liverpool - 2021

Jürgen Klopp Practices: Diamond Passing Combinations

6. Diamond with One-Two, Give & Go + Final Pass for Third Man Run

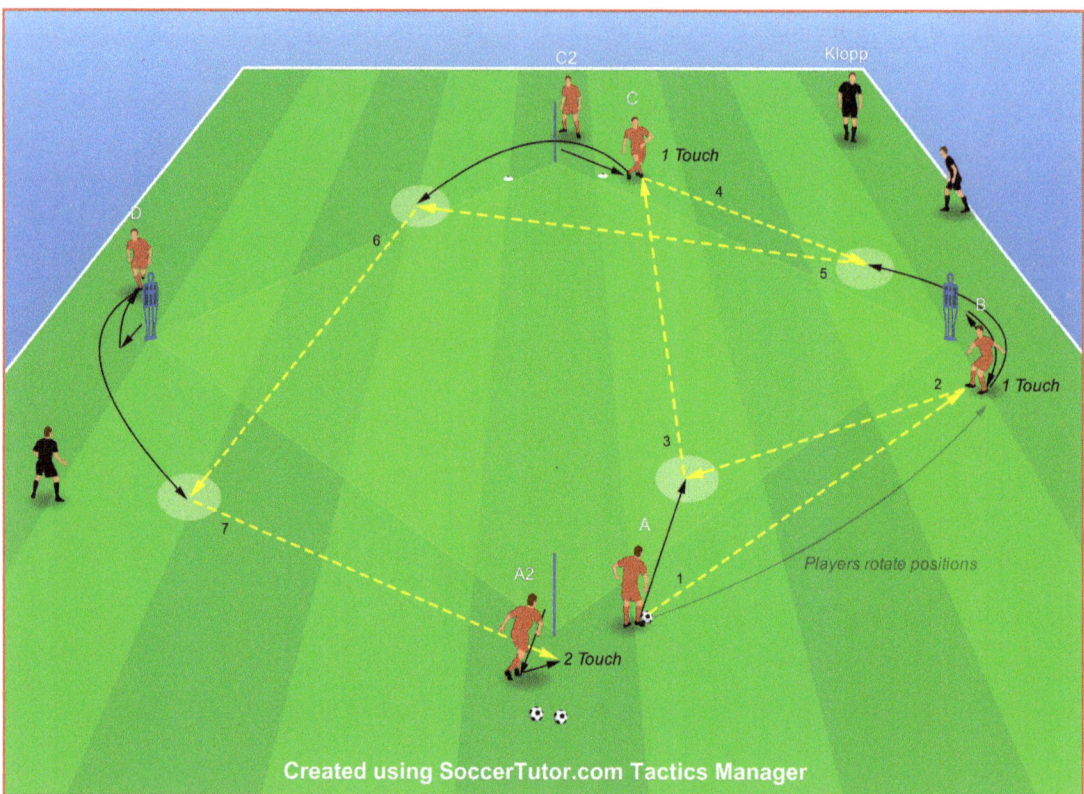

All players check away before moving to receive and rotate their positions:
A → B → C2 → C → D → A2.

Practice Description

1. **A** passes to **B**.
2. **B** passes back to **A**.
3. **A** passes to **C**, who moves at an angle to receive.
4. **C** passes to **B**, who moves around the mannequin to receive.
5. **B** passes across for **C**, who moves around the mannequin to receive and complete the give & go.
6. **C** plays a final pass well-timed for the run of **D** around the mannequin.
7. **D** passes to **A2**, who starts the next repetition of the same sequence.

Source: Jürgen Klopp's Liverpool training session at Anfield, Liverpool - 2021

Jürgen Klopp Practices: Diamond Passing Combinations

7. Diamond with One-Two + Two Give & Goes

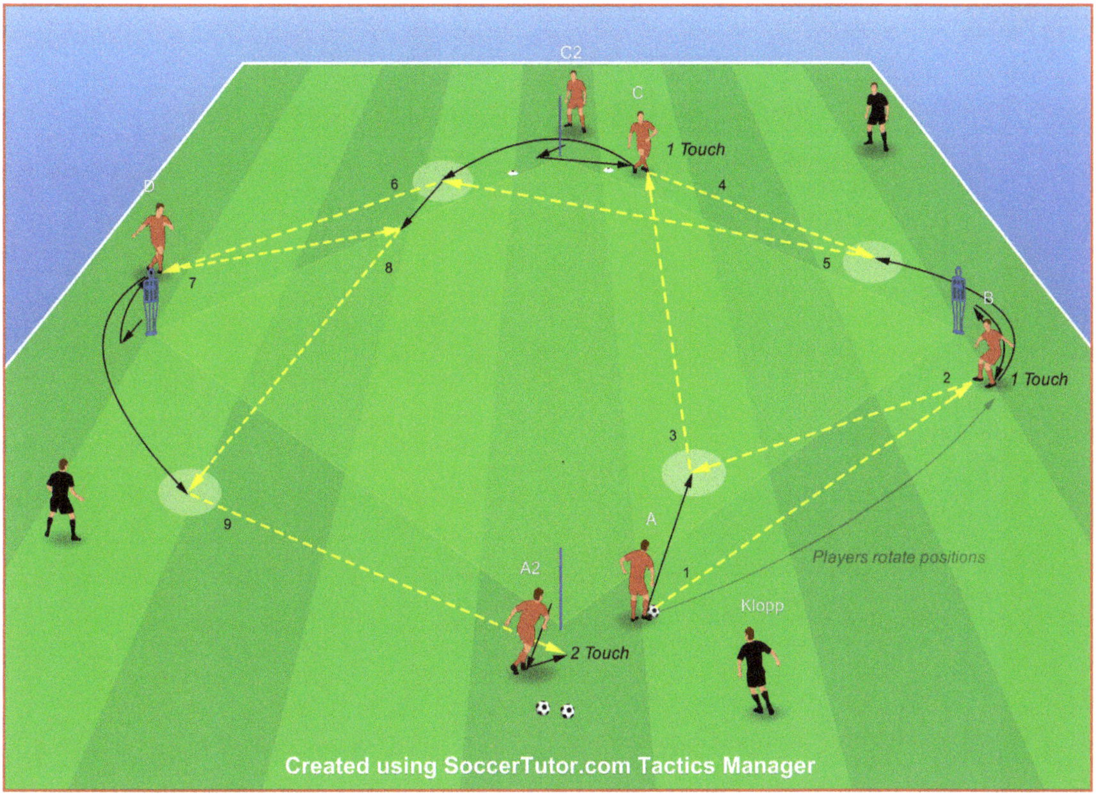

All players check away before moving to receive and rotate their positions:
A → B → C2 → C → D → A2.

Practice Description

1. **A** passes to **B**.
2. **B** passes back to **A**.
3. **A** passes to **C**, who moves at an angle to receive.
4. **C** passes to **B**, who moves around the mannequin to receive.
5. **B** passes across for **C**, who moves around the mannequin to receive.
6. **C** passes to **D**.
7. **D** passes back to **C**.
8. **C** passes to **D**, who moves around the mannequin to receive.
9. **D** passes to **A2**, who starts the next repetition of the same sequence.

Source: Jürgen Klopp's Liverpool training session at Anfield, Liverpool - 2021

Jürgen Klopp Practices: Diamond Passing Combinations

8. Diamond with One-Two, Lay-off, Switch + Give & Go

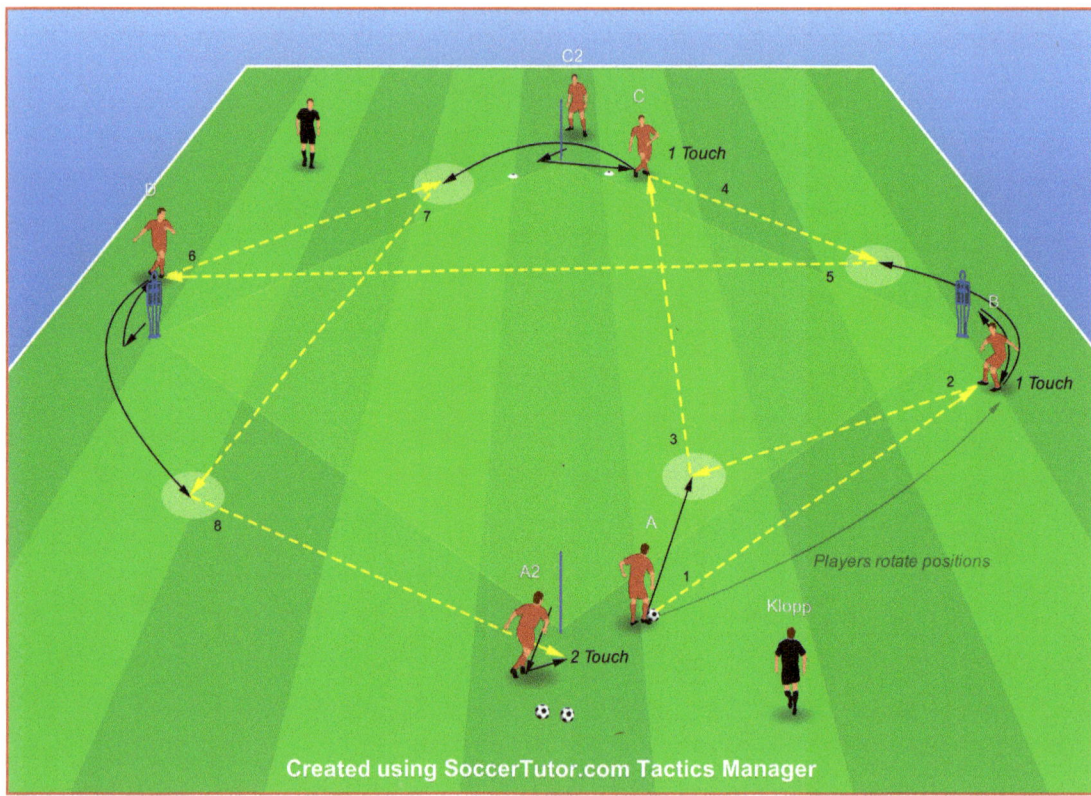

All players check away before moving to receive and rotate their positions:
A → B → C2 → C → D → A2.

Practice Description

1. **A** passes to **B**.
2. **B** passes back to **A**.
3. **A** passes to **C**, who moves at an angle to receive.
4. **C** passes to **B**, who moves around the mannequin to receive.
5. **B** passes across to **D**.
6. **D** sets the ball back for **C**, who moves around the mannequin to receive.
7. **C** passes to **D**, who moves around the mannequin to receive.
8. **D** passes to **A2**, who starts the next repetition of the same sequence.

Source: Jürgen Klopp's Liverpool training session at Anfield, Liverpool - 2021

Jürgen Klopp Practices: Diamond Passing Combinations

9. Diamond with Central Link Player: One-Twos & Opening Up to Receive

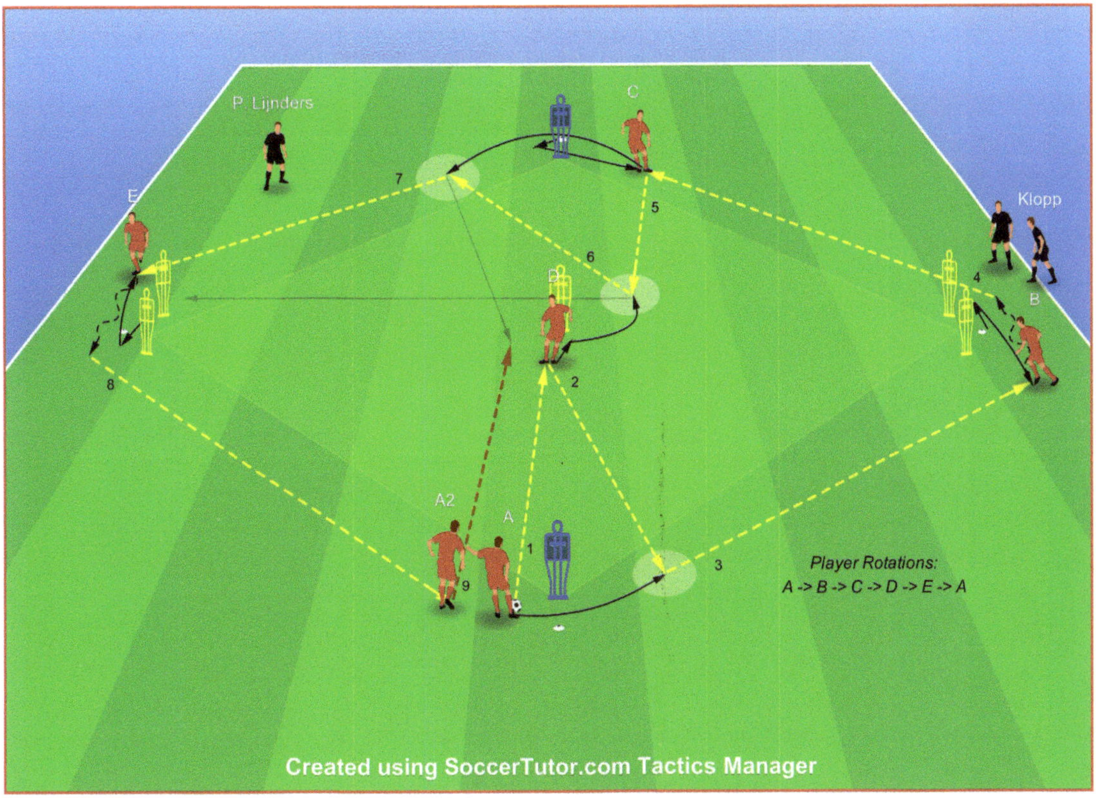

All players check away before moving to receive and rotate their positions:
A → B → C → D → E → A2.

Practice Description

1. **A** passes to the middle player **D**.
2. **D** passes back to **A**, who moves around the mannequin to receive.
3. **A** passes to **B**, who opens up and carries the ball past the 2 mannequins.
4. **B** passes to **C**, who moves at an angle to receive.
5. **C** sets the ball back for **D's** turn and movement to receive.
6. **D** passes to **C**, who moves around the mannequin to receive.
7. **C** passes to **E**, who opens up and carries the ball past the 2 mannequins.
8. **E** passes to **A2**, who starts the next repetition of the same sequence.

Source: Jürgen Klopp's Liverpool training session at Melwood Training Ground, Liverpool - March 2017

Jürgen Klopp Practices: Diamond Passing Combinations

10. Diamond with Central Link Player: Lay-offs and Support Play

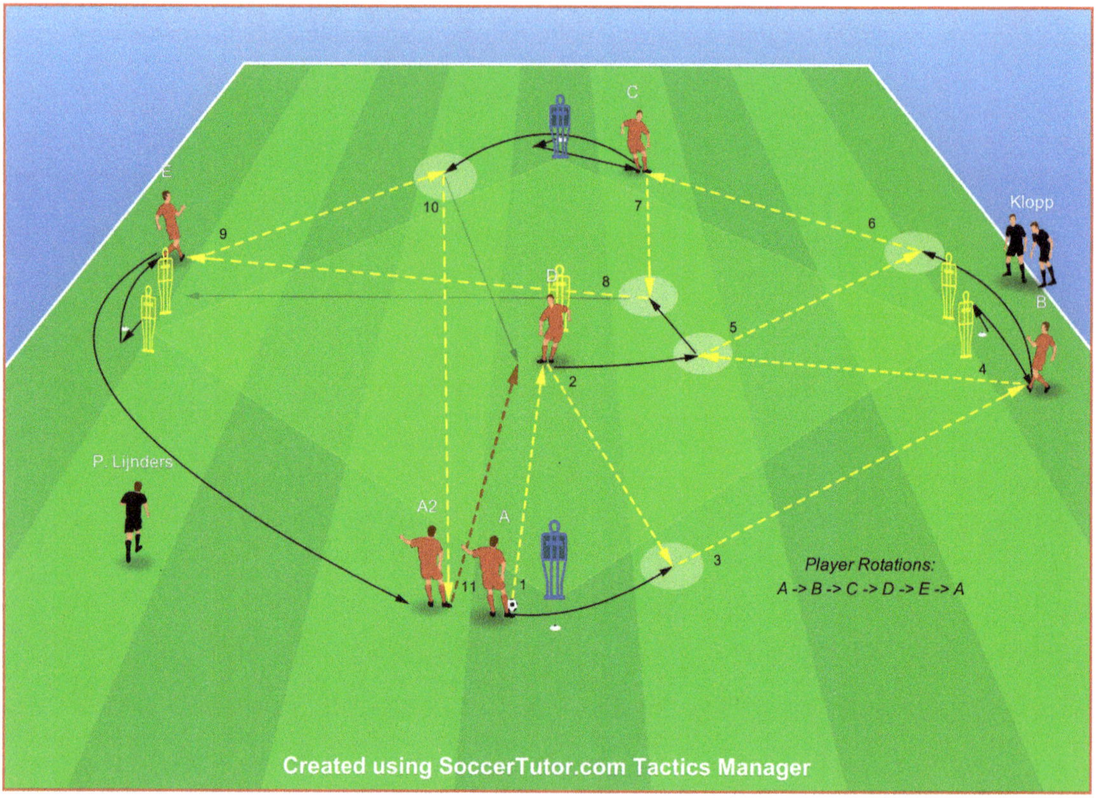

All players check away off their cone before moving to receive and rotate their positions: A → B → C → D → E → A2.

Practice Description

1. **A** passes to the middle player **D**.
2. **D** passes back to **A**, who moves around the mannequin to receive.
3. **A** passes to **B**.
4. **B** passes inside to the middle player **D**.
5. **D** passes back to **B**, who moves around the 2 mannequins to receive the return pass.
6. **B** passes to **C**.
7. **C** sets the ball back for **D**.
8. **D** passes across to **E**.
9. **E** sets the ball back for **C's** movement around the mannequin.
10. **C** passes to **A2**, who starts the next repetition of the same sequence.

Source: Jürgen Klopp's Liverpool training session at Melwood Training Ground, Liverpool - March 2017

Jürgen Klopp Practices: Diamond Passing Combinations

11. Diamond with Central Link Player: Support Play for Give & Goes

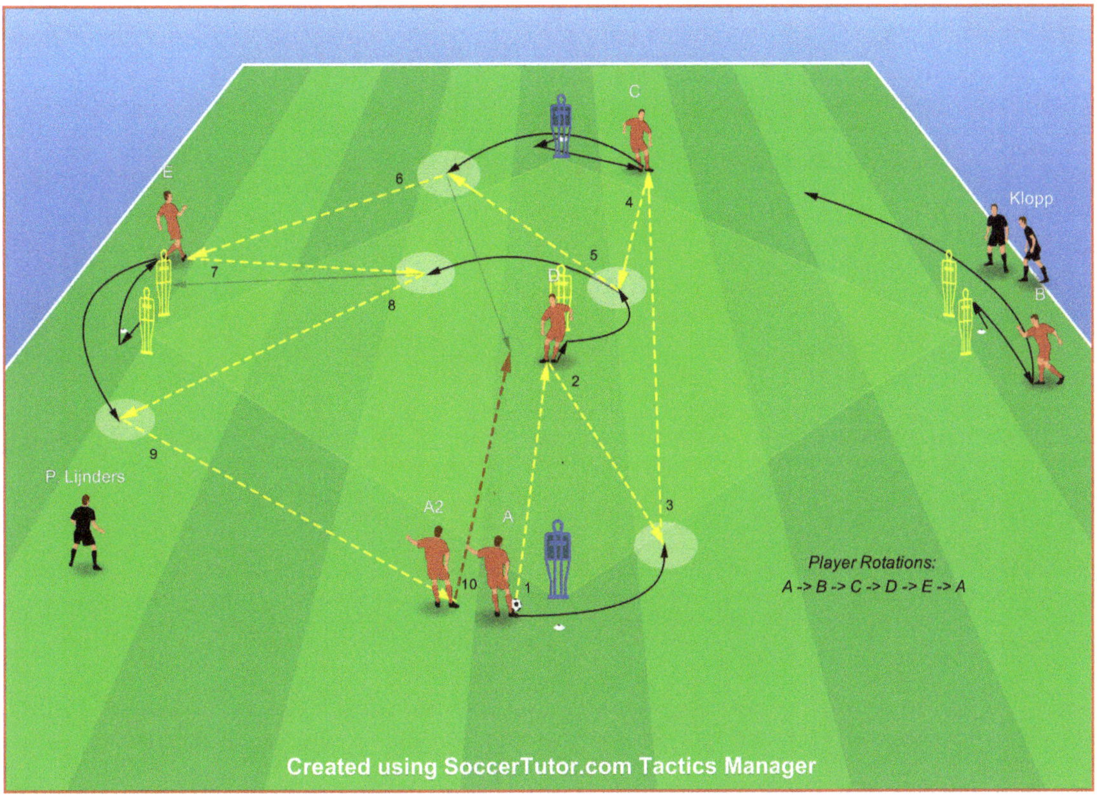

All players check away off their cone before moving to receive and rotate their positions: A → B → C → D → E → A2.

Practice Description

1. **A** passes to the middle player **D**.
2. **D** passes back to **A**, who moves around the mannequin to receive.
3. **A** passes to **C**.
4. **C** sets the ball back for **D's** turn and movement to receive.
5. **D** passes to **C**, who moves around the mannequin to receive.
6. **C** passes to **E**.
7. **E** passes inside to **D**, who moves across to provide support.
8. **D** passes to **E**, who moves around the 2 mannequins to receive.
9. **E** passes to **A2**, who starts the next repetition of the same sequence.

Source: Jürgen Klopp's Liverpool training session at Melwood Training Ground, Liverpool - March 2017

Jürgen Klopp Practices: Diamond Passing Combinations

12. Diamond with Central Link Player: Support Play to Left and Right Sides

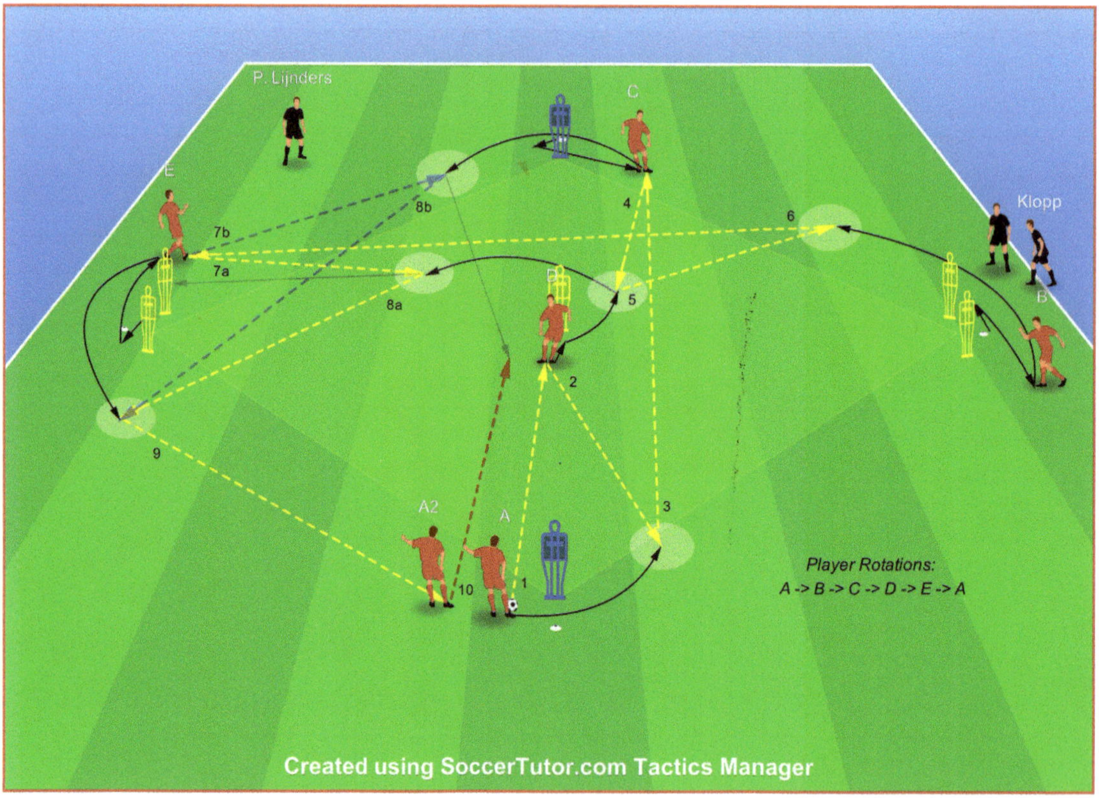

All players check away off their cone before moving to receive and rotate their positions: A → B → C → D → E → A2.

Practice Description

1. **A** passes to the middle player **D**.
2. **D** passes back to **A**, who moves around the mannequin to receive.
3. **A** passes to **C**.
4. **C** sets the ball back for **D's** turn and movement to receive.
5. **D** sets the ball for the run of **B** around the 2 mannequins to receive.
6. **C** passes across the diamond to **E**.
7. **E** either sets the ball for **D** (7a) or **C** (7b).
8. **D** (8a) or **C** (8b) pass back to **E**, who moves around the 2 mannequins to receive.
9. **E** passes to **A2**, who starts the next repetition of the same sequence.

Source: Jürgen Klopp's Liverpool training session at Melwood Training Ground, Liverpool - March 2017

Jürgen Klopp Practices: Diamond Passing Combinations

13. Diamond + Triangle with Quick Changes of Direction

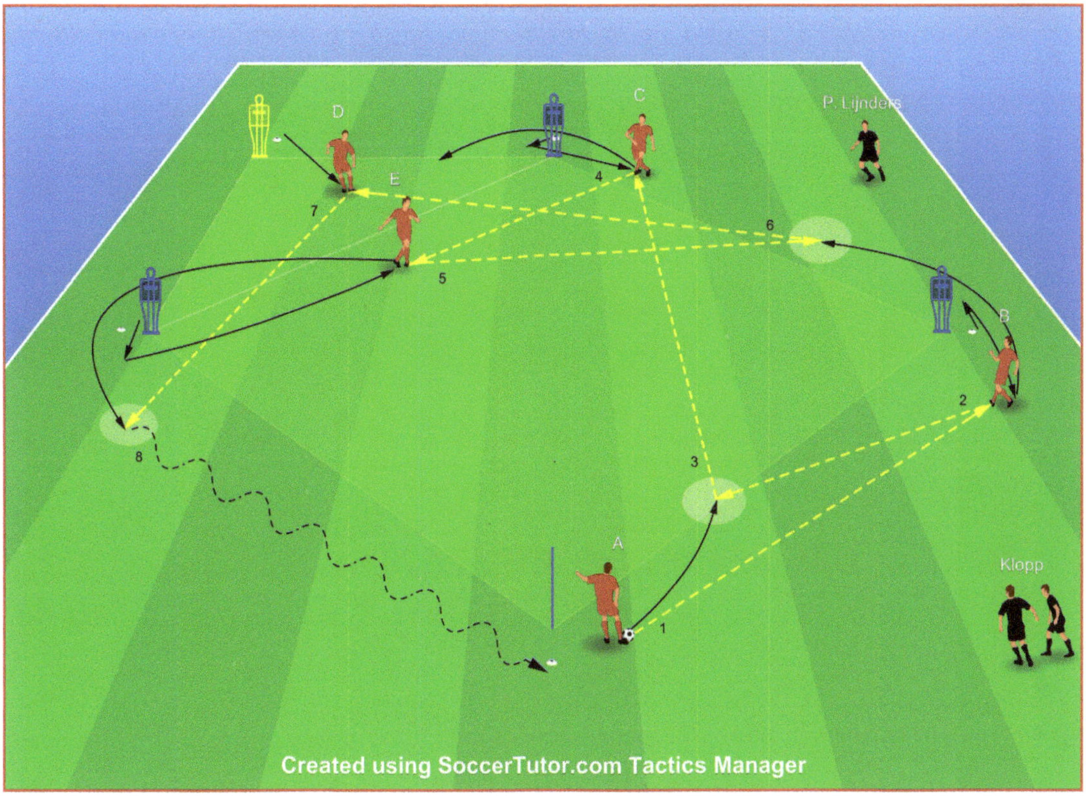

All players check away off their cone before moving to receive and rotate their positions:
A → B → C → D → E → A.

Practice Description

1. **A** passes to **B**.
2. **B** passes back to **A**, who moves forward.
3. **A** passes to **C**.
4. **C** passes to **E**, who moves inside to receive.
5. **E** passes back across the diamond to **B**, who moves around the mannequin to receive.
6. **B** passes back across the diamond again to **D**, who drops off the yellow mannequin to receive.
7. **D** plays the final pass for the run of **E**, who moves back outside and runs around the mannequin to receive.
8. **E** dribbles to Position A and starts the next repetition of the same sequence.

Source: Jürgen Klopp's Liverpool training session in La Manga, Murcia, Spain - February 2017

Jürgen Klopp Practices: Diamond Passing Combinations

14. Diamond + Triangle with Short and Quick Combination Play

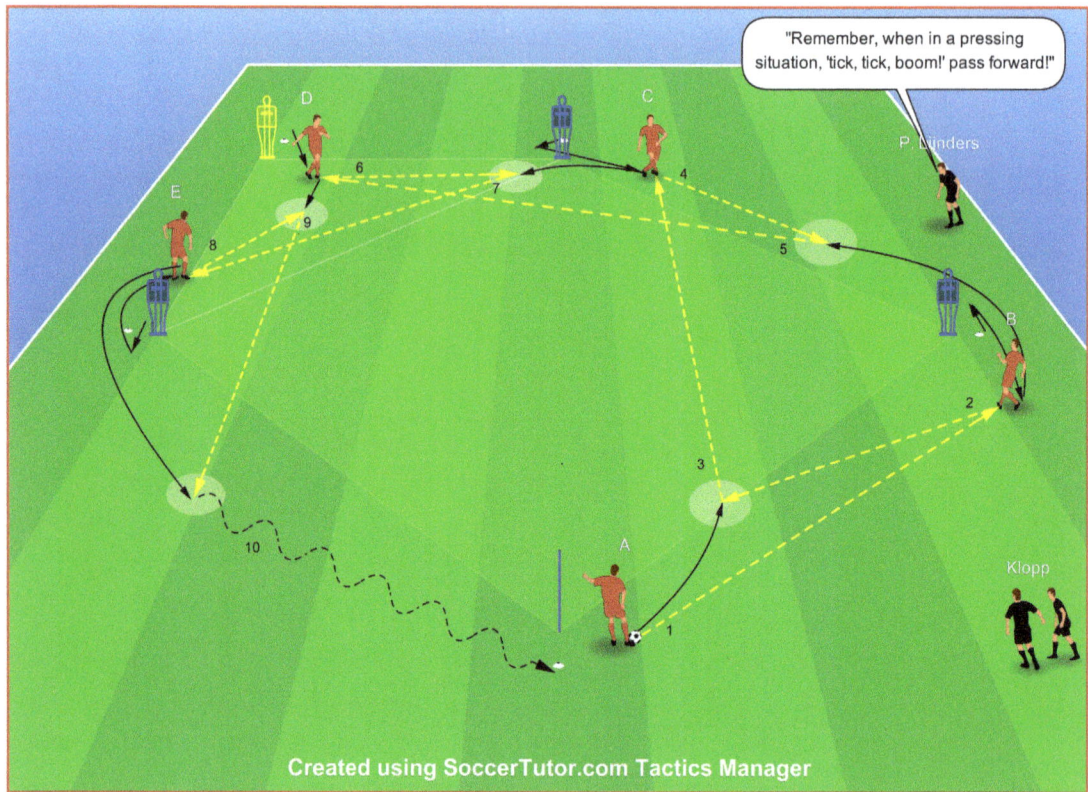

All players check away off their cone before moving to receive and rotate their positions: A → B → C → D → E → A.

Practice Description

1. **A** passes to **B**.
2. **B** passes back to **A**, who moves forward.
3. **A** passes to **C**.
4. **C** passes to **B**, who runs around the mannequin to receive.
5. **E** passes across the diamond to **D**, who drops off the yellow mannequin to receive.
6. **D** sets the ball back to **C**, who shifts across in front of the mannequin.
7. **C** passes to **E**.
8. **E** sets the ball back for **D**.
9. **D** plays the final pass for the run of **E** around the mannequin.
10. **E** dribbles to <u>Position A</u> and starts the next repetition of the same sequence.

Source: Jürgen Klopp's Liverpool training session in La Manga, Murcia, Spain - February 2017

Jürgen Klopp's Pressing and Counter-pressing Philosophy

Direct from
Jürgen Klopp's
Training Sessions

JÜRGEN KLOPP: PRACTICES FROM KLOPP'S SESSIONS

PRESSING AND COUNTER-PRESSING

PRESSING

Pressing is when pressure is applied by the defending team on a player or team that has possession of the ball.

Pressing is used to rush the opponent's next action and limit the time and space available for good decision making.

The aim is to force the ball away from dangerous areas and win the ball from your opponents.

However, pressing is not only a defensive tactic used to stop your opponent from creating chances and scoring goals.

Pressing, counter-pressing and counter attacks provide defending and attacking tactics for a team, with the aim to apply pressure, win the ball and then launch a quick counter attack to score.

The higher a team recovers possession, the nearer the opposition goal is and the faster the ball is recovered after its loss.

In addition, the opposition may be unbalanced with limited time to cover space, which leaves gaps and lines available. In this way, counter attacks become a natural consequence of ball recovery.

COUNTER-PRESSING

Immediate pressing around the ball area just after losing possession to win the ball back as quickly as possible.

By using counter-pressing, your team are pressing a transition from defence to attack or counter attack from the opposition without retreating back, thus stopping their attack before it starts.

Counter-pressing Tactics

1. Overload the space around the ball.
2. Press the ball carrier while he is receiving and/or controlling the ball with one or two players.
3. Block passing lines for potential receivers.
4. Be compact around the ball area.
5. Try to force a mistake or at least force the play wide.

Jürgen Klopp's Pressing and Counter-pressing Philosophy

JÜRGEN KLOPP'S COUNTER-PRESSING

Jürgen Klopp: *"The best moment to win the ball is immediately after your team just lost it. The opponent is still looking for orientation where to pass the ball. He will have taken his eyes off the game to make his tackle or interception and he will have expended energy. Both make him vulnerable."*

JÜRGEN KLOPP'S COUNTER-PRESSING

Liverpool are and have been the best counter-pressing team in world football for a few years.

Jürgen Klopp wants his players to:

1. Play with a high defensive line.
2. Play with a high intensity.
3. Play with a fast and exciting all-action attacking style.
4. Attack the space in front after losing the ball (aggressive counter-pressing).
5. Surround the man with the ball.
6. Win the ball back as quickly as possible!

Jürgen Klopp explains that:

"The closest player goes 100% and puts total effort into the press."

"One player can always defend two opponents by blocking the line, pressing the ball carrier and checking over the shoulder."

"The last two yards of the press define everything. As far as aggression goes, yes please, but this must be controlled with an anticipation of where the next pass will go, and with teammates reorganising as a group constantly and quickly."

BENEFITS OF LIVERPOOL'S COUNTER-PRESSING STYLE

1. Regaining possession high up the pitch.
2. Gaps in opposition's disorganised shape can be exploited.
3. More chances created as they are closer to the opposition's goal.
4. More goals scored!
5. Continuously win the ball back quickly = longer spells of possession.
6. Stop the opposition from having successful counter attacks.
7. Improve work rate, teamwork and motivation for the whole team with a very positive style of play (on the front foot).
8. Excite the crowd and create high energy, engagement and noise to encourage the team further.

Jürgen Klopp's Pressing and Counter-pressing Philosophy

PRESSING AND COUNTER-PRESSING FOCUS IN LIVERPOOL'S TRAINING

Jürgen Klopp: "We want to attack the opponent non-stop when we have the ball, when we lose it and when the opposition have it."

RONDOS

The emphasis of Rondos is normally expected to be about possession, but at Klopp's Liverpool the focus is on pressing and counter-pressing.

As Klopp has talked about, defending is Liverpool's first attacking action. Their playing style is with a high line and pressing with high intensity to win the ball as quickly as possible.

Klopp's Assistant Coach Pep Lijnders has explained how rondos and possession games are all about pressing in Liverpool training sessions, explaining that they must "stimulate our counter-pressing vision where we try to disrupt the build-up of the opponent inside their first few touches."

When referring to the Rondos which are part of all of Liverpool's training sessions, Pep Lijnders remarks that the 5v2 rondo is a **Pressing Rondo**. He goes on to say:

"Our game is about movement and speed, and with only five players, those five have to run non-stop."

"The two guys in the middle are encouraged to intercept within the first six passes. If they succeed, they can both go out at the same time. Otherwise, only the player who intervened is allowed to leave the middle."

POSSESSION GAMES

Liverpool's possession games are focused on immediate fast transitions and making sure to never pause or delay after losing the ball, even for a second.

Pep Lijnders explains that *"The players first have to understand the importance of counter-pressing to our team - that element comes back in every exercise."*

"When a team lose the ball in training, you will hear me, Jürgen or Pete (Krawietz) screaming: 'Go! Get it back! Don't stop!'"

When observing Liverpool's rondos and possession games in their training sessions, the following is clear:

- The players keep count of the passes to maintain a high level of competition.
- In the rondos, the motivation to win the ball within 6 passes increases the speed and intensity of the pressing to replicate Liverpool's non-stop running counter-pressing philosophy.
- The Liverpool players react immediately to press the new ball carrier.
- The Liverpool coaches and players really focus on the counter-press, to act collectively as a team and try to win the ball back immediately after losing possession.

Pep Lijnders Quotes from: Renard, A - The Guardian. 2019. Interview with Liverpool's Pep Lijnders [Online]. [Accessed 30th October].
Available from: https://www.theguardian.com/football/2019/dec/02/liverpool-pep-lijnders-jurgen-klopp-assistant-paddle-tennis-james-milner

Pressing Rondos and Possession Games

Direct from Jürgen Klopp's Training Sessions

©SOCCERTUTOR.COM

JÜRGEN KLOPP: PRACTICES FROM KLOPP'S SESSIONS

"Attack the opponent with, but especially without the ball - a chasing attitude over 95 minutes."

Jürgen Klopp: Pressing Rondos and Possession Games

1. 4 v 2 Rondo to Find the Free Player and Pressing to Close Passing Lines

Reds = Break out of pressure and find free player

Yellows = Press together and close passing lines

Practice Description

- In this 4v2 Rondo, the players work in groups of 6 in an 8 yard square.
- There is 1 player in the possession team on each side of the square. They are positioned on the outsides but must still play within the area.
- The 4 outside players aim to keep possession of the ball and are only allowed to use **1 touch**.
- Success comes from quick passing, good angles and breaking through pressure to move the ball to a free player.

- The 2 inside players (yellow bibs) work together to press, close the angles for the potential passing lines and win the ball.
- **RULE:** The player that loses the ball switches roles with the player that wins the ball.
- **COACHING POINT:** Encourage the players to keep count of the passes to maintain a high level of competition.

Source: Jürgen Klopp's Liverpool training session at AXA Training Centre, Liverpool - August 2022

Jürgen Klopp: Pressing Rondos and Possession Games

2. 4 v 2 Pressing Rondo +1 Middle Floating Player

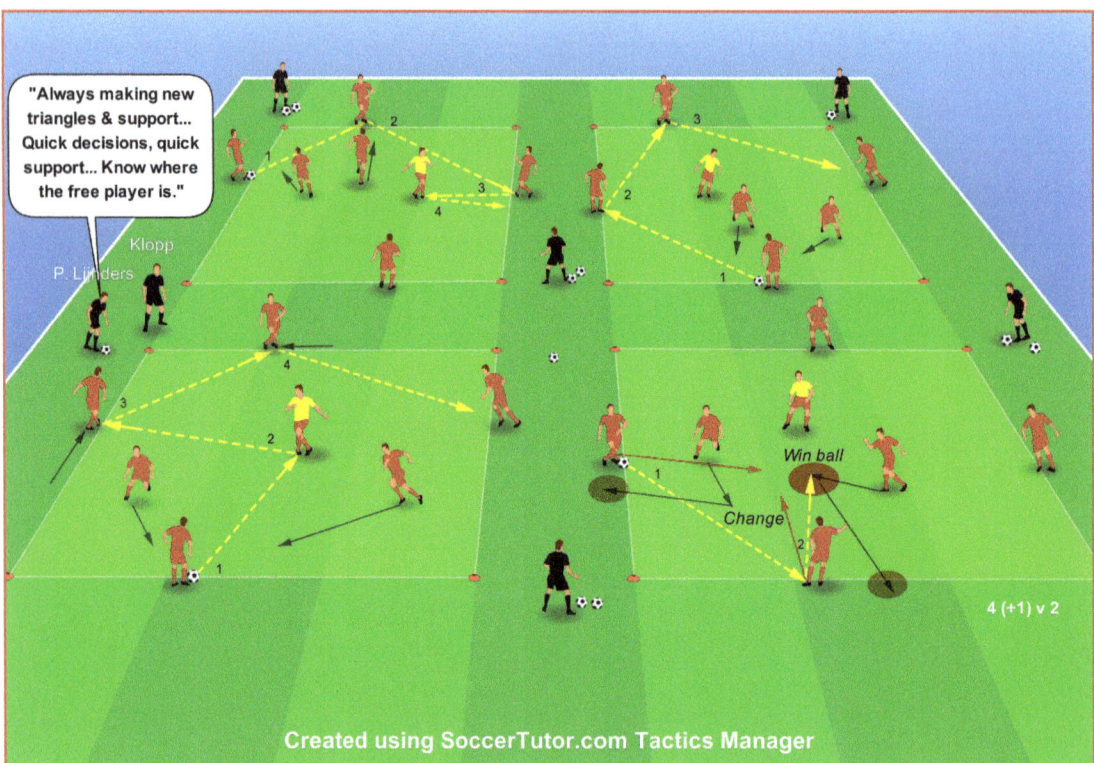

Practice Description

- In this variation of the traditional 4 v 2 Rondo, there is an additional floating player (yellow) in the middle who helps the 4 outside players keep possession.

- There is 1 player in the possession team on each side of the square. They are positioned on the outsides but must still play within the area.

- The **4 outside players have 1 touch** and aim to keep possession of the ball with help from the **yellow floating player**, who is allowed to use **2 touches**.

- The 2 inside players (yellow bibs) work together to press, close the angles for the potential passing lines and win the ball.

- **RULE:** The 2 players that touched the ball last when the ball is lost switch roles with the 2 defending players.

- **COACHING POINT:** The players set targets for number of completed passes and celebrate when they achieve it.

Source: Jürgen Klopp's Liverpool pre-season training session in Salzburg, Austria - July 2021

Jürgen Klopp: Pressing Rondos and Possession Games

3. 5 v 2 Intense Pressing Rondo to "Win the Ball within 6 Passes"

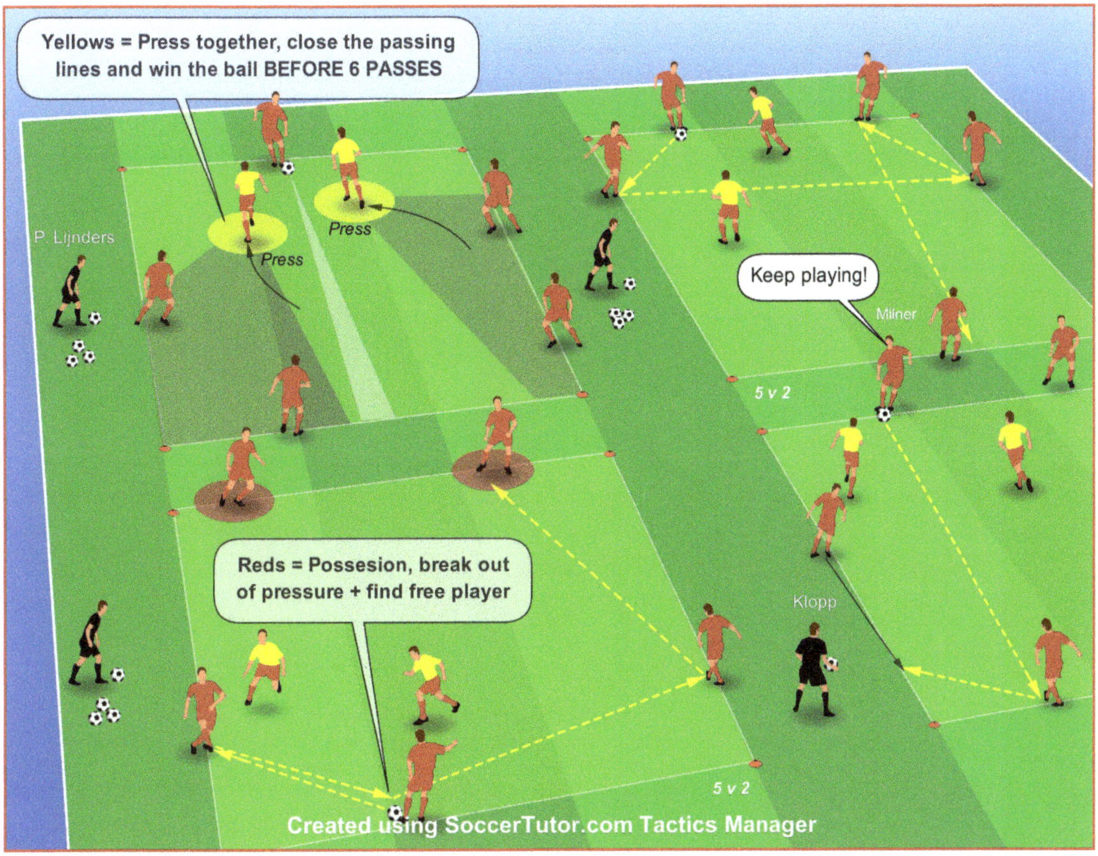

Practice Description

- In this 5v2 Rondo, the players work in groups of 7 in a 10 yard square. The 5 outside players aim to keep possession of the ball and are only allowed to use **1 touch**.

- The 2 inside players (yellow bibs) work together to press, close the angles, and win the ball. If they win the ball within the first 6 passes, they BOTH switch roles with 2 outside players.

- If the middle players win the ball after 6 passes, only the player that loses the ball switches roles with the player that wins the ball.

- **KEY POINT:** The motivation to win the ball within 6 passes increases the speed and intensity of the pressing to replicate Liverpool's non-stop running counter-pressing philosophy.

Source: Jürgen Klopp's Liverpool training session at AXA Training Centre, Liverpool - October 2021

Jürgen Klopp: Pressing Rondos and Possession Games

4. Transition from Attack to Defence in Simultaneous 5 v 2 Rondos

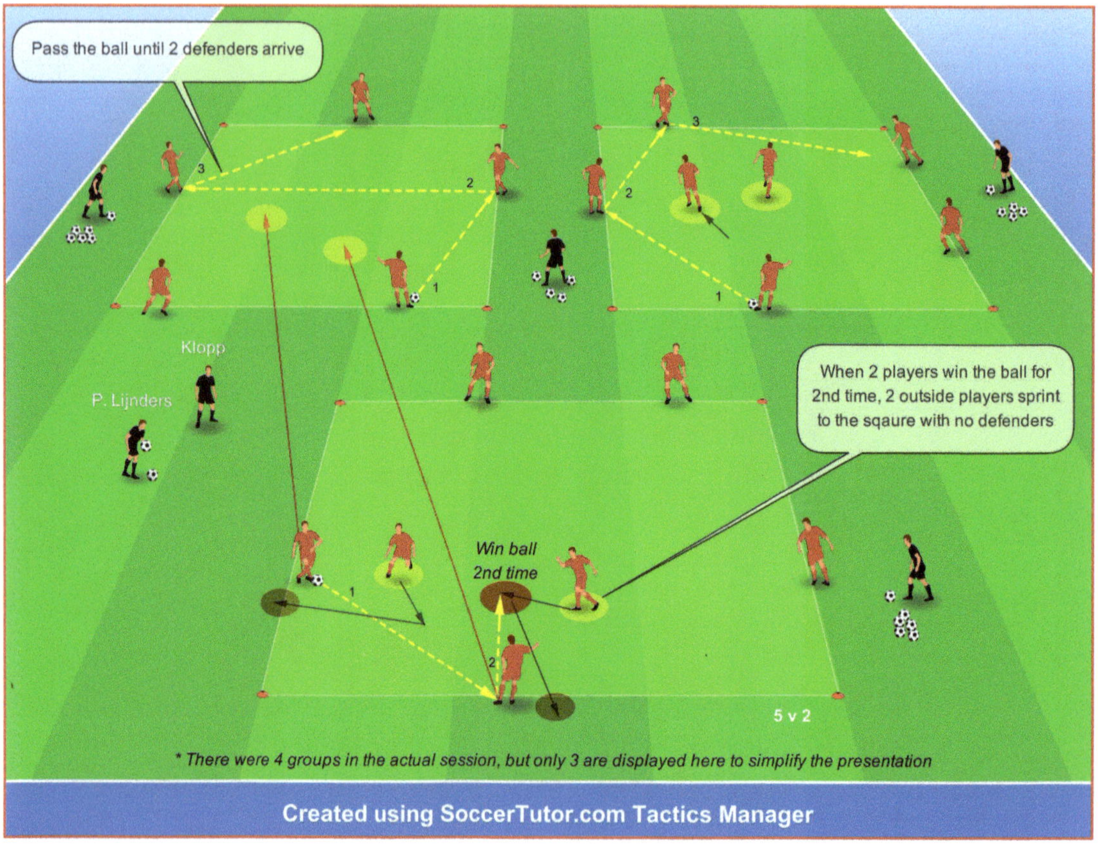

NOTE: *In the actual session there were 4 groups, but only 3 are displayed in the diagram to simplify the presentation.*

Practice Description

- The groups play a normal 5v2 Rondo except for 1 group which simply has 5 players all passing to each other, waiting for 2 defenders to arrive.

- Once the 2 middle players win the ball for a second time in any group, 2 of the outside players in that group have to sprint quickly to the square without any defenders. That group then have 5 outside players passing to each other waiting for 2 defenders to arrive.

- The 2 players who have sprinted across work together to try and win the ball 2 times in their new group before they can switch roles again.

Source: Jürgen Klopp's Liverpool pre-season training session in Salzburg, Austria - July 2021

Jürgen Klopp: Pressing Rondos and Possession Games

5. 6 v 2 Rondo to Find the Free Player and Pressing to Close Passing Lines

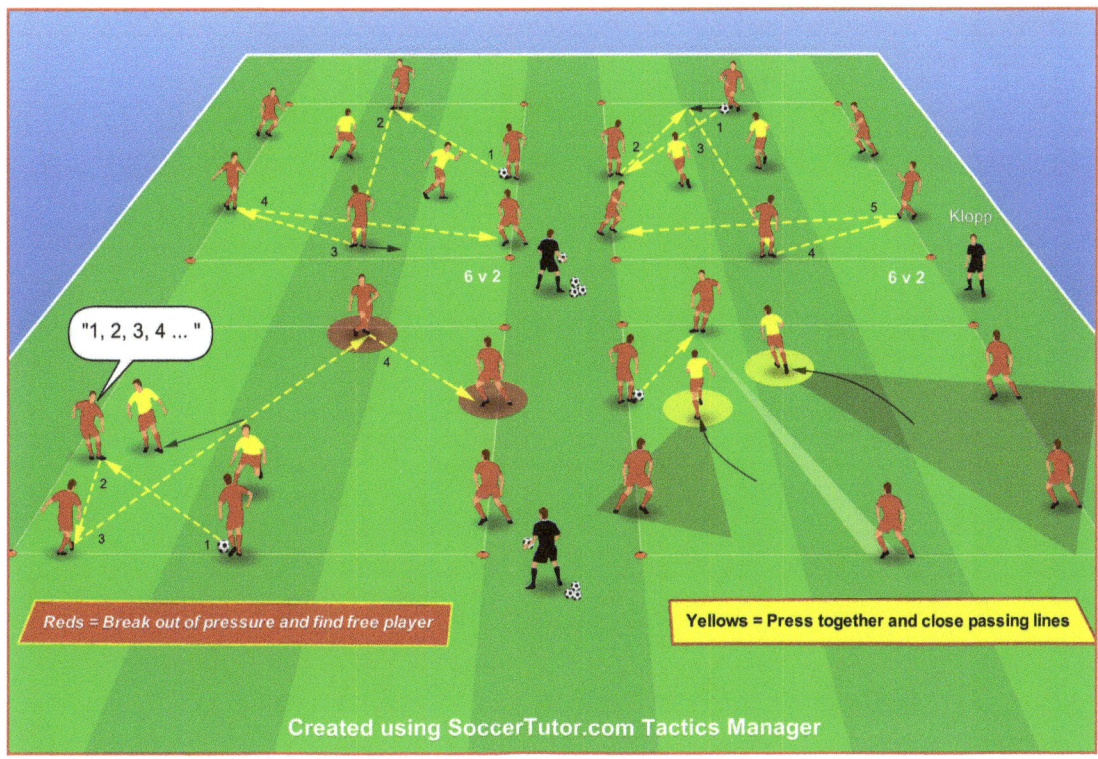

Reds = Break out of pressure and find free player

Yellows = Press together and close passing lines

Practice Description

- In this 6 v 2 Rondo, the players work in groups of 8 in a 10 yard square.

- There are 2 players on 2 sides of the square and 1 player on the other 2 sides. They are positioned on the outsides but must still play within the area.

- The 6 outside players aim to keep possession of the ball and are only allowed to use **1 touch**.

- Success comes from quick passing, good angles and breaking through pressure to move the ball to a free player.

- The 2 inside players (yellow bibs) work together to press, close the angles for the potential passing lines and win the ball.

- **RULE:** The player that loses the ball switches roles with the player that wins the ball.

- **COACHING POINT:** Encourage the players to keep count of the passes to maintain a high level of competition.

Source: Jürgen Klopp's Liverpool training session at AXA Training Centre, Liverpool - April 2022

Jürgen Klopp: Pressing Rondos and Possession Games

6. 6 v 2 End to End Rondo with Support Play and Constant Pressing

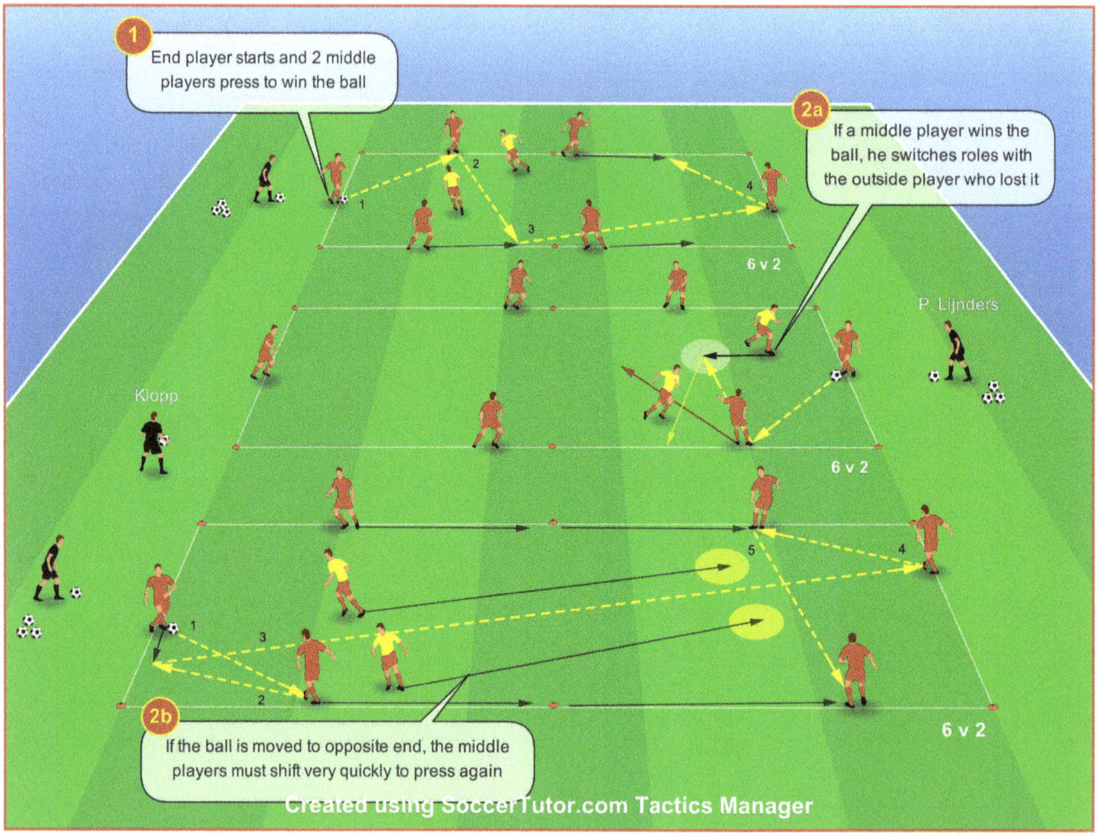

(Diagram annotations:)
1. End player starts and 2 middle players press to win the ball
2a. If a middle player wins the ball, he switches roles with the outside player who lost it
2b. If the ball is moved to opposite end, the middle players must shift very quickly to press again

Practice Description

- In this 6 v 2 Rondo, the players work in groups of 8 in a 5 x 15 yard area.

- There are 2 players on each of the 2 longer sides and 1 player at each end, as shown. They are positioned on the outsides but must still play within the area. There are also 2 inside players.

- The 6 outside players keep possession of the ball using **1 touch** and try to move the ball from one end to the other.

- The **4 red players on the sides work hard to create angles for the players at the ends, constantly moving up and down**.

- The 2 inside players (yellows) work together to press, close the angles, and win the ball. **If they fail to win the ball with their press and the ball is played to the other end, they must quickly sprint across to apply pressure again**.

- The player that loses the ball switches roles with the player that wins the ball.

Source: Jürgen Klopp's Liverpool pre-season training session at Notre Dame University, Indiana, USA - July 2019

Jürgen Klopp: Pressing Rondos and Possession Games

7. 4-Team 2+2+2 v 2 Rondo with Fast Pressing and Transitions

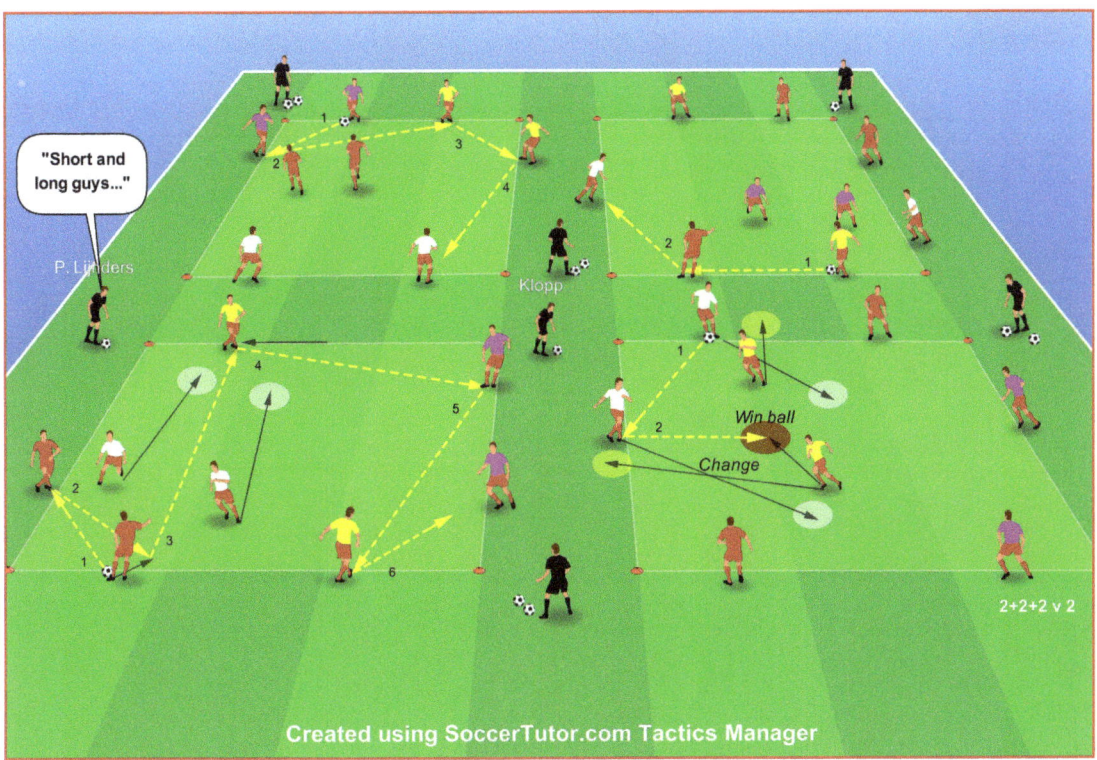

Practice Description

- In this 6 v 2 Rondo (2+2+2 v 2), the players work in groups of 8 in a 10 yard square. There are 4 teams of 2 players

- There are 2 players on 2 sides of the square and 1 player on the other 2 sides. They are positioned on the outsides but must still play within the area.

- The 6 outside players (3 teams of 2) aim to keep possession of the ball and are only allowed to use **1 touch**.

- The 2 inside players work together to press, close the angles for the potential passing lines and win the ball.

- **RULE:** If the defending team win the ball, they switch roles with the team that lost it and move to the outside. The team that lost the ball become the defending team in the middle.

Source: Jürgen Klopp's Liverpool training session at AXA Training Centre, Liverpool - October 2021

Jürgen Klopp: Pressing Rondos and Possession Games

8. 7 v 7 Pole Gates Possession Game

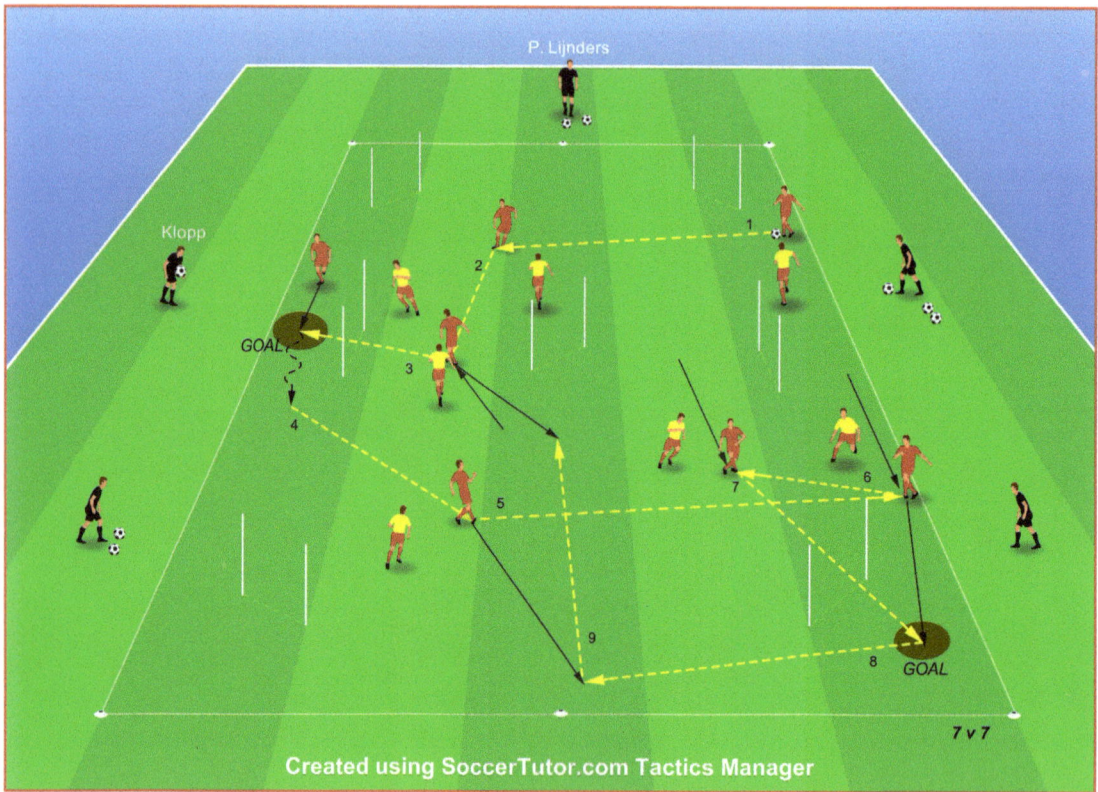

Practice Description

- The practice starts with one team in possession (reds in diagram example) vs. the yellow defending team.

- Each time a team is able to successfully pass and receive through a pole gate a GOAL is scored. The team with the most goals at the end of the game wins.

- The reds try to maintain possession and successfully pass through any of the pole gates for a teammate to receive.

- The diagram example shows the reds scoring a GOAL twice, so the score would already be 2-0.

- If the yellow defending team win the ball, they switch roles with the reds.

- The yellows will then have the aim to keep possession and score goals by successfully passing through the pole gates for a teammate to receive.

Source: Jürgen Klopp's Liverpool training session at AXA Training Centre, Liverpool - December 2021

Jürgen Klopp: Pressing Rondos and Possession Games

9. 7 v 7 Pole Gates Possession Game with End Zone Players

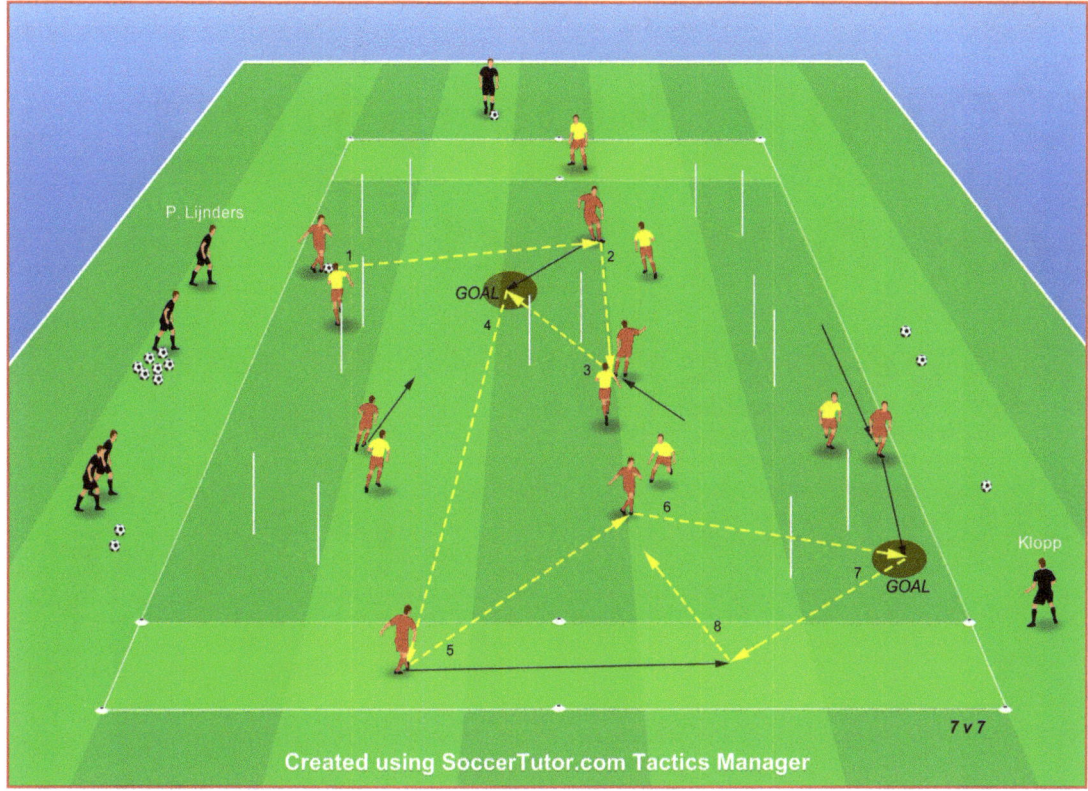

This is a variation of the previous practice, and we mark out end zones. One member of each team's players is now positioned in an end zone and no other players are allowed to enter these zones.

Practice Description

- The practice starts with one team in possession (reds in diagram example) vs. the yellow defending team.

- Each time a team is able to successfully pass and receive through a pole gate a GOAL is scored.

- If the yellow defending team win the ball, they switch roles with the reds.

- The yellows will then have the aim to keep possession and score goals by successfully passing through the pole gates for a teammate to receive.

- The team with the most goals at the end of the game wins.

Source: Jürgen Klopp's Liverpool training session at AXA Training Centre, Liverpool - September 2021

Pressing and Counter-pressing Rondos and Possession Games

Direct from Jürgen Klopp's Training Sessions

"The best moment to win the ball is immediately after your team just lost it. The opponent is still looking for orientation where to pass the ball. He will have taken his eyes off the game to make his tackle or interception and he will have expended energy. Both make him vulnerable."

Jürgen Klopp: Pressing and Counter-pressing Rondos and Possession Games

1. "Hunt the Ball" 3 (+3) v 3 Tactical Rondo to Train Counter-pressing

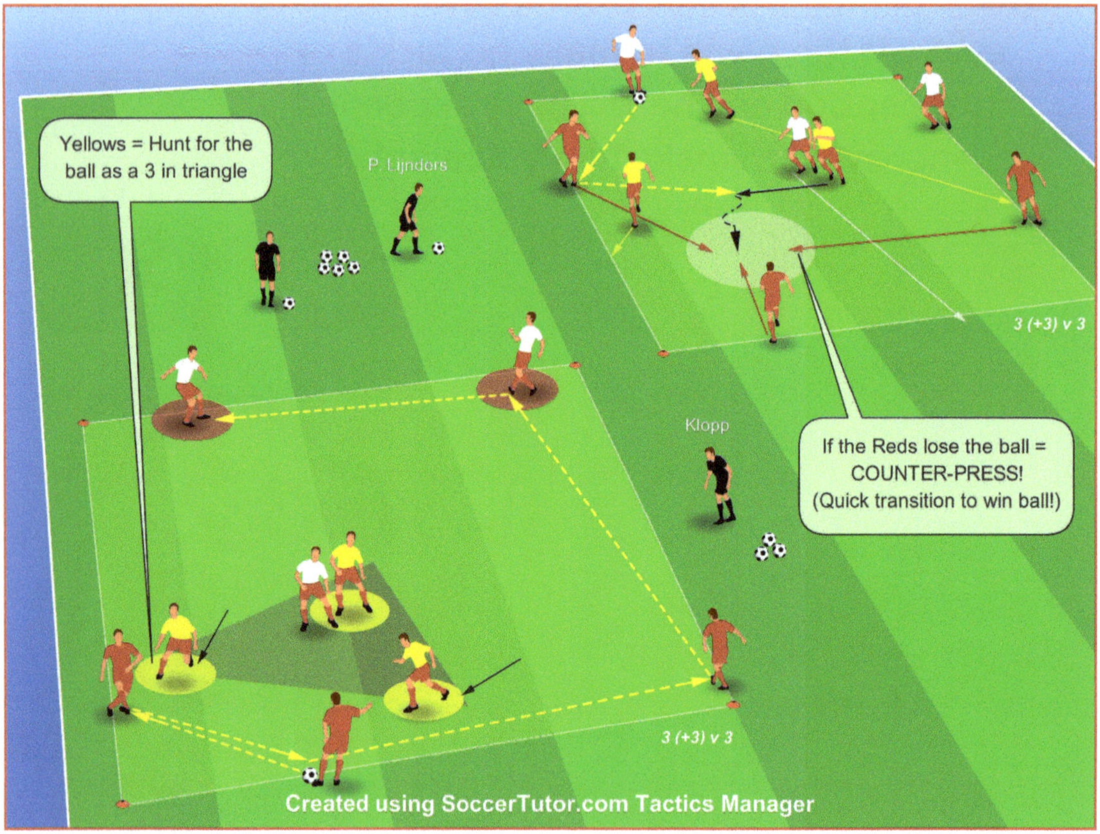

Practice Description

- In a 12 yard square, this Rondo is focused on continuous pressing at high intensity. There are 3 teams of 3 players.

- The **3 defending players constantly "hunt the ball" to practice Klopp and Liverpool's intense pressing and counter-pressing style**.

- We start with 3 red outside players and 2 white outside players + 1 middle player vs. 3 yellow inside players.

- The 3 yellow players press in a **triangle shape** and try to win the ball.

- If a red or white player loses the ball, the 3 players of that colour switch roles with the yellow players who have won the ball.

- In the example at the top, the yellows win the ball and switch roles with the reds. The reds **react immediately to press the new ball carrier and win the ball back as quickly as possible (counter-pressing)**.

Source: Jürgen Klopp's Liverpool training session at AXA Training Centre, Liverpool - July 2022

Jürgen Klopp: Pressing and Counter-pressing Rondos and Possession Games

2. High Intensity 3 (+2) v 3 Pressing & Counter-pressing Possession Game

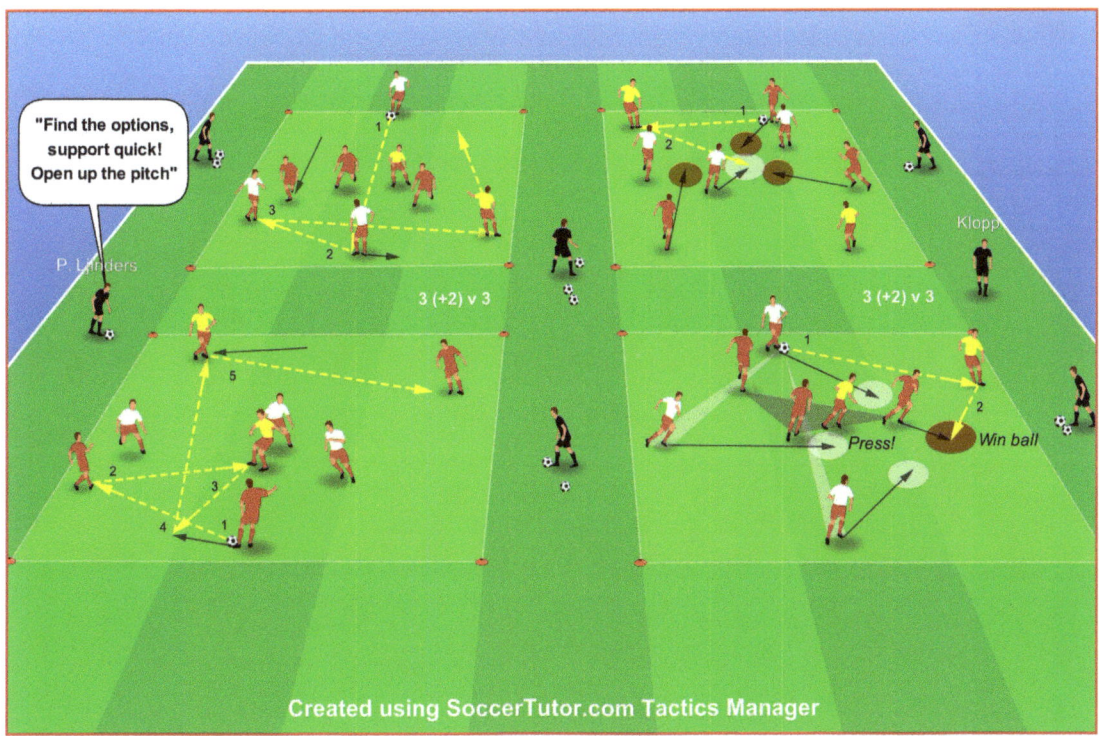

Practice Description

- In a 12 yard square, there are 2 teams of 3 players (red and white) + 2 yellow jokers who play with the team in possession.

- All the players can move freely inside the area and mostly use **1 or 2 touches**.

- The 3 defending players work together to press, block off passing lines and try to win the ball.

- The team in possession look to move the ball quickly and keep the ball.

- **COACHING POINT:** The focus of the practice is to on high intensity pressing for the defending players, but also maximising the space and good support play for the possession players.

- If the defending team win the ball, they switch roles with the other team and try to maintain possession with help from the 2 yellow jokers.

- The team that lost possession react immediately to try and win the ball back **(counter-press!)**.

Source: Jürgen Klopp's Liverpool training session at Melwood Training Ground, Liverpool - July 2019

Jürgen Klopp: Pressing and Counter-pressing Rondos and Possession Games

3. 4 (+2) v 4 Pressing & Counter-pressing Possession Game

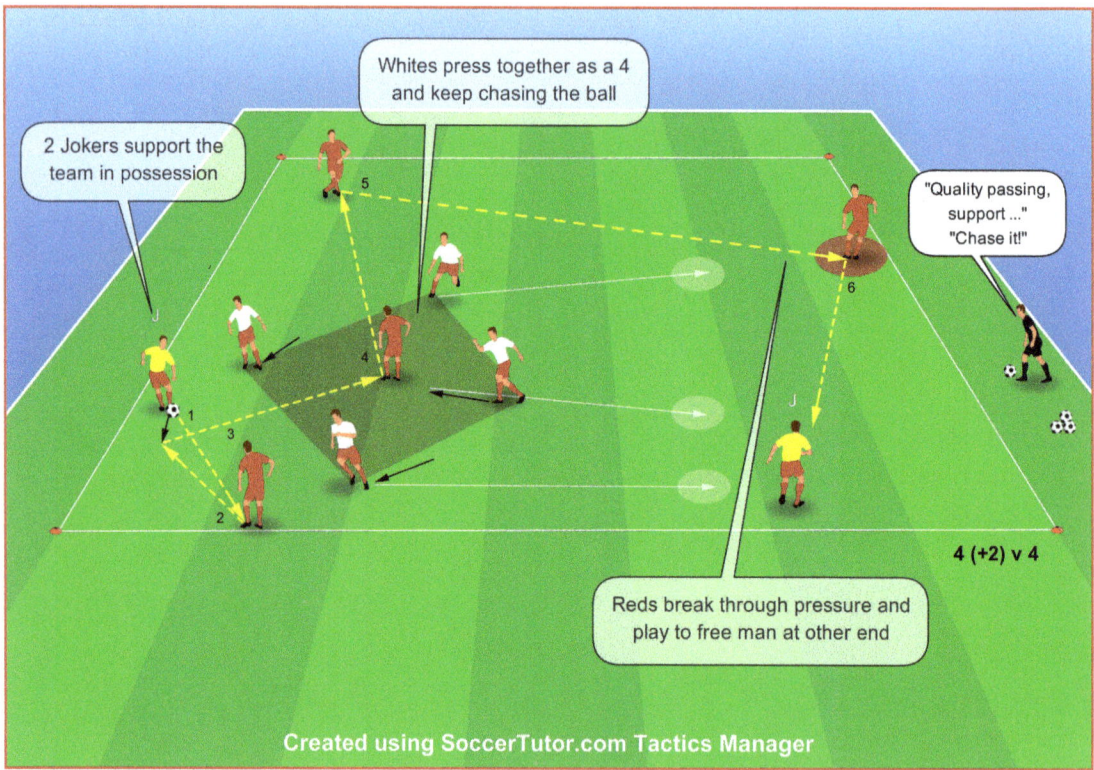

Practice Description

- In a 15 x 20 yard area, there are 2 teams of 4 players (red and white) + 2 yellow jokers who play with the team in possession.
- All the players can move freely inside the area and mostly use **1 or 2 touches**.
- The 4 defending players (whites in diagram) work together to press, block off passing lines and try to win the ball.
- The team in possession (reds) look to move the ball quickly and keep the ball.

- **COACHING POINT:** The focus of the practice is to play through the press and move the ball from one end to the other to the free player.
- If the defending team (whites) win the ball, they switch roles with the reds.
- The white players then try to maintain possession with help from the 2 yellow jokers.
- The reds react immediately to try and win the ball back **(counter-press!)**.

Source: Jürgen Klopp's Liverpool pre-season training session at Notre Dame University, Indiana, USA - July 2019

Jürgen Klopp: Pressing and Counter-pressing Rondos and Possession Games

4. 4 (+2) v 4 Possession Game with Intense Counter-pressing Focus

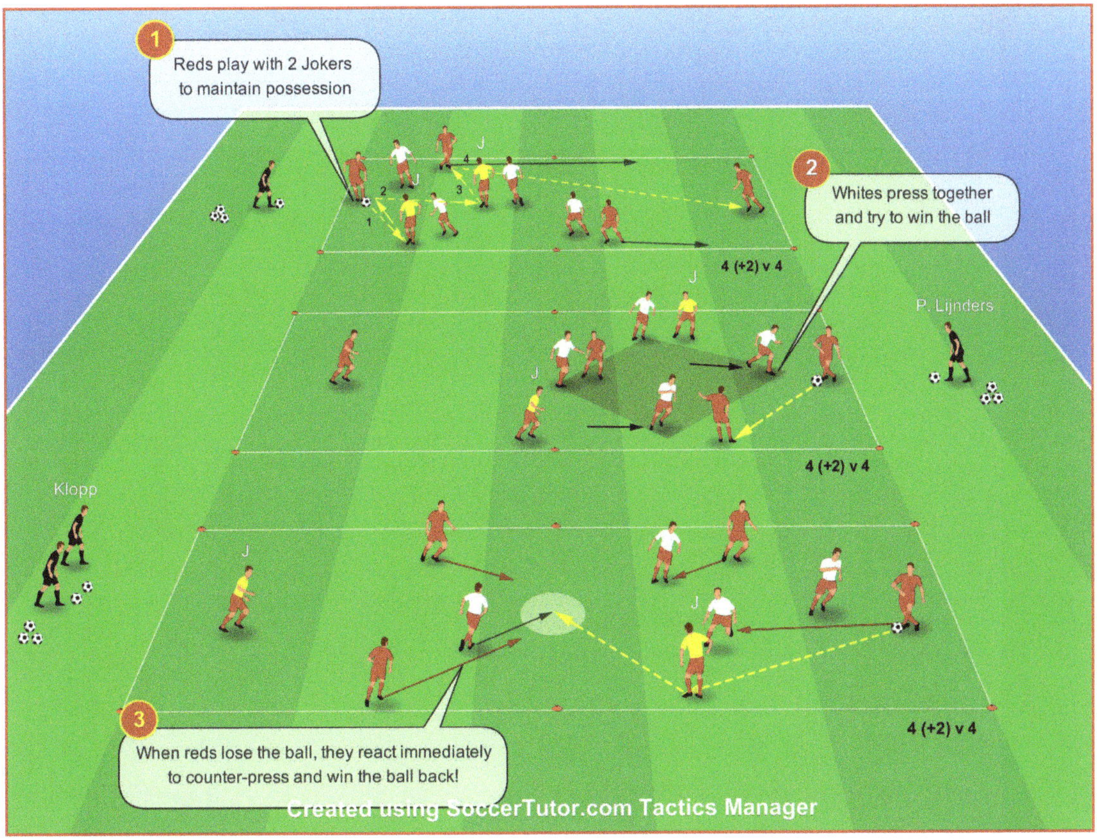

1. Reds play with 2 Jokers to maintain possession

2. Whites press together and try to win the ball

3. When reds lose the ball, they react immediately to counter-press and win the ball back!

Practice Description

- This is a variation of the previous practice in a smaller 5 x 10 yard area, so there is <u>MORE</u> counter-pressing.

- It is harder to maintain possession compared to a 15 x 20 yard area, so the players move the ball even quicker and **mostly use 1 touch**.

- It is easier for the defending team to win the ball than in the previous larger area, so there are more transitions.

- **COACHING POINT:** In this smaller area, there are many more opportunities for counter-pressing to win the ball back immediately after losing it!

Source: Jürgen Klopp's Liverpool training session at AXA Training Centre, Liverpool - November 2021

Jürgen Klopp: Pressing and Counter-pressing Rondos and Possession Games

5. 3(+2) v 3(+2) Possession Game with "Free" Outside Support Players

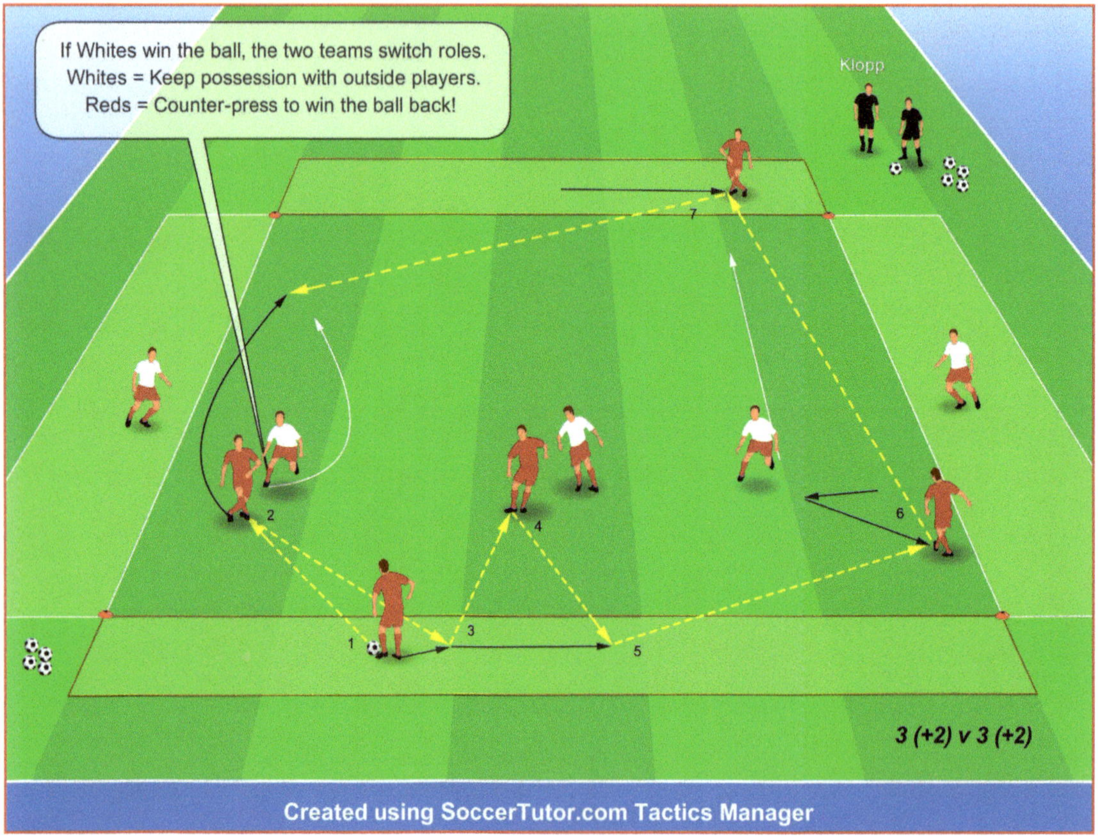

If Whites win the ball, the two teams switch roles.
Whites = Keep possession with outside players.
Reds = Counter-press to win the ball back!

3 (+2) v 3 (+2)

Practice Description

- In a 10 yard square, we have 2 teams of 5 players (red and white). 2 of each team's 5 players are positioned outside the square as shown.

- The practice starts with one team (reds in diagram) trying to maintain possession.

- **COACHING POINT:** The key is to utilise the outside players to keep the ball, as they are always free to receive.

- The defending team (whites) work together (pressing) to close off the passing angles and try to win the ball.

- If the whites are able to win the ball, the two teams switch roles and the white team continue the practice trying to maintain possession by utlising their 2 outside players.

- The reds will then make a quick transition and try to win the ball back as quickly as possible **(counter-press!)**.

Source: Jürgen Klopp's Liverpool training session at Melwood Training Ground, Liverpool - March 2019

Jürgen Klopp: Pressing and Counter-pressing Rondos and Possession Games

6. High Intensity 4 (+2) v 4 Pressing & Counter-pressing in Centre Circle

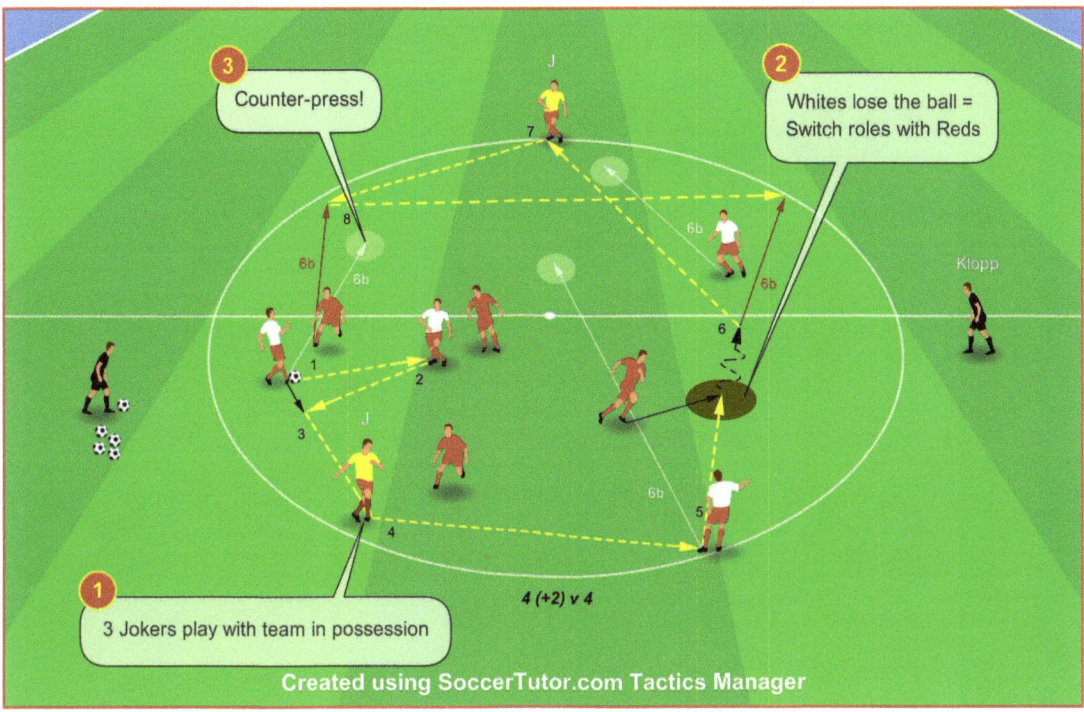

Practice Description

- In the centre circle (radius = 10 yards), there are 2 teams of 4 players (white and red) + 2 yellow jokers who play with the team in possession.
- All the players can move freely inside the area and mostly use **1 or 2 touches**.
- The 4 defending players (reds in diagram) work together to press, block off passing lines and try to win the ball.
- The team in possession (whites) look to move the ball quickly and keep the ball.
- If the defending team (reds) win the ball, they switch roles with the whites.
- The red players then try to maintain possession with help from the 2 yellow jokers. The whites have to make a quick transition to try and win the ball back immediately **(counter-press!)**.

Source: Jürgen Klopp's Liverpool training session at AXA Training Centre, Liverpool - December 2021

Jürgen Klopp: Pressing and Counter-pressing Rondos and Possession Games

7. High Intensity 4 (+3) v 4 Pressing & Counter-pressing in Centre Circle

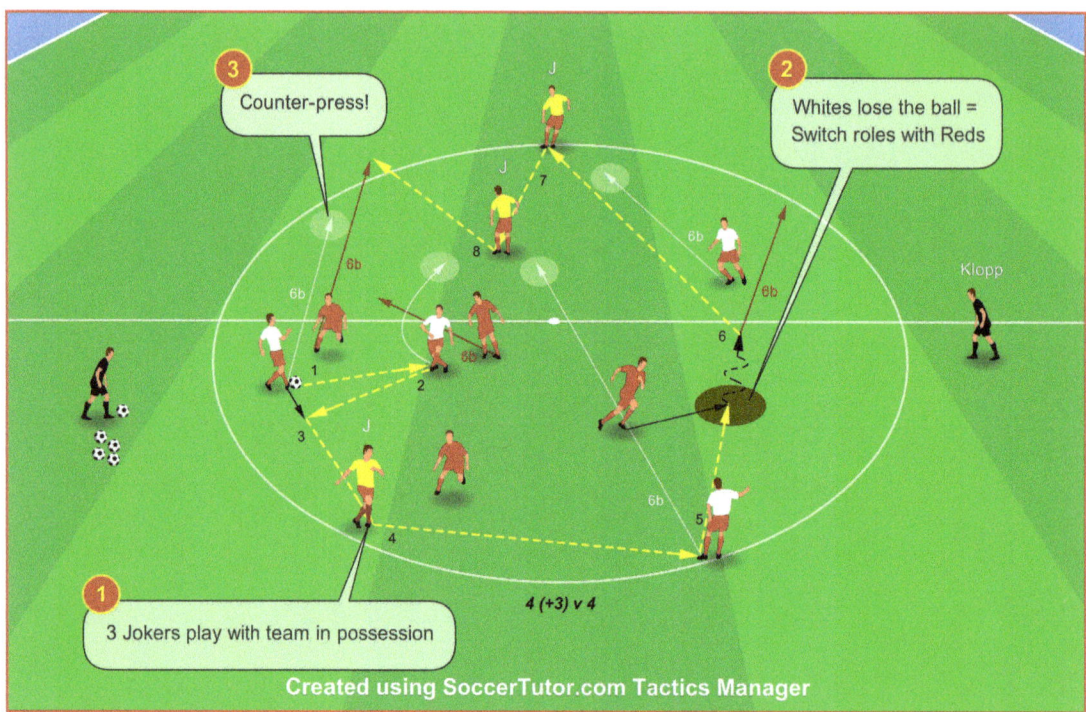

Practice Description

- This is a simple variation of the previous practice with 1 more joker added.
- There are still 2 teams of 4 players (white and red) but now there are 3 yellow jokers who play with the team in possession.
- The objectives and rules remain exactly the same (see previous page).

- **COACHING POINT:** The Liverpool coaches and players really focus on the counter-press, to act collectively as a team and try to win the ball back immediately after losing the ball.

Source: Jürgen Klopp's Liverpool training session at AXA Training Centre, Liverpool - December 2021

JÜRGEN KLOPP: PRACTICES FROM KLOPP'S SESSIONS

Jürgen Klopp: Pressing and Counter-pressing Rondos and Possession Games

8. Support Play + Continuous Pressing 4 (+6) v 4 Hexagon Possession Game

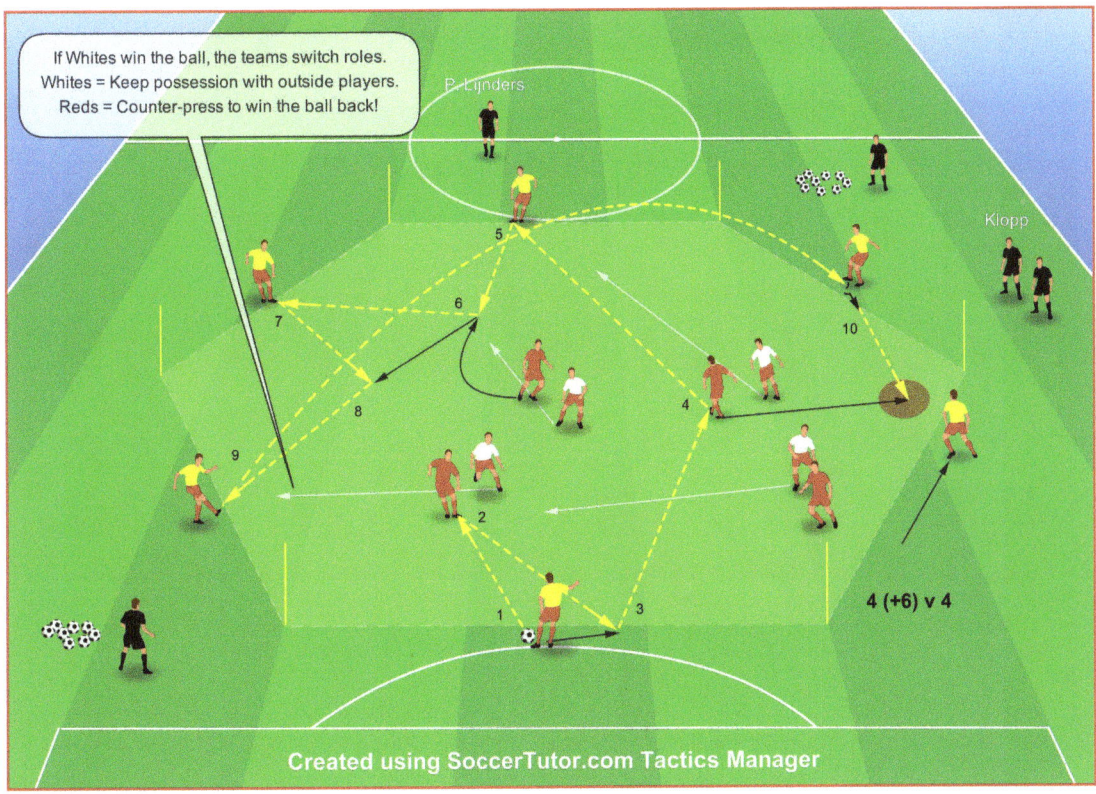

Practice Description

- In the hexagon area shown which is marked out with poles, there are 2 teams of 4 players (red and white) + 6 yellow outside players who play with the team in possession.

- **Inside players mostly use 1 or 2 touches.**

- **Outside players are limited to 1 touch.**

- The 4 defending players (whites in diagram) work together to press, block off passing lines and try to win the ball.

- The team in possession (reds) look to keep the ball using their 10 v 4 numerical advantage. They move the ball quickly which can be very tiring for the defending players, who have to continuously keep pressing.

- If the defending team (whites) win the ball, they switch roles with the reds. The white players then try to maintain possession with support from the 6 yellow outside players.

- The reds react immediately to try and win the ball back **(counter-press!)**.

Source: Jürgen Klopp's Liverpool training session at AXA Training Centre, Liverpool - November 2021

Jürgen Klopp: Pressing and Counter-pressing Rondos and Possession Games

9. Pressing & Counter-pressing in a 3-Team 4 (+4) v 4 Possession Game

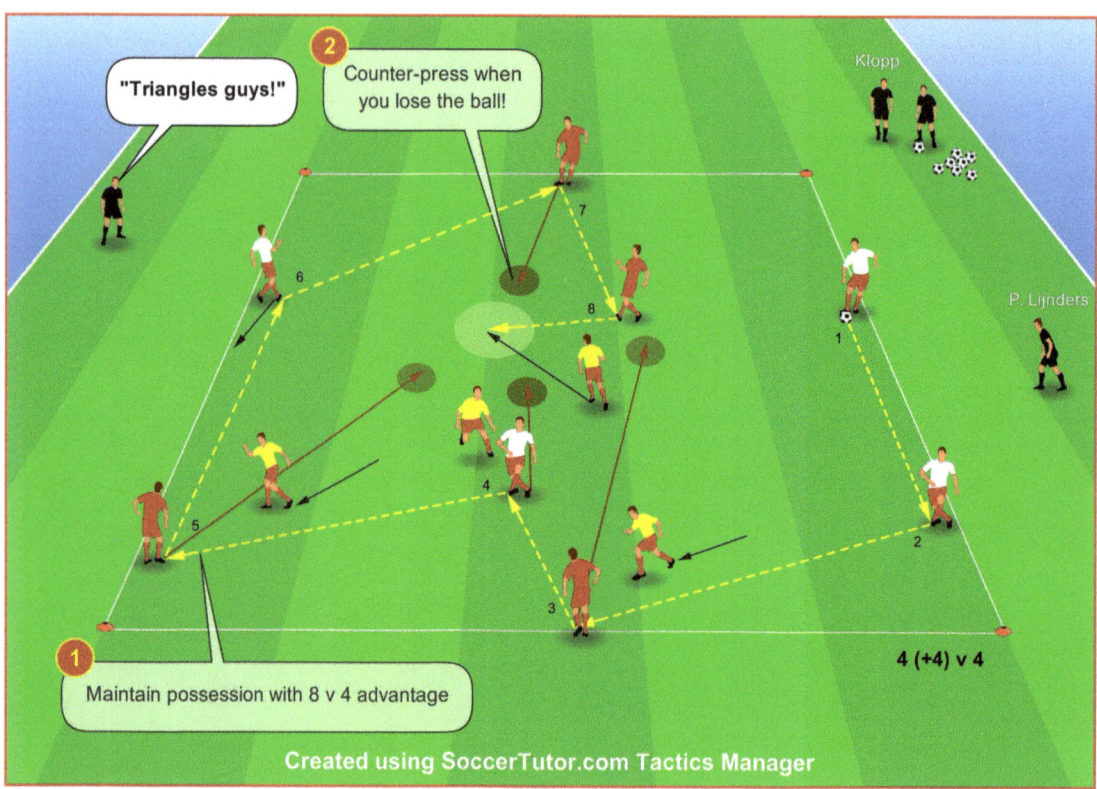

Practice Description

- In a 10 yard square, there are 3 teams of 4 players (red, white, and yellow). 2 teams start in possession with 3 outside players and 1 inside player each. The other team defends with all 4 players operating inside the area.

- The players mostly use **1 or 2 touches**.

- The 4 defending players (yellows in diagram) work together to press, block off passing lines and try to win the ball.

- The reds and whites look to move the ball quickly and maintain possession. If the defending team win the ball, they switch roles with the team that lost it.

- In this example, the yellows win the ball, switch roles with the reds and try to keep possession with the whites. The reds must react very quickly to try and win the ball back **(counter-press!)**.

- **COACHING POINT:** The coach's focus is triangle shapes in possession and the counter-press, for the outside players to compress quickly and win the ball back immediately after losing the ball.

Source: Jürgen Klopp's Liverpool training session at AXA Training Centre, Liverpool - July 2022

Jürgen Klopp: Pressing and Counter-pressing Rondos and Possession Games

10. Dynamic 4 v 4 v 4 Three-Zone End to End Possession Game

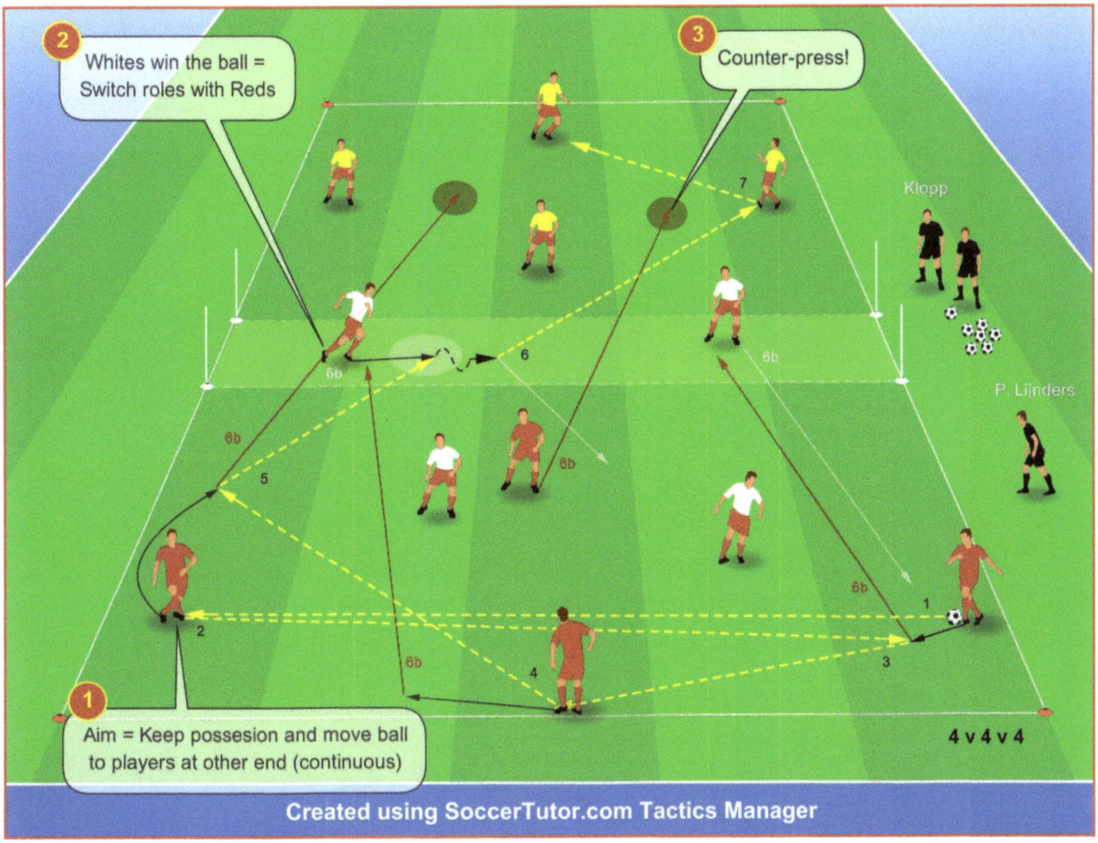

Practice Description

- In a total 10 x 15 yard area, mark out a 2 yard zone in the centre, as shown.
- There are 3 teams of 4 players (red, white, and yellow).
- The practice starts with a 4v2 situation in an end zone. The reds start in the diagram example and their aim is to keep possession and move the ball to yellows in the opposite end zone. The yellows then have the same aim.
- The white team defend with 2 players in the end zone who try to stop the reds progressing the ball + 2 players in the middle zone who try to intercept passes.
- When the whites win the ball, they switch roles with the red team and pass to a yellow player.
- 2 red players move to the middle zone and the other 2 make a fast transition and move into the opposite end zone to press the yellow players **(counter-press!)**.

Source: Jürgen Klopp's Liverpool training session at AXA Training Centre, Liverpool - December 2021

Jürgen Klopp: Pressing and Counter-pressing Rondos and Possession Games

11. Pressing and Counter-pressing in a 4 (+3) v 4 Positional Possession Game

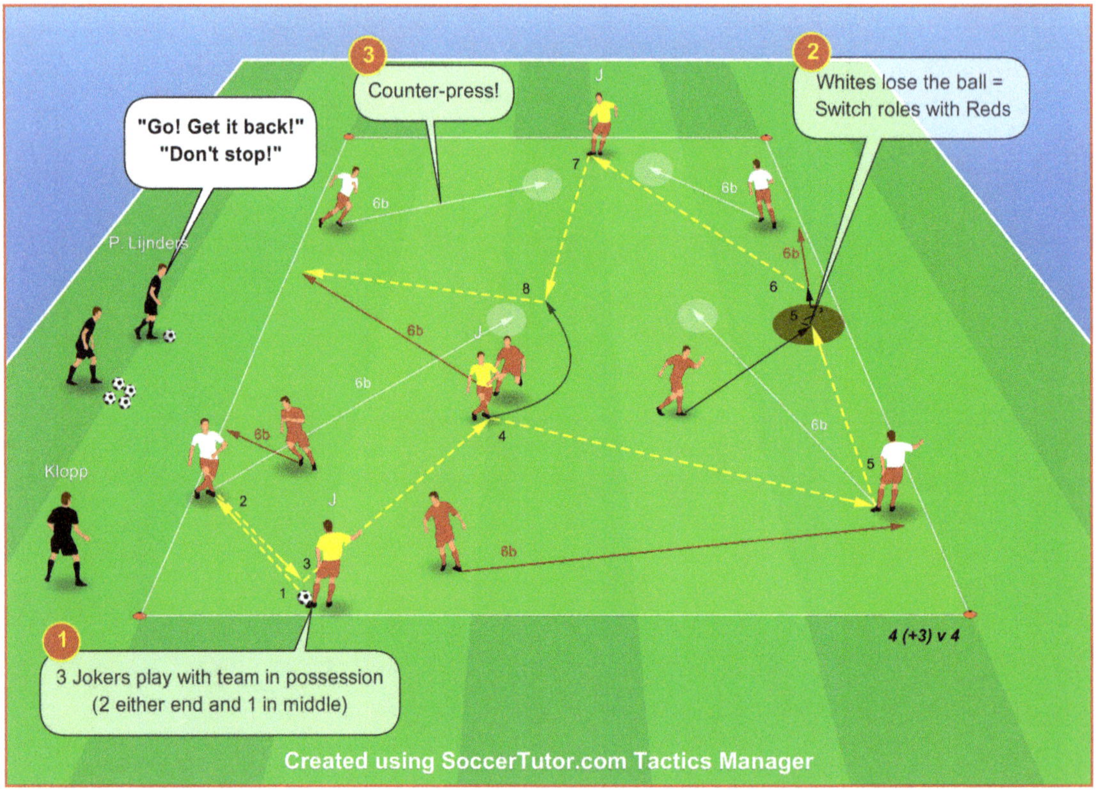

Practice Description

- In a 10 x 15 yard area, there are 2 teams of 4 players (white and red) + 3 yellow jokers who play with the team in possession.

- All 4 white players are positioned on the long sides (2 on each side) and all the red players start inside the area. There is 1 yellow joker at each end and 1 inside.

- The practice starts with one team (whites) who try to maintain possession with help from the 3 yellow jokers.

- The red team work together (pressing) to close off the angles and try to win the ball. If the reds are able to win the ball, the teams switch roles.

- The reds move to the outsides and try to maintain possession with help from the 3 jokers.

- The whites all move inside and work together to try and win the ball back immediately **(counter-press!)**.

Source: Jürgen Klopp's Liverpool training session at Melwood Training Ground, Liverpool - July 2018

Jürgen Klopp: Pressing and Counter-pressing Rondos and Possession Games

12. Pressing and Counter-pressing in a 4 (+4) v 4 Positional Possession Game

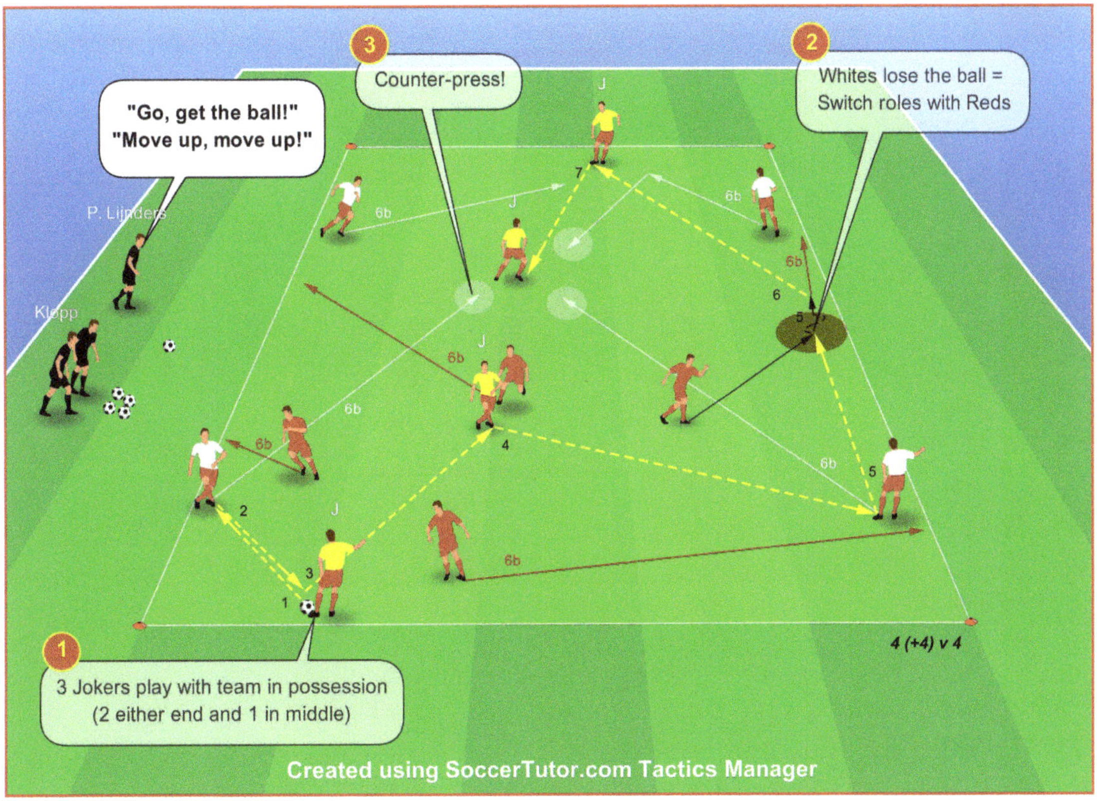

Practice Description

- This is a simple variation of the previous practice with 1 more joker added to create a 4 (+4) v 4 positional possession game.

- The objectives and rules remain exactly the same (see previous page).

- **COACHING POINT:** The Liverpool coaches and players really focus on the counter-press, to act collectively as a team and try to win the ball back immediately after losing the ball.

Source: Jürgen Klopp's Liverpool training session at Melwood Training Ground, Liverpool - July 2018

Jürgen Klopp: Pressing and Counter-pressing Rondos and Possession Games

13. Pressing and Counter-pressing in a 7 (+3) v 7 Positional Possession Game

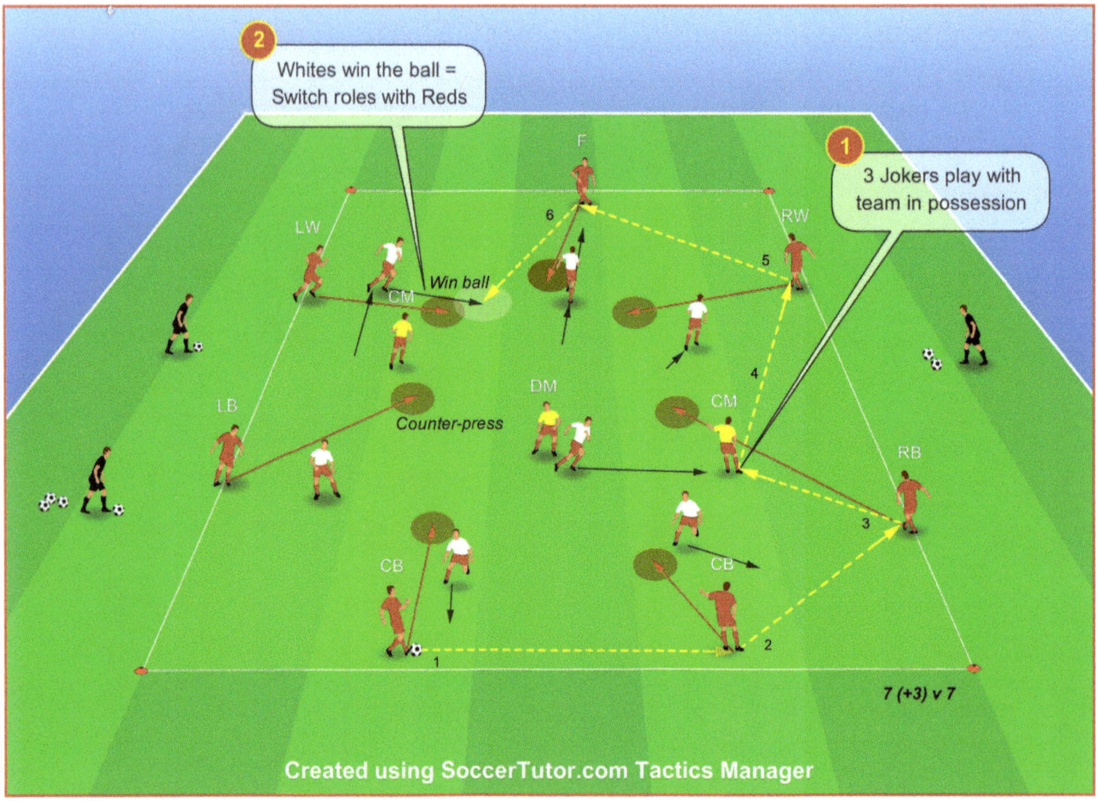

Practice Description

- In a 25 x 30 yard area, there are 2 teams of 7 players (white and red) + 3 yellow jokers who play with the team in possession.
- **POSITIONAL GAME** = Centre backs at the base, the forward at the top, the wide players on the sides, and the central midfielders (jokers) in the middle.
- The practice starts with one team (reds) trying to maintain possession with help from the 3 yellow jokers.
- The white team work together (pressing) to close off the angles and try to win the ball. If the whites are able to win the ball, the teams switch roles.
- The whites move to the outsides and try to maintain possession with help from the 3 jokers.
- The reds all move inside and work together to try and win the ball back immediately **(counter-press!)**.

Source: Jürgen Klopp's Liverpool training session at AXA Training Centre, Liverpool - January 2021

Coming Soon!

Football Coaching Specialists Since 2001

Jürgen Klopp

Attacking Patterns & Combinations, Finishing, Transition & Small Sided Games Direct from Klopp's Training Sessions

Vol. 2

Available in Full Colour Print and eBook!

Football Coaching Specialists Since 2001

PEP GUARDIOLA
88 Attacking Combinations and Positional Patterns of Play Direct from Pep's Training Sessions
Vol. 1

PEP GUARDIOLA
85 Passing, Rondos, Possession Games & Technical Circuits Direct from Pep's Training Sessions
Vol. 2

Coaching Books Available in Full Colour Print and eBook!
PC | Mac | iPhone | iPad | Android Phone / Tablet | Chromebook

 **FREE** Coach Viewer **APP**

SoccerTutor.com

Free Trial

Football Coaching Specialists Since 2001

Tactics Manager
Create your own Practices, Tactics & Plan Sessions!

Tactics Manager App

 Soon!
 Soon!

SoccerTutor.com

www.ingramcontent.com/pod-product-compliance
Lightning Source LLC
Chambersburg PA
CBHW061209230426

43665CB00028B/2963